JOAN DENISE MORIARTY
FOUNDER OF IRISH NATIONAL BALLET

JOAN DENISE MORIARTY
FOUNDER OF IRISH NATIONAL BALLET

Material for a History of Dance in Ireland

Edited by

RUTH FLEISCHMANN

MERCIER PRESS

IRISH AMERICAN BOOK COMPANY (IABC)
Boulder, Colorado

MERCIER PRESS
PO Box 5, 5 French Church Street, Cork
16 Hume Street, Dublin 2

Trade enquiries to CMD DISTRIBUTION,
55a Spruce Avenue, Stillorgan Industrial Park, Blackrock, Dublin

Published in the US and Canada by the
IRISH AMERICAN BOOK COMPANY
6309 Monarch Park Place, Niwot, Colorado, 80503
Tel: (303) 652 2710, (800) 452-7115
Fax: (303) 652 2689, (800) 401-9705

ISBN 185635 234 X

10 9 8 7 6 5 4 3 2 1

Printed in Ireland by Colour Books Ltd.

CONTENTS

ACKNOWLEDGMENTS

Ninety-five people responded to my request for an account of their association with Joan Denise Moriarty; they have thus created this book. In addition, many others have given invaluable help of various kinds, without which it could not have been produced. To all these I wish to express my deep gratitude. Because of the number of contributors, I have had to shorten many of the articles. The original texts have been placed with the Fleischmann Papers in the archives of University College Cork.

I am indebted to Michael D. Higgins, who as Minister for Arts, Culture and the Gaeltacht granted me access to the Arts Council's Irish Ballet Company/Irish National Ballet files; to David McConnell, then acting director of the Arts Council, for study and photocopying facilities and Phelim Donlon of the Arts Council for his courteous help in locating documents; I thank The Royal Academy of Dancing in London for study facilities given to me in their library, in particular the librarian Mandy Payne; Molly Webb, the librarian of the Imperial Society for Teachers of Dance, for access to their library in London; Jane Pritchard, the archivist of the Rambert Dance Company of London for information about the Rambert School records; Peter Bassett, archivist and librarian of the Laban Centre for Movement and Dance of London for study facilities and access to the Brinson papers; Christina Darby of the Calouste Gulbenkian Foundation London for help in trying to locate the Brinson papers connected with the report on dance in Ireland. I am particularly obliged to Virginia Teehan, director of the archives of University College Cork, for all the help and good counsel I was given during my studies of the Fleischmann Papers there; also to Rachel Granville for her unfailing cooperation.

With regard to copyright I thank: Breda Brophy and Aideen Rynne for permission to quote Miss Moriarty's papers; the Arts Council for permission to quote from documents in their files; Marshall Hutson for permission to reproduce his portrait of Miss Moriarty and his *Macha Ruadh* design; the Cork Arts and Theatre Club for permission to quote and reproduce material from the tribute it offered to Miss Moriarty on 24 February 1988: *This Is Your Life*; in particular thanks to Michael Twomey, who presented the show, for lending me the script he had prepared; to Jo White for information and advice; and to Hilda Buckley, Monica Gavin and Ann Quain for the video made of the evening, from which the texts were transcribed. I am grateful to Werdon Anglin for permission to quote a letter by the late Dr Peter Brinson; to *The Examiner* for permission to reproduce Declan Hassett's obituary of Miss Moriarty; to Mary Colley, Jack Lynch, the Earl of Rosse, Dame Ninette de Valois' lawyer (M. R. Macfadyen, who is acting under Enduring Power of Attorney) for permission to quote letters; to Senator Michael Yeats for permission to quote W. B. Yeats' poem 'Sweet Dancer'.

I thank *The Examiner* and the *RTE Guide* for permission to use their photographs. Every effort has been made to establish sources of all photographs used and acknowledgement given – should a source have not been acknowledged, I take this opportunity of apologising for such an oversight and will make the necessary correction at the first opportunity.

For interviews I thank Martin Drury, Arthur Lappin, Colm Ó Briain, the late Professor Ó hEocha and Dr David Nowlan, the registrar of the National University of Ireland.

I thank very specially: Séamas de Barra, Ethel Beare, Sister Angela Bolster, Hilda Buckley, Jonathan Burnett, Canon Jerram Burrows, Michael Casey, William Cogan, Maria and Joe Cunningham, Charles Czarny, Geoffrey Davidson, the late Norris Davidson, Tom Donnelly, Caoimhe Ní hEinigh, Pat Fleming, Monica Gavin, Gerald Y. Goldberg, Esther Gyves, Richard Henchion, Charles Hennessy, Beatrice Hunt, Nóirín Hurley, Muriel Large, Pat Leonard, Pat and Jim McCarthy, Derek McCoy, Mairtín McCullough, Catherine McMahon, Donn McMullin, Patrick Murray, Colum Ó Cléirigh, Betty and Shane O'Connor, the late Madeleine O'Connor, Robert O'Donoghue, Joahne O'Hara, Angela O'Keeffe, Cherry O'Keeffe, Máirín O'Rourke, Domini and Michel Paschoud de Lutry, Ann Quain, Breda Quinn, Helen Quinnell, Domy Reiter-Soffer, Aideen Rynne, Etienne Rynne, Carolyn Swift, Kieran Tunney, Maureen Weldon, Patrick Zuk.

I am grateful to Ursula Stiller and Gráinne Delany of the Faculty of Linguistics and Literary Studies at the University of Bielefeld, who helped with the typing, deciphering of handwriting and transcribing from tapes.

This book has been a family undertaking. Those involved were: my brother Neil Fleischmann of Victoria, British Columbia; my sisters Anne Fleischmann of Killarney and Maeve Fleischmann of Cork; my brother Alan Fleischmann and his wife Vanessa of Caledonia, Minnesota; my husband Rainer Würgau.

Ruth Fleischmann

Introduction

The Relevance of Miss Moriarty

THIS BOOK IS ABOUT a remarkable Irish woman, a pioneer who brought classical and modern dance all over Ireland, and who founded the first professional ballet company in the country. Not only did she introduce a new art form: she created just over a hundred original works for her companies. In those choreographed for her two professional groups, she ventured out into a new type of dance, drawing on themes from Irish mythology and legend and fusing traditional dance forms with ballet. She wanted to create an original Irish form of this European art. She had studied ballet with Marie Rambert, spent her youth in England and became champion Irish stepdancer of Britain as well as an accomplished traditional musician: a prize-winning war pipes player.

Just what a feat it was to bring ballet to Ireland in the 1950s must be called to mind. The arts had had a hard time during the first decades after independence, being generally regarded as anti-national and a luxury for the rich. Ballet was unknown and bound to come in for a particularly rough ride, given the puritanism which had become established in the nineteenth century. Miss Moriarty began her work during the era when the censors decided what books people might read, what films they might view; much of the great literature of Europe was prohibited, including some of the best Irish works of the century. Those who tried to lift that green curtain sometimes heard their efforts denounced from the pulpit, as Miss Moriarty was to experience. But she prevailed and brought ballet to every town in Ireland, north and south, that had a hall with a stage on which her company could dance.

This book begins with an account of dance in Cork by Aloys Fleischmann, the musician and composer who was involved in the Cork ballet from the first performance in 1947. He began writing this article the year before his death in 1992. It is based on his personal recollections as well as on his extensive collection of documents and goes up to 1960. Two other documents written by him sketch the subsequent development of the professional companies up to 1985, the end of Miss Moriarty's directorship of Irish National Ballet. The story of ballet in Ireland is one of astonishing successes, but also of tragedy, as fifteen years after the establishment of the national ballet company, the Arts Council ceased funding it. The editor has been granted access to the relevant Arts Council files, and outlines the reasons for that controversial decision.

The main part of this book consists of accounts given by ninety-five people from all walks of life of their association with Miss Moriarty. Among the contributors are professional dancers, members of the amateur Cork Ballet Company, guest choreographers, producers and teachers, critics, former pupils, those who supplied the music for the ballet, those who supported her artistically, financially, technically and as friends. Her nearest relatives have also contributed, a cousin outlining what can be documented about her early life. These are accounts of first-hand experience: this is authentic material for future studies. From it a number of features stand out.

We are reminded by articles describing the 1940s and 1950s of how different life was in post-war Ireland. Prospects, resources and therefore horizons were restricted, compared to what we have become accustomed to; travel for pleasure within the country was rare, not to mind outside it – most of those undertaking journeys across the water went for good. Fine music had become technically accessible outside the concert hall, but record-players and records were expensive and not many people in Cork had them. The widening of horizons, which so many experienced through Miss Moriarty, is a leitmotif of the articles in this book dealing with the early years of the Cork Ballet Company. She not only introduced her dancers to ballet but, through the Cork Symphony Orchestra, to the repertory of classical and modern music; their experience of costume-designing and stage scenery often awakened their interest in painting. They describe the excitement, the colour and new quality of experience brought into what for many was a drab and enclosed world. Through these articles we see what a wealth of talent lies within such a community, which can be activated with the right incentive.

Furthermore, the dancers came into contact with the creative process and saw that their own city could produce not only poets, novelists and dramatists, but original choreography and modern ballet music. The dance produced was European in origin, but also Irish; it made many of the young dancers for the first time aware of the richness of the Irish heritage, brought a new dimension of the Irish folk tradition to them and gave them a pride in that tradition long before the general revival of interest of the 1960s. However, Miss Moriarty did not only give her dancers access to the Irish heritage, but also to other European folk traditions, bringing many on their first trip abroad. Furthermore, she built bridges within Ireland:

her first professional company went on regular tours to Northern Ireland from the end of the 1950s when links of any kind were rare indeed. Her work won support from people from all over the country, and from people of the main religious denominations in Ireland, north and south. Her supporters were to be found in large and small houses in Cork city, in many convents and schools across the country, in small towns from County Cork to County Donegal, and in buildings as diverse as the Lota School of the Brothers of Charity in Cork, Birr Castle in Offaly and Dáil Éireann in Dublin. The range of her co-operation with people working in other art-forms is striking: she and her dancers appeared in opera, theatre, musicals, pantomime, folk dance.

Miss Moriarty's Cork dancers nearly all speak of the quality of the friendships formed during their time in the Cork Ballet Company. A further leitmotif is that of Miss Moriarty's quiet kindnesses to people in trouble – among her papers there is documentation of many more. Perhaps the most significant evidence of the depth of her impact on their lives is that so many of them have followed her example and taken an active part in the cultural life of their communities, furthering music, dance, theatre and literature. This bears witness to the quality of her motivation and the role model she gave. The Appendices (compiled by Hilda Buckley and Monica Gavin) list the ballets created by Miss Moriarty, and the repertoire of her companies: they convey an idea of the enormous amount of work which she accomplished in her lifetime.

The dancers in the professional companies were given a far wider range of roles than they would have had in the well-known companies; they were also encouraged to choreograph. But they had to work under very difficult conditions. The culture-shock suffered during the beginning of their time in Cork is a leitmotif in their accounts. It is not surprising that in the articles of the professional dancers critical elements are more frequent than in those of the amateurs. When Miss Moriarty was young ballet schools and companies were run autocratically and she did not adopt modern management techniques when she founded her company. This often led to friction and dissatisfaction among the dancers, many of whom criticise her difficulty in communicating and what they saw as rigidity. However, running such a company on the very limited resources available could probably not have been done without friction even under ideal management; and she won respect from all for the valiant struggle she had put up for ballet. Many of the guest artists marvel at what she achieved on such a small budget and under such difficult conditions.

It is characteristic of Miss Moriarty that, despite the destruction of part of her life's work, she continued working with her amateur company until shortly before her death on 24 January 1992, touring whenever possible to small towns within reach of Cork. Irish National Ballet was disbanded, but Miss Moriarty's legacy was not destroyed. Against all odds, she had managed to secure recognition on the national level for dance and to keep professional ballet in Ireland for over twenty years all told. She made it possible for thousands of young people in the south of Ireland to receive dance training; she supplied a prospect of a professional career in Ireland for the most talented. She also provided a model of selfless service to her community. It is unlikely that anybody in Ireland has done more for dance than she. Carolyn Swift, the *Irish Times* dance critic, wrote in an obituary of Miss Moriarty that the only memorial worthy of her would be the re-establishment of a state-funded ballet company. May the twenty-first century in Ireland not be poorer with regard to dance than was the twentieth.

1: THE BALLET IN CORK

(1) The Amateur and Professional Companies 1947–1985

Aloys Fleischmann

1945 was the centenary of the death of Thomas Davis, the poet of the Young Ireland movement. Having been commissioned by Radio Éireann to write one of the works for a centenary concert, I thought of setting Thomas Davis' poem 'Clare's Dragoons' for baritone solo, mixed choir, orchestra and war pipes. Miss Moriarty agreed to play the war pipes and helped with the ornamentation of the part. The first performance took place in the Capitol Theatre in Dublin and in the Cork City Hall shortly afterwards, where it received a tumultuous reception. Not very long afterwards, she decided that her ballet group were sufficiently advanced to put on a programme of ballet; she asked whether I would conduct the Cork Symphony Orchestra, which had been founded in 1934, for a ballet performance in June of that year. After some hesitation, I agreed. This was the start of a collaboration which was to last a lifetime.

The plan was to give the performance in the Capitol Cinema Theatre in Cork, the manager of which agreed to sponsor the show. But the stage proved to be far too small, and the concrete floor unsuitable for the dancers. The manager then very generously agreed to sponsor the performance in the Opera House. The programme included a solo dance, La Calinda, from the Delius opera *Koanga*, in which Miss Moriarty danced to her own choreography, depicting a slave casting off her bonds – a theme which symbolised what she herself was about to achieve in liberating dance from the shackles of ignorance and prejudice.

Despite the general scepticism that an amateur ballet company could acquit itself creditably in an art form new to Cork, the general consensus in the press was that the performance exceeded even the most optimistic expectations. Mr P. J. Little, Minister for Post and Telegraphs, attended and at the end addressed the audience from the stage. He was reported in *The Irish Press* three days later as saying that the standard was 'astonishingly good'; the local press added that in this he was endorsed by two eminent musicians, the composer E. J. Moeran and the Cork pianist Charles Lynch. Among the chief members of the committee who organised the event was Mrs Jane Dowdall, a close friend of the then Taoiseach, Mr de Valera, who was godfather to her son. She was later to become the first lady

Lord Mayor of Cork, a Senator and member of the Council of State.

Prices in those days at the Cork Opera House in the 1940s ranged from 5/- for the dress circle to 1/6 for the gallery; despite the full house there was a loss of £43, equivalent to about £400 in today's terms. But Mr Patrick Farrell, manager of the Capitol Cinema Theatre, paid the loss. The performance was so successful that it was decided to risk a full week in the following season. So Cork's annual ballet week was born.

It would be difficult to imagine a more formidable task than organising and maintaining a dance company in a country with but little interest in the arts. Up to now the only form of ballet seen in Cork had been the odd interlude in the course of an opera, which was endured with as much patience as possible until the singing started again. Apart from this, ballet proper was regarded as being something dubious if not downright immoral. In 1929 one of the first ballet companies to visit Ireland, an off-shoot of Anna Pavlova's company, had a nightly attendance in the Cork Opera House of a few dozen people, the performances having been denounced from several pulpits, and the unfortunate company had to wire to London for money to take them home. It was this event which prompted Seán Ó Faoláin to write his play *She Had To Do Something*, produced at the Abbey Theatre in 1937.

Recruiting boys for the performance in 1947 had been a struggle. Three had been prevailed upon to take character parts, which could be managed without much training. Even with Miss Moriarty's considerable powers of persuasion, the struggle continued in each successive season. To the young men of Cork, any form of dance other than that of the ballroom was 'sissy', for girls only, and her argument that ballet training leads to increased prowess in sport fell on deaf ears. However, a handful were always secured, often at the last moment, through the good offices of the girls of the company. In the course of the years to follow quite a number of romances blossomed, some leading to marriages.

Miss Moriarty had to work hard to increase the numbers of pupils attending her dance school. One of her students, Lavinia Anderson, aged seven, later to become a solicitor and ballet mistress of the company, was so much in awe of her tall, strict teacher that for five years she never opened her mouth in class, leading Miss Moriarty to ask the mother whether her daughter had a speech defect. Soon the studio became somewhat overcrowded, with about two hundred students coming once or twice a week to a dozen different classes.

During the war years the Cork Orchestral Society was forced to cease activities, though its orchestra continued to give symphony concerts and participated in oratorios. With improved conditions in the post-war years it was decided to revive the society, and in view of the success of the Cork Ballet Group's performance at the Opera House, to combine with the group as a joint venture in 1947. So in December of that year the society and the group co-operated in a production of Milton's masque *Comus*, directed by Alec R. Day, a Cork business man, and his friend Leslie Horne, manager of an insurance company, both of whom had a special love of the theatre. From now on they were to set new standards in Cork for staging and lighting.

In May 1948 *The Cork Examiner* announced that for the first time a local company would give a week of ballet at the Opera House with a full symphony orchestra and choir – about 250 performers in all. Since Miss Moriarty felt that the company was not yet sufficiently developed to tackle one of the major classics, she used her choreographic skills to suit the capabilities of her dancers in five short ballets. Along with extracts from *Nutcracker*, she danced herself in *Valse Triste* (Sibelius) and *Bolero* (Ravel), and in the *Polovtsian Dances* from Borodin's opera *Prince Igor*.

Two works by Irish composers were also presented. *Puck Fair*, written by the Dublin-born composer Elizabeth Maconchy to a libretto by the poet F. R. Higgins, had already been staged by the Dublin Ballet Club at the Gaiety Theatre, with choreography by Cepta Cullen and designs by Mainie Jellett. Re-choreographed by Miss Moriarty, it was a vivid portrayal of the famous fair in Killorglin, Co. Kerry, at which a mountain goat is hoisted on to a platform high above the main street, presiding over three days of revelry of every kind. In this ballet farmers and tinkers are in conflict because a farmer's daughter is found dancing with a character know as the Fiery Tinker. A black-coated gentleman appears, who calls in the guards to arrest the tinker. In the long run the tinker wins out, and as a last defiant gesture prepares to steal the goat.

The second work, with music written by me for the occasion, was *The Golden Bell of Ko*, based on a Chinese legend. The idea came from Marten Cumberland, a writer temporarily living in Cork and an enthusiastic admirer of Miss Moriarty's efforts. He had got the story in China from a Buddhist monk: a tyrannical mandarin commands a local bell-maker to cast a great bell of gold within a certain time, or forfeit his life. The time-limit expires, and the bell has not been cast. To save their father his three daughters cast themselves into the furnace of the bell-foundry; the bell is miraculously cast and to its pealing angelic voices ring out triumphantly.

As so often with elaborate productions of this kind, there was a last-minute hitch. A large church-bell was found locally, pitched to the note D, the tonality of which the whole closing scene was geared. At the second-last rehearsal the bell sounded magnificent, filling the hall with its resonance and almost drowning choir and orchestra. When moved to the Opera House it could not be accommodated in the pit, and was mounted in a box adjoining the stage. On being struck, it emitted not the full tone of the previous rehearsal but a dull thud: it had been dropped and badly cracked in the course of transit to the Opera House. However, a tam-tam made up for the lack of carrying-power, and the ballet succeeded thanks to the exotic choreography, the striking designs and costumes by Marshall and Clare Hutson and the lighting by Leslie Horne. Quidnunc (Seumas Kelly) of *The Irish Times* reported that no similarly ambitious venture had ever been staged in this country, while *The Cork Examiner* commented 'never in history has there been such a show'.

In December of the same year the Cork Ballet Group co-operated with the university and Aeolian choirs and the Cork Symphony Orchestra to put on for the first time in Ireland Henry Purcell's masque *The Fairy Queen*. In addition to those who had organised the previous week of ballet, there was a company of actors headed by Dan Donovan and Lorna Daly. In a humorous description of the masque, Tatler's Leader Page Parade of *The Irish Independent* suggested that Cork had 'mustered for this occasion all its cultural batteries ... So there you have it, acting, song, dance and instrumental music rolled into one, a sign that some brave spirits are keeping the south awake.'

The ballet week of May 1949 included scenes from Ibsen's *Peer Gynt* devised by Leslie Horne to Grieg's music and *William Tell*, with scenario and music derived from Rossini's opera. Members of the company still remember the clever stage trick by which the apple, placed on the head of William Tell's son, was already split in half, and then pulled apart by threads held in the wings when, on the orders of the tyrant Gessler, Tell shoots an arrow at the apple. But at one of the performances, the arrow, instead of speeding into the wings above the boy's head, shot sideways and smashed one of the footlights, to the great amusement of the audience. A letter which appeared subsequently in *The Irish Independent* queried whether anyone could devise a way of bringing the company to Dublin to allow Miss Moriarty's work to be appreciated by a wider audience, 'and (whisper it!) allow perhaps some of our producers to see how a show should be put on.'

The programme of May 1950 included *Hommage à Chopin*, a slightly belated tribute to the composer, whose centenary was celebrated in 1949; *Capriccio Espagnol* to the music of Rimsky-Korsakov; and the first performance of *The Children of Lír*, libretto by Patricia O'Reilly and music by Éamonn Ó Gallchobhair. *The Cork Examiner* reported that this work strengthened the belief that ballet in Ireland has a rich source of material in its folklore. The opening performance was attended by the Taoiseach John A. Costello and his wife, and a reception was held afterwards in the house of the President of the Cork Orchestral Society, Séumas Fitzgerald, who was Chairman of the Cork Harbour Commissioners and a leading figure of the Fianna Fáil party in Cork. A magnificent cake was produced by Mrs Fitzgerald in the shape of a swan, for according to the legend the four children of King Lír had been changed by his second wife into four swans. The cake was cut jointly by the Taoiseach and Miss Moriarty, but the photo which appeared in the press on the following day led to a great deal of acrimony. The bitterness arising out of the civil war was still so ingrained that for a senior Fianna Fáil politician to entertain the leader of Fine Gael in his house was unacceptable to the rank and file of Fianna Fáil, and his generous gesture nearly cost Mr Fitzgerald his membership of the party.

At this time a number of medical students joined the company. They used to bring their text books with them so that they could study during breaks and they took special pleasure in scaring the girls with pictures of deformed babies and lurid illustrations of the results of various diseases. Two of them, Reginald Armitage and Horace Townsend, donated a trophy to be awarded annually to the most promising dancer. A year later Michael MacConaill, the son of the Professor of Anatomy at University College, joined the company. When in May 1951 Miss Moriarty decided that the company was now capable of attempting one of the standard ballets, she chose the second act of *Coppélia* reproducing as far as possible the original choreography of Marius Petipa, with Reginald Armitage as Dr Coppélius, the wizard toy-maker, Patricia O'Gorman and Betty Long alternately as Swanhilda. The dark interior of Dr Coppélius' workshop with its fantastic dolls, designed by Marshall and Clare Hutson, must have been one of the most original stage-pictures ever seen in the Cork Opera House.

The same programme included the first performance of *An Cóitín Dearg* (The Red Petticoat), the scenario and costumes for which were devised by Micheál Mac Liammóir, and the music written by me. The libretto, written in Mac Liammóir's gayest and raciest vein, tells of a Connemara boy and girl who fall in love but are separated by the boy's mother, who wants him to marry a well-to-do crone. Each emigrates to the USA, but they are ultimately reunited in Connemara. The part of the crone was danced by Miss Moriarty and the cast included a comical cow, to which some of the critics took the greatest exception. Whereas the first and third acts were folk-inspired in both dance and music, the music of the second New York act was described by one critic as 'academic jazz'. Summing up the achievements of the Cork Ballet Group to date, Eric Cross, author of *The Tailor and Ansty*, wrote the following letter to *The Cork Examiner* on 27 May 1951:

BALLET IN CORK

> Sir – Ballet Week is an event in the life of Cork of which its citizens should be very proud. For the past four years a group of the young people of Cork have worked with enthusiasm, idealism and no small measure of courage to create this annual event and have thereby established Cork as the artistic capital of Ireland. Ballet is not highbrow – whatever that may mean. It requires no specially-cultivated taste for its enjoyment beyond eyes which can see and ears which can hear and an imagination which can still be caught up and enthralled in the passing wonder of the moment. Ballet is the champagne of all the arts and of entertainment. It is the gayest, most lighthearted and exhilarating of all the products of the theatre. It is an expression of the young of heart, clinging still to the wondering imagination of childhood: recapturing the immediate delight of childhood and renewing the heart again. It has no dull message or sententious propaganda, teaching only, by the way, the wisdom of the moment's joy.
>
> This present ballet week offers samples of almost the entire range of the art of the ballet ... The curtain comes down too soon: on a riotous, rapturous swirling, whirling rhapsody of colour and light and dancing and music and exhilaration of a Hungarian fantasy. The young of heart have done their part.

On the Sunday morning after the final performance, Miss Moriarty, attending mass at the church of SS Peter and Paul, heard the preacher denounce the scandalous scenes at the Cork Opera House where a semi-nude female figure had offended against all normal codes of decency. He was referring, of course, to the tutu worn by Swanhilda, and it took some years before tutus and leotards were no longer regarded as indecent by even a minority of the audience.

Enthusiasts for Cork's ballet week often went to see the programme twice or even thrice and, to encourage this, for the first time in May 1952 there was a variation on alternate nights. In addition to the rest of the programme, there was either *Papillons*, to Schumann's music scored by Seán Ó Riada, who was studying at that time for his degree at the university, or *Scheherazade* – not based on Fokine's ballet, but on the titles which appear at the head of each movement in Rimsky-Korsakov's symphonic suite, including 'Shipwreck on the Rock' as the final climax. Invited to contribute a work for this occasion, the composer Éamonn Ó Gallchobhair produced *The Singer*, based on Pádraic Pearse's play of the same name, which deals with a young poet who hears the cries of the people and is profoundly disturbed. He first writes patriotic songs for them, but in the end throws in his lot with the active combatants in a rising against the occupying power. In this short and dramatic ballet the composer and choreographer achieved an intensity of expression which was heightened in the minds of the audience by its association with the rising of 1916. Pádraic Pearse's sister attended the opening and Miss Moriarty and Éamonn Ó Gallchobhair received an ovation after the closing performance.

Five weeks later the entire company and orchestra embarked on their first venture outside Cork, when they brought the programme to the Savoy Cinema in Limerick for a performance on Sunday 29 June. The cinema had a seating capacity of close to 2,000 and a large orchestral pit: but there was an organ in the centre dividing the pit into two separate sections. However, the stage and lighting facilities were adequate and the big audience enthusiastic. Miss Moriarty remembers on the night prior to the performance the rather eerie experience of ironing the costumes on stage, alone in an empty house, until the dawn broke. This was the first performance of ballet in Limerick; that year there was a three-week season of Mona Inglesby's International Ballet in Dublin, followed by a two-week season in Belfast, which testified to a growing interest in ballet. Among those who attended the Limerick performance were the author Seán Ó Faoláin, who was to become chairman of the Arts Council, and the painter Cecil Salkeld, executive officer of the cultural activities of An Tóstal, a new national venture.

A short time before this the Minister for Industry and Commerce, Seán Lemass, had come to the conclusion that the country was half asleep and to arouse it from its lethargy he conceived the idea of stimulating every city, town and even village to have its own Tóstal, that is its assembly or festival. So the Cork programme for An Tóstal of 1953 consisted of High Mass in the Catholic Cathedral, a military parade through the town, exhibitions, recitals, lectures and sporting fixtures of every kind, and for good measure Handel's *Messiah* with Our Lady's Choral Society and the Hallé Orchestra conducted by Sir John Barbirolli. In the centre came Ballet Week at the Opera House, for which Miss Moriarty had devised *Tableau for An Tóstal* as a salute to what within the next seven years was to become a large-scale Festival of Cork. The tableau was followed by *Suite Symphonique*, based on Tchaikovsky's Serenade for Strings, *Vanity Fair*, a light-hearted ballet to music by Offenbach, and no less than four revivals of earlier works, namely *Puck Fair*, *The Singer*, the *Polovtsian Dances* from *Prince Igor* and *The Golden Bell of Ko*, with *The Singer* and *Puck Fair* on alternate nights.

An amusing mishap occurred in connection with the revival of *The Golden Bell of Ko*. On Friday night the bulb of the lamp suddenly blew which was illuminating the copies of the music for the offstage choir. Knowing their parts well enough by the end of the week, the choir was able to keep going, but the resultant tension in the complete darkness became so great that the pitch gradually rose, until by the final bars the choir was a good semitone sharp to the orchestra. The composer was afterwards complimented by several members of the audience on achieving such a remote and ethereal effect in writing for distant angelic voices! The whole production was subsequently brought as part of Killarney's An Tóstal to the town hall there, where a largely tourist audience headed by some Americans sitting in the front row made loud comments during the performance.

With increasing confidence The Cork Ballet Group now changed its title to The Cork Ballet Company, with Miss Moriarty as artistic director, myself as chairman, and Leslie Horne as manager, all in a voluntary capacity. The company came under the patronage initially of Dame Marie Rambert and Dame Alicia Markova and subsequently of Dame Ninette de Valois. Headquarters were now in Emmet Place, facing the Cork Opera House, for in 1953 Miss Moriarty had moved from her Patrick Street studio to a building which had wardrobe rooms on the ground floor, a large studio on the first floor, and a smaller studio, office and dressing-room facilities on the second floor.

An Tóstal of 1954 was marked by the first Cork International Choral and Folk Dance Festival of which I was at first chairman and ultimately director. For the inauguration of each Choral Festival from now on the Cork Ballet Company formed part of the ceremonial procession into the hall and before the official opening contributed a short dance, often a dramatised version of a subject from Irish folklore, such as *The Planting Stick* or *The Straw Boys*, or an excerpt from a ballet such as *The Seasons* (Glazounov), or *The Dance of the Apprentices* and final chorus from *Die Meistersinger*. Its 1954 programme included as a special contribution to An Tóstal Éamonn Ó Gallchobhair's *Casadh an tSugáin* (The Twisting of the Rope), based on the play by Douglas Hyde, the scholar and president of Ireland, which deals with a vagabond poet who nearly upsets the marriage of a farmer's daughter. The programme was probably the most varied yet presented, with *A la Dégas*, modelled on the famous painting by Dégas of a ballet class at the Paris opera; *The Haunted Inn* to music by Kachaturian; and *Half Moon Street*, a narrow street at the back of the Opera House, which was a skit on the company itself to music by Rossini with the stage as a stage seen from the wings and an imaginary audience to the left, and the artistic director, conductor and leading dancers all guyed. Quidnunc in his Irishman's Diary commented that twelve or fourteen years previously Dubliners could see the occasional ballet production in their city, but that they now had to travel to Belfast (where Patricia Mulholland directed a company based on traditional Irish dance), or to Cork to do so. The actor Jack MacGowran wrote to the *Cork Examiner*:

Dear Sir, – Through the courtesy of your paper, I would like to put on record my appreciation of the great work that Joan Denise Moriarty is doing for the dance in Cork City. It is a pity that her field is so limited, as she is deserving of a wider recognition considering the fact that there has been no tradition of ballet in this country up to now.

As a Dubliner, one felt that somewhere down south an attempt was being made to promote ballet, but without seeing there is no real believing.

I was happy to be part of the audience that saw her latest presentation in the Cork Opera House, wherein she built original choreography around the personalities of her dancers, and used as her themes subjects culled from real life and from reflections.

Such enterprise and genuine feeling would be sadly rewarded if it did not get the chance to expand further. I hope that Dublin will give this lady the opportunity to grow. The material is there. All it needs is support and recognition – Yours faithfully Jack MacGowran, (Dublin Globe Theatre) Opera House Cork, 28 April 1954.

Apart from International Horse Jumping, which took place in Cork for the first time, the most prestigious event of the 1955 An Tóstal was a gala performance of the full three-act *Coppélia* before President and Mrs O'Kelly in the Opera House. The entire house was in evening dress and during the final bars of the ballet the applause was so thunderous that the dancers could not hear the orchestra. Though the president was not in good health, he insisted on coming backstage and addressing the company, saying that their dancing had given his weak old heart a new lease of life. Since Cork audiences at that time felt cheated unless they were entertained until at least 10.30pm, Coppélia was preceded by two short ballets – *Macha Ruadh*, an ancient tale of how a king's daughter overcame her rivals for the throne, set to my music, and *Cameo*, three miniatures to Tchaikovsky's music suggesting the design on a cameo brooch, both ballets choreographed by Miss Moriarty.

At one of the performances during the week an unprecedented calamity arose. The third act of *Coppélia* had been in progress for about five minutes when the lights in the orchestral pit suddenly failed. The orchestra played on for a short time, but one by one the instruments fell silent, until even the leader gave up. The dancers were transfixed on stage, not knowing whether to keep moving or remain still. At last the curtain came down. Realising that the audience in the parterre could not have seen what had happened, I addressed the house, explained that the players were in total darkness and asked for their indulgence until the difficulties were sorted out. After a few minutes the lighting was restored, and the third act was started again. At the end of the performance the Opera House electrician tore down to make the charge that some member of the orchestra had been responsible for disconnecting the current. But years afterwards it transpired that in reaching out from his box he himself had inadvertently pulled the relevant plug out of its socket.

Some members of the company regarded the black-out as a portent, for this was the last ballet performance in Cork's quaint Victorian opera house. Built originally in 1854 as the Athenaeum, a multi-purpose hall with a seating capacity of 2,000, it was re-built in 1875 as the New Theatre Royal and Opera House, soon shortened to Cork Opera House. While rehearsals were proceeding for its 1955 pantomime, the building went on fire and while the dancers of the ballet company watched from the windows of their studio directly opposite, to their consternation and grief it was completely gutted, with only the outer walls left standing. Immediately efforts were made to acquire the site and to raise funds to enable the Opera House to be rebuilt.

In the meantime, undaunted, the company went ahead with plans for its 1956 season, now to be held in the City Hall, as part of the new Festival of Cork. For the first time guest artists from abroad were engaged, namely Domini Callaghan, a member of Mona

Inglesby's International Ballet, and Peter Darrell of Sadler's Wells and also of London's Festival Ballet, later to become the founder of Western Theatre Ballet and later again artistic director of Scottish Ballet. Peter Darrell directed the second act of *Swan Lake*, with Domini Callaghan as Odette and himself as Prince Siegfried. In the same programme Miss Moriarty mounted her first large-scale ballet *The Seal Woman*, to Hamilton Harty's Irish Symphony; it was based on the legend of how a seal adopts a human form and lures a young fisherman to his destruction. The part of the Seal Woman was danced by Cherry Hutson, with decor by Frank Sanquest, and evocative costumes designed by Clare Hutson. The evening was completed with a lively circus ballet, *The Big Top*, to the music of Rossini.

In a press interview Domini Callaghan said that the warmth of the reception by the huge audiences exceeded all expectations and that the company were 'extremely professional'. It was estimated that some 8,000 people attended the performances during the week. Immediately after the Ballet Week, as part of the festival, the Vienna Philharmonic Orchestra under André Cluytens gave a memorable concert in Cork's Savoy Cinema, followed by the Third Cork International Choral and Folk Dance Festival in the City Hall, and then by the first Cork International Film Festival, founded by Dermot Breen, who was also general organiser of An Tóstal.

After the company had taken the City Hall with some trepidation in 1956, it transpired that the hall allowed some three hundred more seats than the Opera House and was acoustically more resonant. The orchestra was seated on a sprung floor below the inset stage and the sight-lines were good from the front half of the parterre. But from the back of the parterre and from the balcony the long distance resulted in a lack of visual intimacy, whereby facial expression was the chief sufferer. However, all staging and lighting difficulties had been overcome, so plans were now laid for 1957, which was to see the first performance in Cork of *Giselle*, the oldest of the classical ballets still in the repertoire. This was directed by Michel de Lutry, the Swiss dancer and choreographer, with his wife Domini Callaghan as Giselle and Miss Moriarty as the Queen of the Wilis. *Giselle* was preceded by *Moy Mell (Magh Meala* – the plain of honey or the happy land), a two-scene ballet in which Miss Moriarty contrasted Irish traditional dance forms, to music by the Dublin composer A. J. Potter, with the new manifestations of jive and crooning to the music of George Gershwin. The programme ended with a rousing performance of *Capriccio Espagnol* (Rimsky-Korsakov).

The first night was attended by Sir Graham Larmor and some

fifty members of the Irish Association for Cultural, Economic and Social Relations, who travelled from Belfast and Dublin as well as by the Minister for Lands, Mr Erskine Childers. A. V. Coton, a well-known English ballet critic who had come to Cork for one of the performances, wrote in *The Daily Telegraph* of *Giselle* that 'within its own terms it was an entirely successful production'; of *Moy Mell* that 'Miss Moriarty was to be highly commended for daring to tackle an up-to-date subject, and doubly so for doing it so neatly'; and of the company as a whole that 'Cork's activities in this non-professional field of ballet are far ahead of all similar efforts anywhere in these islands. No other ballet company within my knowledge has produced a programme of such magnitude, and, within the special conditions, quality.'

Also included in the 1957 Festival were two different programmes given in the City Hall by the Philharmonia Orchestra conducted by Efrem Kurtz, with Louis Kentner as soloist in the first and Yehudi Menuhin in the second concert; the Fourth Cork International Choral and Folk Dance Festival opened by the Minister for Education, Jack Lynch; a celebrity recital by Joan Hammond; a book exhibition opened by Seán Ó Faoláin, and a host of other events. At a press conference in the Gresham Hotel, Dublin, the details of Cork's programme for the 1958 An Tóstal were announced, which included a production of *The Sleeping Princess* by Michel de Lutry, with Domini Callaghan as Aurora, and five other imported professional dancers; the BBC Symphony Orchestra conducted by Rudolf Schwarz and Nina Milkina as soloist, to be broadcast live from Cork by the BBC; Anthony Hopkins' Intimate Opera, and the Choral and Film Festivals. Quidnunc commented that the programme should bring a blush of shame to many a leathery Dublin cheek.

When asked by the opera and ballet expert Norris Davidson whether *The Sleeping Princess* was not too ambitious, Miss Moriarty would not agree and said she knew what they could do. In a recorded interview during one of the performances, Norris Davidson asked how they had ever thought of attempting this difficult work, which had never been staged by an amateur company before. I replied that the answer was the same as when Sir Edmund Hillery was asked why he attempted to climb Mount Everest – because it was there. Despite the initial scepticism, the production was generally regarded as an immense success and a documentary by Norris Davidson, which included scenes from the ballet, excerpts from rehearsals and interviews with both visiting and local dancers, was broadcast by Radio Éireann.

Not content with what had already been achieved, Miss Moriarty now decided to form a folk dance group consisting of members of her company. Six male and six female dancers were chosen together with five musicians, with whom she travelled in August 1958 to the International Folk Dance Festival of Wewelsburg in central Germany. Though the framework consisted of traditional step-dancing, the movements of her group were ballet-based, looser and more vivacious, a development which did not find favour with the followers of orthodox Irish dance. The repertoire included dances based on what was known about early occupational dances, and dances based on local customs such as the Cake Dance and the Fire Dance. Miss Moriarty performed herself in her green kilted costume as the pivot of the group, while the girls wore red skirts with two black bands near the hem and white crochet shawls such as can be seen on the Aran Islands. The men wore hand-knit bawneen jumpers, grey pants and white woollen caps. Sometimes she accompanied the dancing on the war pipes and when there were processions she headed her group playing the pipes, creating a sensation wherever she went.

Already she had received special grants from the Arts Council to bring Patricia Mulholland's Belfast company to Cork and Fr Ahern's Siamsa Tíre group from Tralee. Now in the following October a 'Grand Gala Ballet Recital' by Anton Dolin, Margit Müller, André Prokovsky and Marina Svetlova was held in the City Hall, to which the Cork Ballet Company contributed the folk ballet *Casadh an tSugáin*.

The arts programme of the 1959 Festival of Cork commenced in the Savoy Cinema on Sunday May 10 with the London Symphony Orchestra led by Hugh Maguire and conducted by Sir Malcolm Sargent, and Claudio Arrau playing Brahms' second piano concerto. On the following night in the City Hall, guest artists Marina Svetlova, prima ballerina of the Metropolitan Opera New York, and Kenneth Melville, a principal dancer of Sadler's Wells ballet and London's Festival Ballet, took part in the Cork Ballet Company's programme, consisting of *Les Sylphides*, a repeat of *The Seal Woman*, the *Don Quixote pas de deux*, and *Aegean Caprice*, specially created for the company by Peter Darrell. Stanley Judson, a member of Anna Pavlova's company and later *premier danseur* of Sadler's Wells, was guest producer and choreographer; he reproduced Fokine's *Les Sylphides* and cooperated with Peter Darrell in the choreography of *Aegean Caprice*. Described as the finest ballet performance yet, the stage seemed now set for the fulfilment of Miss Moriarty's dream, the creation of a professional company in Cork.

Realising she had brought her amateur dancers as far as they could go, Miss Moriarty now directed all her energies to mobilising the support necessary for the provision of full-time professional training for a small company which would give performances all through the season and would tour the cities and provincial towns. To this end she invited Stanley Judson, who had partnered Pavlova and Markova, and had considerable experience as ballet master and choreographer in Britain and the USA, to join her as associate director of the projected company. He had been impressed by what he had seen of the company's work during his previous visit and he agreed, saying it would bring back for him the exciting pioneering days of Vic Wells Ballet.

But the first major problem was, of course, finance. The Arts Council was approached and promised to give a grant of £25 for each of the fifty programmes planned for the first season. Representatives of major companies such as The Irish Dunlop Company and The Irish Refining Company pledged support and contributions came in from fourteen further firms, from thirteen life members and thirty-four annual subscribers. Miss Moriarty remembers journeying to Dublin with Senator Mrs Dowdall, now Lord Mayor of Cork, and myself to interview the directors of Arthur Guinness and Co. at their headquarters, where we were entertained to a sumptuous lunch and presented with a cheque for £500. The total funding amounted to about £8,000, equivalent to £80,000 in today's terms, and this seemed adequate to justify a start. It was thought, moreover, that with the advent of television it would be important that a professional ballet company be available for its programmes, and that some additional funding might be secured through its agency.

There were, of course, sceptics who kept on saying that there was no future for ballet in Ireland. Had not Ninette de Valois failed, even with the support of the Abbey Theatre? But the lady whom Quidnunc nicknamed the 'red-haired de Valois of the South' remained undaunted. In the teeth of the Jeremiahs, Irish Theatre Ballet was launched at a press conference in the Studio, Emmet Place Cork, on 16 September 1959, with Senator Mrs Dowdall, Marie Rambert and Alicia Markova as patrons, Miss Moriarty as director, Stanley Judson as associate director, Yannis Metsis of Athens Opera Ballet as ballet master and choreographer, Leslie Horne as manager, Mrs Maeve Coakley as wardrobe mistress, and a board of which a Cork solicitor, James W. O'Donovan, was elected chairman. There were twelve dancers, eight of whom had graduated from the Cork

Ballet Company. The services of Ireland's most renowned pianist, Charles Lynch, were secured for performances, while three other pianists played for rehearsals. The average salary for the dancers was £5 per week, with shoes and costumes supplied. Four of the girls had actually resigned from lucrative positions to join the company. Miss Moriarty, Mrs Coakley and Leslie Horne worked in a purely voluntary capacity.

After three months of intensive rehearsal, the opening performance took place in the Palace Theatre on 14 December 1959. Of the eleven ballets which comprised the repertoire for the season, seven were chosen for the opening, three choreographed by Miss Moriarty – *Súgraí Sráide* (Street Games) inspired by seeing children and teenagers playing on the gallery steps of the old Cork Opera House, to music by T. C. Kelly and E. J. Moeran; *Peter and the Wolf*, to music by Prokofiev; and *Voice in the Wilderness* to music by Bloch – and four choreographed by Stanley Judson – *Springtime in Vienna*, to music by Johann Strauss; *Crown Diamonds* to music by Auger; *Pas de Quatre* to music by Chopin; and the reproduction *La Spectre de la Rose* to music by Weber. *The Cork Examiner* reported that 'Irish Theatre Ballet made its debut before a distinguished audience and scored a remarkable first-night triumph, a triumph for this new company, a triumph for Cork and a red-letter occasion in our cultural history. The young people had an insight beyond their years and there was a freshness and a rapture about the manner in which they presented the various ballets which roused the enthusiasm of so many experienced firstnighters.' In *The Irish Times*, in 'An Irishman's Diary' Quidnunc reported:

> Cork was specially illuminated by a brilliant frosty moon for the debut of ITB. The artificial Christmas illuminations along Patrick Street added to the festive air that the Leeside city assumes so gracefully and gratefully on any occasion of this kind. The sixty-two year old Palace had had a face-lift for the occasion, too, and with its red, pale blue, and gold decor and its new amenities, it looked once more like a real theatre, part Covent Garden in miniature, partly a Baroque and friendly Brighton Pavilion, with Byzantine boxes added. It was a gala night, and the audience lived up to its mood as they chattered in the foyer, watching the distinguished visitors arrive with Marina Svetlova conspicuous among them in magnificent blue mink.

Also present were A. V. Coton representing *The Daily Telegraph*, and W. Bridges Adams, the former Director of the Shakespeare Memorial Theatre in Stratford-upon-Avon. A. V. Coton suggested that the evening represented another cultural march stolen on Dublin, and that it crowned a dozen years of hard pioneering by Miss Moriarty. Among the ballets singled out for praise in *The Cork Examiner* report was her *Sugraí Sráide*, 'this gay, happy lively impression with its overtones of tenderness, which caught the spirit of the city of St Finbarr, and rang as true as footsteps on the pavements of the old city.' Her other ballet, *Voice in the Wilderness* was described in another report by Séumas Kelly (Quidnunc) as 'a torrid Maugham job about three memsahibs, two of whom carry the white man's burden in the teeth of emancipated native temptations, while the third gives up and goes native, in a Van Gogh setting by Patrick Murray'. This was the first appearance on the scene of an artist who was to dominate theatrical design in Ireland for a generation to come. A special ovation was accorded to Charles Lynch for his playing of the Bloch score, and to the cello soloist in it, Gwenda Milbourn, a member of the newly-formed RTE String Quartet. *Springtime in Vienna* was hailed as 'taking us back to a sedate age ... when waltz-time was new, and our ears had not been assaulted by rock'n and roll'; while *Crown Diamonds* was regarded as 'a colourful and witty piece which provided a grand finale to the night.'

After the first battle had been won, the campaign started to tour the company to the various centres already planned. When asked about Dublin at the initial press conference, Miss Moriarty smiled a sphinx-like smile: 'I'll take my time,' she said. 'I've waited fourteen years for this, and I can wait a few more.' To help the launching of the tour she had received generous gifts from the Gulbenkian Foundation – a mini-bus for the dancers and mini-van for the transport of sets, props and costumes. Unlike any union-ruled professional company of today, every member was expected to take on additional tasks. Cyril Daunt, the touring manager, drove the bus; one of the boys drove the van; and everyone helped to set up when arriving at a hall, often for a one-night stand. The boys unpacked the van and assisted in preparing the stage and lighting, while the girls ironed costumes. Before the performance anyone not involved in the early part of the programme would stand by at the box office, act as usher and sell programmes. After the show, if they were not staying overnight, all would make quick work of stripping the stage and loading the van.

Editor's note: Aloys Fleischmann's text[1] breaks off here. Having discovered in the spring of 1992 that he was seriously ill, he had to devote all his energies to finishing his project on Irish folk music, hoping to be able to return to the account of the ballet once the research was over. He died on 21 July 1992, three days after the com-

pletion of his Sources of Irish Folk Music.

In a Memorandum written in December 1971 to the Minister of Finance in Jack Lynch's government making a case for a state-subsidised ballet company, Aloys Fleischmann sums up the work and end of Irish Theatre Ballet as follows:

From 1959 to 1964 the company toured the entire country, giving seasons in Cork, Dublin, Belfast, Limerick, Galway, Waterford, including two tours of Northern Ireland, and annually visiting over seventy towns and villages, most of which had never seen ballet before but gave a most enthusiastic reception to our performances. During this period the company was engaged four times by Radio Telefís Éireann, and twice by Ulster Television. The repertoire consisted of a wide range of ballets, including the classical repertoire, mime dances, modern dance dramas, Irish folk ballets (for two of which music was specially commissioned from the late Seán Ó Riada) and educational programmes for schools. The first ballet master was Stanley Judson, one of the founder members of Vic-Wells Ballet – the predecessor of the Royal Ballet – and a member of the Anna Pavlova Company. Mr Judson remained as ballet master for two years, and was succeeded by the Greek choreographer Yannis Metsis, now ballet-master at the Royal Opera House, Athens. He in turn was succeeded by Geoffrey Davidson, who subsequently became ballet master of Ballet Rambert and is now ballet master of the Gulbenkian Ballet Company of Lisbon. Among the guest artists who appeared with the company were Marina Svetlova (prima ballerina of the Metropolitan Opera New York), Domini Callaghan (Zürich Opera Ballet), Kenneth Melville (London Festival Ballet), Joseph Gavino (New York City Ballet) and the British dancers Belinda Wright and Yelko Yuresha.

The company derived two-thirds of its income from private sponsorship, and received a small Arts Council of Ireland grant. But it became more and more difficult to make ends meet, and late in 1963 to avoid closure, a merger was effected with Patricia Ryan's amateur National Ballet of Dublin: the new company was named Irish National Ballet. This partnership only lasted some months, and as a result of renewed financial difficulties then had to be disbanded.

Editor's note: Most of the dancers emigrated, and joined various continental ballet companies. Norris Davidson gave an account of the beginning of the company in Dance and Dancers *of January 1961; Fay Werner wrote about its end in* The Dancing Times *of June 1964. The work the company did is described below by several former members.*

31

In an article written in 1989[2] after the final decision of the Arts Council not to support Irish National Ballet, Aloys Fleischmann sketched the development of the second professional company as follows:

The Cork Ballet Company in the meantime had continued to flourish. The company toured to Killarney, Clonmel, Limerick, and played for a week in three consecutive years to packed houses in the Gaiety Theatre, Dublin. In 1972 *Swan Lake* evoked such enthusiasm that the then Taoiseach, Mr Jack Lynch, and his finance minister, Mr Colley decided that Ireland should now have a professional company. Although there was a change of government before this decision was implemented, the new government honoured the commitment of its predecessor. So the Irish Ballet Company, later to be named Irish National Ballet, came into being. Miss Moriarty produced a number of Irish ballets, in particular *The Devil to Pay* to music by Seán O Riada, and a full-length ballet based on Synge's *Playboy of the Western World* to music by The Chieftains, which was received with the greatest enthusiasm at the Dublin Theatre Festival in 1978, so much so that the audiences danced in the aisles at the end of each performance. This production was taken by Mr Noel Pearson to the City Center, New York, for a fortnight's run, and later to the Sadler's Wells Theatre in London, which was booked out for the week before the production opened. For her services to ballet here Miss Moriarty was awarded an honorary doctorate by the National University of Ireland on the very day on which her *Playboy* opened in New York.[3]

For the Dublin Theatre Festival of 1981 Miss Moriarty then created a further full-length ballet based on the *Táin*, which with the co-operation of the RTE Concert Orchestra played to full houses for a week in the Gaiety Theatre. Reviewing the festival as a whole the *Irish Times* theatre critic, Dr David Nowlan, stated:

> The Irish production in which form and substance seemed most successfully to reflect and support each other was the Irish Ballet Company's *The Táin*, where Joan Denise Moriarty managed to create a new choreographic 'vocabulary' with which her dancers could express the pagan vitality of this great Irish legend. Here was an Irish company, to an excellent score, moving itself into a marginally new area of expression.

Fernau Hall, in *The Daily Telegraph*, wrote that this work had now established itself as the Irish Ballet Company's finest achievement.

Apart from her Irish folk ballets, Miss Moriarty produced work in a variety of genres, including *Reputations*, the first and only ballet commissioned by RTE, shown several times on TV, and *Diúltú* (Renunciation), commissioned by the government for the Pádraic Pearse Centenary, based on a poem by Pearse, to an imaginative score by John Buckley, and performed at the Abbey Theatre in 1979. In 1985 for a festival in Rennes, designed to celebrate the twinning of this city with Cork, *Playboy* was performed by the Ballet Company and The Chieftains on two nights in the open, before audiences of several thousand.

But all this was not good enough for the Arts Council, which proceeded to dismantle the company, first by bringing in an outside consultant, Mr Peter Brinson, who declared in his report on dance in Ireland that 'a new policy' was needed for Irish National Ballet, without giving any indication as to the direction to which such a policy should lead. Miss Moriarty and most of the board were forced to resign, and for the next two years a new board obeyed every behest of the Arts Council, only to find in 1988 that its subsidy was cut almost without notice. The Taoiseach's office then made a grant available to enable the company to survive until a new Arts Council was appointed, and in Domy Reitei-Soffer's magnificent *Oscar*, a theatrical experience of the highest order was created for audiences in Cork, Dublin and Belfast. The obvious compromise would have been to award a sufficient subsidy which would enable INB to put on a performance as fine as *Oscar* in Cork, Dublin and Belfast say twice a year. This would maintain continuity, even if it meant a new combination of dancers for each occasion, and would cost about half of the grant necessary to maintain a permanent company. [But the Arts Council withdrew its subsidy] ...

In a previously published article I had advocated that the Arts Council would show a more humane image. The new council has now begun its term of office by projecting an image of Baal, and effectively killing professional dance in Ireland for the coming generation. Arts Council subsidised bodies can begin to shiver in their shoes. A mockery has also been made of the original plan to build the Firkin Crane as a home for INB, on which half a million has already been spent, and for which a further half million has just been voted by the European Community.

Perhaps in the course of the third millenium someone will again arise with the creative ability, the dedication and the stamina to awaken a lethargic public to the stimulation and delights of dance as a theatrical art form.

In the meantime, yes, we have disgraced ourselves again.

(2) The Arts Council and Irish National Ballet 1985–1989

Ruth Fleischmann

The Ballet Company was dramatically successful between 1978 and 1981, such a short time after its founding in 1973. In 1983, on the strength of Miss Moriarty's achievements with the *Playboy* and the *Táin*, the government agreed to allow the company to change its name from 'The Irish Ballet Company' to 'Irish National Ballet' – the Arts Council was consulted and agreed to the proposal, the dance officer responding to the query from the Taoiseach's office as follows:

> I am pleased to confirm to you that the Arts Council considers it entirely appropriate that this change in title should be effected, as the council considers this company to be the premier dance company in the country with responsibility for providing performances throughout the country.[4]

Such a level of activity gave rise to high Arts Council expectations; when the company did not sustain its exceptional international touring, dissatisfaction began to set in. The national status accorded to the company led to recriminations from new Dublin dance groups excluded from or given only small council grants.

A journalist noted the irony that the innovative activities of the council in the 1970s had in the 1980s 'generated a momentum which they cannot service and an appetite which they cannot satisfy'.[5] In those years Ireland suffered a serious recession coupled with inflation and soaring unemployment; the European Community insisted on monetary discipline to prepare for the closer union agreed. The council found itself with a smaller budget, many more clients and would-be clients clamouring vociferously for aid, and coming in for harsh criticism no matter what steps it took in these difficult circumstances.

The documents in the Arts Council Irish Ballet Company/Irish National Ballet files show that when in the 1980s difficulties began to arise between the Arts Council and the ballet company, finances were the overriding problem: the high cost of running a touring ballet company. The council was aware that the company's budget was small given its objectives; the company had an accumulated debt to service; there was no prospect that it could become self-supporting as audiences were small, tickets inexpensive and therefore the box office takings modest whereby expenses were considerable. The professional ballet company was indeed a financial problem for the Arts Council, as were the four big theatrical organisations it looked after: the Abbey/Peacock and Gate Theatres, the Dublin Theatre Festival, and the touring Irish Theatre Company. In 1982 the council received four million pounds from the government, but due to inflation that meant a cut of 8% in real terms over the previous year.[6] It therefore removed the grant from three of the four major Dublin theatrical institutions, continuing to support only the Abbey Theatre. That meant the end of the Irish Theatre Company, the only organisation of the four that served audiences outside Dublin.[7] It was an ominous sign for the Cork company.

As well as being worried about the heavy cost of maintaining the ballet company, the Arts Council was dissatisfied with the size of the company's audiences. In 1983 20,000 people paid to see it perform; that meant a subsidy of £16 per head.[8] The ballet company board argued that building audiences inevitably took time and that it had an extensive schools programme designed to arouse interest among the young, and was thus undertaking long-term audience creation. That year a national public opinion inquiry commissioned by the council showed very low public participation in the arts generally – of the people questioned, 21% had attended a traditional music concert during the previous year, 20% a play, 9% a classical concert, 8% had visited an exhibition, 5% had attended a ballet performance.[9] Given that ballet was such a recent arrival on the artistic scene in Ireland that nobody had thought of including dance in the Arts Act of 1973, the fact that the ballet company attracted an audience of 20,000 per annum at the end of the first decade could have been seen as something of an achievement.

From 1980 the board of the ballet company begins to appear as a problem in Arts Council files. One of the main objections raised by the council was the preponderance of Cork members: in 1980 there were only two outsiders among the nine. The dance officer in that year criticised what he called a 'woolliness' of the board of Irish National Ballet concerning administrative and financial matters.[10] An occasional memo shows irritation with the board: meetings tended to be lengthy, and they were held in the evenings. This meant that the Dublin members had to stay overnight, which one of the dance officers told me he had found tiresome.

Miss Moriarty's sometimes strained relations with the dancers were a further problem. The council was critical of communication structures: the first dance officer told me he thought Miss Moriarty directed the company like 'a Victorian boarding school'. The Dublin

35

board member Loretta Keating, who has a high regard for Miss Moriarty, writes that on the whole 'there was not a great rapport between Miss Moriarty and the dancers', that she tended to be dismissive of their worries and grievances. Loretta Keating, having the dancers' confidence, saw her role as mediating on their behalf. She says the Cork board members welcomed this.[11]

Before the Brinson Report, the question of the company's artistic policy does not figure as a problem in the council's files: in 1980 the dance officer praised the 'high level of artistic input to board discussions' at Irish National Ballet meetings, and noted that Miss Moriarty and Pat Murray had the 'breadth of vision' which directors of such a company required.[12] At an Arts Council meeting with the board of the company in June 1982, the chairman Dr James White said the council 'had the highest opinion of the work of the Irish Ballet Company', and that it was 'anxious to promote it in every way'.[13] But as competition for funding grew fiercer during the 1980s, the council came under great pressure to justify its expenditure. It adhered to new cultural theories and its empathy with a classical company operating along more or less traditional lines began to wane. The first dance officer said to me that he came to regard Miss Moriarty as being inflexible and unwilling to discuss policies. His successor told me the council expected new policies, which were not forthcoming, and that the board had 'no culture of self-criticism'. As we shall see, the council's prime interest lay in contemporary and community dance, which were not central concerns of the ballet company.

In 1984 the Arts Council commissioned Peter Brinson to write a report on dance in Ireland. The council had been sharply criticised by Dublin companies for supporting Irish National Ballet to the detriment of others without being competent to judge the quality of the major client. Arthur Lappin was the council's first dance officer, but his competence lay in the field of drama, and he had to acquire a knowledge of dance after his appointment. The second dance officer, Martin Drury, was an expert on education, both men having done outstanding work in their respective fields. Naturally, in selecting an outside authority for the report on dance, the council chose somebody with whom there had been a long association, whose views it knew and shared, and who had had a decisive influence in forming its views on the arts.[14] It chose somebody who had moved away from classical ballet, and whose professional and personal interest was centred on promoting community dance, contemporary dance, and dance in education.

Peter Brinson (1923–1995) was an English academic who developed interest in ballet far too late to become a dancer, but who became a distinguished theorist of dance. He set up the famous 'Ballet for All' movement in 1964 for the Royal Academy of Dancing, which until 1979 toured England with a small group of young Royal Academy graduates introducing, illustrating and explaining the classical ballets to new audiences in small places. He wrote extensively on the history of dance and made a most persuasive case for giving dance and the other arts a full place in education. In 1968 he became head of the Royal Academy of Dancing. He planned dramatic innovations within the dance profession and embarked on a large-scale building programme; by the following year Brinson and the Academy had parted company, the latter now close to bankruptcy due to what its president Margot Fonteyn called the 'folly' of the ambitious expansion plans.[15] In 1972 he became director of the British Gulbenkian Foundation, achieving much improvement in the status of the arts in British education. In 1982 he became director of research and community development at the Laban Centre for Movement and Dance, a centre for contemporary dance training. He had had links with the Dublin dance world since 1969.[16]

Brinson's report *The Dancer and the Dance: Developing Theatre Dance in Ireland* was published in May 1985. He had examined the three main dance companies in the country as well as half a dozen community arts dance groups, and made recommendations concerning all of them. A draft of his report was sent in late March for comment to the groups concerned, but the Cork company (and presumably the other groups too) had barely a week in which to study and respond to it; there was never any discussion of the draft with Brinson, and before publication none with the council.

Brinson diagnosed the main problem facing dance in Ireland as government underfunding, the Arts Council's total grant amounting to a mere 0.037% of gross national product – one of the lowest arts fundings of Europe. He underlined the urgency of promoting dance in primary and secondary education. He proposed that the grant to Dublin City Ballet be stopped, that to Dublin Contemporary Dance Theatre increased. He advocated that Irish National Ballet be maintained, but its grant cut because of the need to distribute more equitably the small amount of money available for dance, and that the company be reorganised so as to survive under the new circumstances. He said it was his most important single recommendation that a national school of dance be established in Ireland, and he commended Miss Moriarty for having proposed one to the Arts Council in 1979 and in 1981 – in both cases, though the council welcomed the idea, it had been unable to provide funding.

He paid tribute to Miss Moriarty's dedicated work for dance, but was critical of the manner in which Irish National Ballet was being run, and stated that the artistic policies pursued were a prime cause of the company's problems. He recommended that a successor be sought at once for Miss Moriarty, indicating that she had mentioned retirement. Wherein the deficiencies of the artistic policies lay, he did not specify. He made no concrete suggestions with regard to the direction the company should take in the future. Irish National Ballet was a classical company whose repertory contained many modern works as well as Irish folk ballets. Brinson's proposals about the type of dance the company should be doing were couched in the most general terms: he said that 'a new repertory appropriate to a smaller company' was needed, and that it should be

... in line with current artistic development in theatre dance to produce new product for marketing which emphasises its national status.[17]

This seems to indicate that he believed the choreographers who had worked for the company up to then were not producing suitable 'product' for marketing. If he felt that the choreography of Toni Beck, Hans Brenaa, Nils Christe, Charles Czarny, Peter Darrell, John Gilpin, Michel de Lutry, Royston Maldoom, Domy Reiter-Soffer was wrong for the company, he did not say why. He welcomed a proposal in the company's five-year plan (drawn up the previous year) announcing that it would invite internationally known choreographers to create works for the company; but he did not say what it was about their work which would be different and would make a more suitable 'product for marketing'.

Though commercial considerations cannot be foreign to dance-company management, a dance consultant can be expected to present sound artistic reasons for his views, and the public body acting on his recommendations must be accountable for them. If the analysis on which the decision is taken is not made public, its validity cannot be tested. The Arts Council had been attacked for giving large grants without being competent to judge the worthiness of the company aided. With Brinson it had an outside critic, but it expected its clients and the public to accept his judgement without knowing how and why he came to it. The lack of concrete criticism and of concrete proposals was pointed out by the board of Irish National Ballet in all its responses to the report. It could have added that the council had not made itself accountable, as the grounds for its decisions were not transparent – it had merely shifted the responsibility for them away from itself. Brinson's analyses of Irish National Ballet and the other groups were not made public at the time: the material concerning the Cork company is not in the council's Irish National Ballet files, nor among Brinson's papers in the Laban Centre in London, nor is it in the files of the Gulbenkian Foundation, which contributed towards the cost of Brinson's Report.[18]

The Brinson Report seemed to demand the impossible of Irish National Ballet in financial terms. Its grant was to be cut substantially,[19] yet more touring was expected, more visits to Dublin with its high theatre rentals, and new works commissioned from internationally-known choreographers. The large sums which the company would have required for such increased activity it was told to procure from the private sector through vigorous fundraising – as though that could be a realistic possibility with the country in recession, having a weak indigenous manufacturing base at the best of times, and no tradition of sponsorship from industry for any of the arts, not to mind for the newest arrival, against which there was still much prejudice. At this time, such sponsorship as was available was already being sought by the Trust Fund for the rebuilding of the Firkin Crane, planned as the company's home. This led the board of Irish National Ballet to ask the council:

> The ultimate question remains: does the Arts Council of Ireland want a National Ballet Company?[20]

The board feared that the council was preparing for the closure of the company by laying down unfulfillable conditions, for non-compliance with which the Cork board could then be blamed, and funding for Irish National Ballet stopped.

Brinson had no brief from the Arts Council to make recommendations about the location of Irish National Ballet. However, the question does play a role in his report. Brinson notes that many of the people he spoke to regarded the company as regional rather than national, since it was based in Cork. It does not seem to have occurred to him to question such attitudes. It is true that many people living in the capital regard only the institutions situated there as being national in character; this could, however, be seen as an unfortunate result of the damaging centralism found in most former colonies. It is a tendency also found in other parts of Europe, and one that the European Union is seeking to redress through its regional policies, particularly in the field of culture, albeit none too successfully.

It is clear from the little Brinson says on the subject that he was in favour of locating the company in Dublin. He describes the touring allowance which had to be paid to each dancer whenever the company performed more than sixty miles away from Cork as being a 'major constraint on touring'. Yet this would also apply to performances given outside Dublin, were a company based there still to feel obliged to serve the four provinces. The main argument in favour of a Dublin location is not that it would have given a better base for touring, but that the largest audience in the country lived there.

The Arts Council was officially committed to an arts policy of regional development. The imbalance between the aid given to the capital and the rest of the country had been greatly reduced; nonetheless, in 1983 57% of all council grants still went to Dublin.[21] At a meeting in December 1984 the director assured the ballet company that the council 'had no reservations about the National Ballet being based in Cork'.[22] However, one year later, on the eve of the Brinson Report, the dance officer told the board that while there was no 'philosophical objection' to the company being based in Cork, there would be many practical advantages if it were in Dublin.[23] Arthur Lappin, who regretted the cessation of funding to Irish National Ballet and had publicly protested against it, told me that he found it hard to forgive Miss Moriarty for having refused to move to Dublin, as if she had consented, the company might have been saved.

THE ARTS COUNCIL'S UNACCEPTABLE TREATMENT OF MISS MORIARTY

In 1985 Miss Moriarty was probably well over 70, and she was not in good health. The Arts Council felt she was overtaxed: it wanted somebody in charge of the ballet company with the appropriate professional background, better managerial skills and rapport with the dancers, and who was more familiar with the international dance scene. It was critical of the fact that she had not found a successor: how difficult a task that was it was to discover after she had gone. Miss Moriarty had tried;[24] she needed somebody of fine professional quality, somebody who would be prepared to put up with difficult conditions, and to fight every inch of the way against apathy, ignorance, envy and officialdom to maintain the company. There were not many Irish people at the time qualified or willing to take on such a task, and even fewer outsiders.

For every founder figure the time comes when they must go. It is often very difficult for them to see this; it was so for Miss Moriarty in particular with no obvious successor in sight, with the future of the company uncertain, and the grave doubts she had about the intentions of the council.[25] The council may well have been right in thinking that the time had come for a change at the top, that the company had become such a big concern (thanks to Miss Moriarty's efforts), that it was now beyond her strength, and that new directions, improvement and innovation were needed. However, even if that were so, the Arts Council was not entitled to treat her as it did: the manner in which she was removed was unjustifiable.

Muriel Large, the company's administrator, told me that the council had on many occasions from 1984 on indicated to the board of the ballet company that it wanted change at the top. But Loretta Keating, who was the Dublin member of the company board since 1980, was unaware of any such dissatisfaction until Brinson told her of it in 1985 – so the officers cannot have spoken out at board meetings. Miss Moriarty did not respond to the council's signals; she did not accept the dance officers as competent judges of dance. As she did not go of her own accord, she was forced out in a most hurtful manner.

The board of the Cork company had in March seen the criticism of her made in the draft of the Brinson Report; they had protested about it in their April submission to the Arts Council; they did not know what changes would be made for the final version of the Report. Three weeks before its publication, *The Sunday Press* of 5 May 1985 published an account of it under the heading 'Final Curtain for Joan Denise?' The council was not responsible for the premature leak (the council files also show that Aloys Fleischmann accepted this); but Brinson's criticism of Miss Moriarty and his view that she would have to go was contained in the report published by the council shortly afterwards on 29 May. The dance officer told me that because it was difficult to get through to the board on the issue of Miss Moriarty's replacement 'the message had to be very strong and very terse'. The 'message', delivered publicly through the published report, was that Miss Moriarty's artistic policies were the company's main problem and that she would have to retire. The dance officer told me he was 'surprised at the level of sensitivity to criticism'. What he describes as 'criticism' was in fact a public humiliation of the founder of professional ballet in Ireland though, no doubt, this will not have been intended. The judgement and sentence were announced publicly, but the trial had taken place *in camera* and the evidence has never been disclosed.

For all the interest the council took in theories of culture, it does not seem to have reflected very much on its complicated role as patron-officials of the arts. It dispensed taxpayers' money to artists, as did the aristocratic patrons of musicians, painters and writers up to the eighteenth century; like them, the officers were not themselves always experts, nor accountable to those they supported. Unlike the patrons of the old days, they owed their interesting positions to their clients, to those dedicated practitioners who created the work capable of receiving Arts Council funding. That alone would demand an attitude of courtesy and respect towards those given grants and a deep-seated awareness that the council is there to serve those working in the arts, just as the latter are servants of their communities.

Furthermore, even if the Arts Council had reached new frontiers in cultural theory, had re-defined art and its function and had worked out new means of bringing larger groups of people to participate actively in the arts, it must have realised that it was those people of the older generation involved in pioneer work who had laid the foundations for this new departure, people who had spent their lives seeking to bring the arts, which they regarded as being among the most valuable of human experience, within the reach of people hitherto deprived of access. This is a fundamentally egalitarian approach and if the council had widened that perspective, surely it could have seen how very recent the new insights of the organisation were, and how much it owed to those of the previous generation on whose shoulders it stood if indeed it did see so much farther.

If the council was right that a new management was essential for the ballet company, it should have been able to persuade the board of the validity of this viewpoint. The council owed it to the board to have presented it with the detailed analysis of the company's shortcomings which it obviously had, and to have worked out with the company an outline of the policies expected. On that basis, it could have convinced Miss Moriarty of its competence to judge, and got her to retire, while paying her due public tribute.

The published Brinson Report should not have contained the negative passages on Miss Moriarty and should not have been made public until the findings had been extensively discussed with those concerned.[26] Outwardly the council appeared to have handed over the responsibility for its decisions to Brinson, but it was the council that decided on the draft of the report, on exactly what was to be published and what not. The scanty correspondence available between Brinson and one of the officers shows this clearly.[27]

By the 1980s the Arts Council was still not accountable to its clients or to the public. In 1987 a White Paper on the government's general cultural policies was published, outlining the overall direction;[28] but the Arts Council had not publicly established its policy towards the various arts through a similar process of democratic consultation and consensus as that leading to the White Paper. Furthermore the Arts Council had not discussed with its clients how an organisation receiving grants should be assessed or evaluated: there were no agreed procedures. The inquiry into dance over which Brinson presided was not transparent: his report presents no analysis of Irish National Ballet's shortcomings; it simply proclaims that policy was wrong.[29] The Arts Council never outlined either publicly or at board meetings what policy it expected the company to adopt. When specifically asked to do so by Aloys Fleischmann at a meeting on 20 May 1985, the dance officer responded that it was not the council's business to lay down policy for the company.[30] Yet the council reserved the right to act as judge of what was correct policy and what not, whereby its own views and criteria were thus exempt from public scrutiny and debate. The council may have believed that in withholding the nature of its criticism it was protecting the reputations of those criticised.[31] It does not seem to have seen that such discretion perhaps protected itself more. Irish National Ballet was thus put in a situation resembling Kafka's novel *The Trial*, in which the accused is not told what the charge is that has been brought against him, nor made acquainted with the law under which he is being charged, nor is he allowed to discover the reasoning on which the judgement is based.

The End of Irish National Ballet

Anneli Vourenjuuri Robinson, a Finnish dancer and choreographer, became artistic director; she had all the qualifications on paper that institutions such as the Arts Council have so much faith in. However, her two-year contract was not renewed – though she was an excellent teacher, the board seemed surprised that she did not have the drive they deemed necessary and were used to from Miss Moriarty. There was now a new board consisting of several business people, many non-Cork members, and Colm Ó Briain of Dublin, who had been director of the Arts Council, and who now became deeply involved in seeking to make the company successful. Radical measures were taken to get rid of the debt within three years; the council agreed that the company would work an eight-month year for two years, the money saved being used to repay the overdraft. The board believed its three-year plan had been accepted by the council, and that it had the council's support and goodwill in its efforts to implement the Brinson recommendations.

However, although the council was willing to give the company a chance, it continued to harbour grave doubts about the likelihood of success and had retained an option to review its position. In March 1988 it used that option, stopping the grant after the first year of the agreed three-year period. The factors which the council saw as justifying that decision were as follows:[32]

First: the issue of cost was crucial. The problem in the council's view was that, although the subsidy the company received was minimal given what it had set itself to accomplish, that subsidy constituted a disproportionate amount of the organisation's dance budget. The council continued to pursue the unrealistic solution of expecting the company to finance a substantial proportion of its costs itself. The new board had aimed at raising £100,000 per annum; the council complained in 1988 that there had been 'almost total failure to raise significant sponsorship funds' from the private sector.[33] What disappears from view in the discussions about Irish National Ballet receiving 80% of dance funding is the inequitable distribution of the council's budget as a whole among dance, drama, music and the visual arts.[34] In 1985 dance received a mere 7.6%; in 1988 the dance budget was halved. A more balanced distribution of resources among the art forms had never been an option: none of the arts had adequate funding; none of the institutions would have been prepared to relinquish any part of what they had in favour of the newest arrival on the scene, the Cinderella of them all: dance. The Arts Council's foremost argument against the ballet company, then, was that it cost too much, and that its external finances had not improved.

Second: that the company had not succeeded in attracting greater numbers of customers; that in 1987 audiences had not been increased beyond the level of the previous year, amounting to a total of 18,500. The council excluded the Cork pantomime audiences from the calculation, presumably because those people had not planned to see ballet but did so involuntarily. However, it could well be argued that introducing around 50,000 pantomime lovers to ballet is effective public relations work.[35] The council furthermore discounted over half of the company's 1987 audiences because they were not adults. That had an impact on the box-office returns as children's tickets are half-price, but it is astonishing to see the fact that the company had succeeded in attracting a young audience of over 10,000 children put on the negative balance sheet for financial considerations.[36]

44

Also excluded from the reckoning were those who attended performances during the company's tour in Northern Ireland, as the tour was financed by the Arts Council of Northern Ireland. But the company's northern tours had a very special social and political dimension. They had begun in the early 1960s before the Troubles, when in the Republic there was virtually no interest in the north; they continued in the dark days of the 1970s after the collapse of the Sunningdale Agreement, when bridge-building operations undertaken from the south were rare events. Desmond Rushe of the *Irish Independent* received a letter from six loyalists after he had written up a visit to Coleraine by the ballet company in 1978. They confirm his positive report:

> We want to endorse what you wrote about the visit to Coleraine and other places in Ulster by the ballet dancers from Cork. As you said, they danced their way into our hearts, and they would have danced their way into all our homes had time permitted. We would have welcomed a longer stay and a change of programme. ... We are moderate loyalists who will have nothing to do with extremists of any kind and who want to live in harmony with people in the south and with those here who differ from us in politics and religion. As you wrote, cultural activity is a very effective way of helping all of us to do this and we sincerely hope that there will be much more cross-border activity in the future.[37]

The council will surely have appreciated as much as these loyalists the potential healing function of the arts in a divided community. Though the council was technically quite justified in excluding the northern figures from the audience reckoning, this and the exclusion of the children illustrate how limited the purely commercial calculation is in assessing the benefit of the company to the community.

Third: the council had doubts about the suitability of the proposed artistic directors of the company. In 1988 the artistic director, the administrator and the ballet master were about to leave. Muriel Large, who had administered the company most efficiently since its founding, was not only an expert in the field of ballet, but had extensive contacts with dancers, teachers and choreographers all over the world, and had given invaluable service to Miss Moriarty and the original board as well as to its successor. Everybody realised she would be very difficult to replace. The Finnish artistic director, who was not being invited to continue, was to be replaced by Patrick Murray, the Cork designer; he did not have the professional dance background which the council felt was needed. He was to be assisted by the choreographer Domy Reiter-Soffer; but, when making the grant application in February to the council, the company could offer no definite proposals about how this was to be organised, a difficult undertaking given Reiter-Soffer's many international commitments. This was a most unsatisfactory situation in the council's eyes. Furthermore, the company had departed (albeit with grudging council consent) from the plans previously submitted for 1988/9: the proposed three weeks of performances with the Dublin Grand Opera Society had fallen through and were to be replaced by three weeks of dance during the pantomime in Cork: a proposed week at the Belfast Festival had not materialised (in both cases for financial reasons) and instead there was to be an extra week's work in schools.

So far the Arts Council's view of the problems of Irish National Ballet is similar to that of the early 1980s during Miss Moriarty's directorship: the company was seen as being too costly, as not paying its way sufficiently via sponsorship, audiences were not increasing, the board was not deemed satisfactory. But for the first time in March 1988, and then again in February 1989 when the Arts Council had to reconsider the issue of funding for Irish National Ballet after the Taoiseach's special grant had come to an end, it added a further reason to justify its decision not to support the company – namely 'poor quality'.

Fourth: in 1988 Irish National Ballet's standards were for the first time said to be inadequate. In the official public statement of February 1989 announcing that a grant would not be forthcoming, the council claimed that it could not countenance the spending of large sums of public money on 'poor quality dance'. This statement was regarded by supporters of Irish National Ballet as offensive and unjustified: it gave rise to intense hurt and indignation. Brinson, the external expert, had said no such thing in any of his public statements. Who in the Arts Council had the competence to make such judgements, what criteria they were following, what comparisons they were making was not divulged. The *Irish Times* dance critic, Carolyn Swift, argued on an RTE broadcast that the company measured up to international standards. The Arts Council dance officer offered no substantive arguments, merely saying that she was entitled to her opinion but that the Arts Council thought differently.

Colm Ó Briain told me that standards had never been an issue raised by the dance officers at board meetings; Loretta Keating confirmed this to me. I have seen no documents in the council's files containing criticism of dance standards, but several praising them. In 1982 the director sent an account to the dance officer of a matinée he had seen in the company of his children. Though the report is not without criticism of didactic aspects of the show, the director said his children 'thoroughly enjoyed it'; he ends:

> ... I hope this is the sort of show for children which the Irish Ballet Company put on during their regular season throughout the country. It's undoubtedly a success.[38]

In 1984 when the council's financial problems had become most pressing, an undated memo entitled 'Thoughts' was sent to the dance officer. It puts the question whether – given the high cost, small audiences, and the council's 'misgivings ... with regard to the Board structure and to standards' it might not make financial sense to close Irish National Ballet and instead bring an international company to Ireland for some weeks every year. In his reply, the dance officer rejected what was said in the memo about unsatisfactory standards. He wrote that he felt it would be a

> ... most regressive step at this stage to consider such radical thoughts. By the way the question of standards in performance I believe does not arise – standards are generally very good.[39]

The dance officer (who took over in 1985) wrote to Peter Brinson in 1987 on the subject of the ballet company: 'I must say I have not seen them dancing as well for a long time. I keep my fingers firmly crossed that it was no fluke but in fact the beginning of a new phase in that company's development.'[40]

The theatre officer Phelim Donlon took the trouble to record his positive view of the company. In August 1985 (some months after the Brinson Report) he attended the last performance of Irish National Ballet under Miss Moriarty's directorship, and wrote of it as follows to the director of the Arts Council:

> I found the programme extremely satisfactory and enjoyable, and it was very well received by an audience of about 60% of the capacity of the Everyman.
>
> [It showed] a wide range of the work and the potentiality of the Company, and it represented for me at any rate the best programme of dance by any Irish company that I have seen to date this year ...
>
> I was extremely interested to see the mix of the audience, which ranged from very young boys and girls to middle-aged people, although it was noticeable that there were not many people of the 20 to 30 age group in the audience. I was also very impressed to see that the range of admission prices was a top of £3, and £1 for senior citizens, for

students and the unemployed. These prices obtained for all performances and represented, to my way of thinking at any rate, the ideal sort of price range for a national company which is in receipt of substantial grant aid.

... The third item was a new ballet by Charles Czarny entitled 'Dreamscapes'. This is a particularly innovative and quite contemporary ballet, and it certainly demonstrates the ability of members of the company to dance in the modern and contemporary idiom to great effect. The standard of dancing demonstrated in this particular item seemed to me to be fully up to anything which a company such as the Dublin Contemporary Dance might legitimately aspire to in this particular idiom.

[The account praises *Enchanté Piaff* by Jonathan Burnett, and the dancer Carol Bryans.] The programme ended with the performance of *Sunny Day* by Charles Czarny based on country and western themes and danced by the entire company. This item is gay and humorous and has the effect of rounding off the programme on a very high up-note and sending the audience home in good mood. ... All in all an excellent evening's dance, a wide-ranging programme and extremely entertaining."[41]

Foreign critics who came to Ireland to see the company dance had generally made very favourable comments on the standards, and the company won an award at the Belfast Festival for its last work, Domy Reiter-Soffer's *Oscar*.

In a letter of 13 April 1988 to the director of the Ballet Company, the Arts Council modified its statement somewhat about the quality of dance being inadequate, now stating that when it spoke of quality it was not merely referring 'to dance performance but to the overall performance of the company as an arts organisation', including audience figures. That was, of course, a rather different matter. Yet the council produced the unqualified statement in 1989 that the company was to be refused funding because of 'poor-quality dance'. The council members who stood over that statement can only have been making unrealistic comparisons, expecting for their money a company such as the Kirov or the Bolshoi, both of which had recently visited Dublin.

An article appeared in the *Cork Examiner* of 25 August 1989 illustrating the false expectations to which the experience of perfect performance could lead, the writer comparing Irish National Ballet dancers unfavourably with the Bolshoi. Aloys Fleischmann wrote to the editor arguing that such a comparison was utterly inappropriate:

To compare this body, with a tradition of over two hundred years, supported by and recruited from a population of several hundred million, costing annually between ten and fifteen million pounds to a fourteen-year old company from our own small population, which had been trying to survive on what would be regarded as a pittance by even the smallest dance company abroad, is much like trying to compare the cities of Moscow or London with Cork.[42]

Both the dance officer and Peter Brinson wrote in their correspondence of 'mediocrity' in connection with Irish National Ballet. It may well be that in 1989 the members of the newly appointed council felt that for such a large proportion of the dance budget they were prepared to settle for nothing less than the best – and what that was they now knew.

In addition to the fourth point about the 'poor quality' of Irish National Ballet there was a fifth issue: Irish National Ballet's artistic policy was not deemed acceptable. This objection had also been raised during the last two years of Miss Moriarty's directorship. The artistic concept submitted by the company board to the council for 1988/9 (together with the programme of performances and tours) was a non-committal two-page sketch of current developments in choreography which showed little trace of the sort of theoretical reflection that Brinson had introduced into the Dublin dance scene; it indicated that those people in Cork who were up to their eyes in practical work for the art of dance had relatively little interest in elaborating theoretical justification for what they were doing, the value of which, they will probably have felt, was self-evident. The council did not express reservations about the dance programmes which the company was proposing, but found the conceptual rationale inadequate.

As we have seen, the council was reticent in giving public expression to its own policies. There are indications, however, that even the most brilliantly formulated case for the Cork company might have had little chance of being accepted by the council, as it may have disapproved of the whole concept of such a company. Two years after the dance officer had left the Arts Council, Martin Drury read a paper to the Thomond College of Education in Limerick, whose community dance and dance-in-education projects the council strongly supported. Having spoken sharply about the failure of the 'dance community' to take an interest in educational issues, he said:

... what was offered by way of public education and most particularly by performances for schools smacked of cultural imperialism: the bringing to small towns and to small people the art of the metropolis, and the reinforcement of the cultural relationship whereby art is special, exclusive, occasional and to be looked at rather than participated in.[43]

Martin Drury's opinion that a performing company which brings the art-form of dance to small towns and schools comes close to practising 'cultural imperialism' was not expressed while he was dance officer of the council; but if this statement reflects the council's thinking during his time of office, it is no wonder that nobody in Cork could come up with a dance policy which met with its approval.

How could it be a form of cultural imperialism for, let us say, a touring theatre company to bring O'Casey's play about life in the Dublin slums, *Juno and the Paycock*, or Samuel Beckett's *Waiting for Godot* to a small town in Mayo? There have always been waves of cultural interaction between the country and the city moving in both directions: for example, much of what we usually regard as authentic Irish folk music did not originate in rural areas but in the courts of Europe, trickling down through the big houses of the ascendancy into the Irish countryside, where it became assimilated. The jigs, reels and laments returned into academic music when Irish composers began to use elements of folk music in their works. A similar interchange can be traced with the folk dances which Miss Moriarty used in her Irish ballets. A large number of the literary masterpieces of the Irish revival owe both their themes and distinctive form to the culture of the Irish countryside. How could it be patronising and arrogant to acquaint people in rural Ireland through touring companies with art deriving from their own culture?

According to Martin Drury, the wrong type of culture is that where art is regarded as something 'special, exclusive and occasional.' Plays such as O'Casey's *Juno*, or Synge's *Riders to the Sea* are indeed 'special'; they are among those miracles that only great artists can achieve of conjuring up for the audience a way of life not our own and yet having us recognise ourselves in it and seeing ourselves all the better for the difference. Is that poem not 'special' which in a few apparently simple lines recreates for us our own experience, the significance of which had not been clear to us or within our powers of expression? A well-choreographed ballet is also 'special', requiring for its creation a sense of form, of movement and performance abilities most of us do not have. Why should the benefit, the pleasure and the stimulation of experiencing something really 'special' be reserved for people living in the small cities of Ireland?

Peter Brinson set up his 'Ballet for All' in order to introduce the classics to people living in areas remote from British theatres, in order to make ballet accessible, to remove its 'exclusiveness'. When Miss Moriarty began her work for dance, ballet was not an art in the 'metropolis' of Cork or in Limerick (nor indeed in Dublin) until, through her efforts, it was made known to a section of the people there and came to be accepted by them. All the touring companies of Ireland aimed at removing the 'exclusiveness' of the theatre, dance and opera, whose unique value is that though many of the greatest works originated in exclusive circles, they speak to all who listen to them. Is it not ironic that the three touring companies whose object was to bring treasures of the European heritage to people hitherto deprived of personal experience of them were disbanded in the name of popular and community art?

In addition to diagnosing the type of art offered in the dance performances of the touring company as 'smacking of cultural imperialism' because its dance was 'special and exclusive', Martin Drury claims that what was offered was objectionable because it did not allow of participation, limiting the addressees to mere watching. He does not only contrast the two aspects, attributing greater weight to the participatory form; he condemns the performing art as damaging, as one establishing domination. The setting up of such exclusive alternatives would seem unwarranted. Are these two aspects not linked and mutually supportive? Is it not in many cases the experience of virtuoso performance which stimulates participation? Anew McMaster brought Shakespeare's dramas to the small towns of Ireland: did not many of the hundreds of amateur drama groups that sprang up all over the country from the 1940s owe their existence to his inspiration? Is it not arbitrary and undialectical to set up such a rigid opposition between art in which untrained addressees participate and art performed with virtuosity?

In his report, Brinson describes ways of community participation in dance which had formed part and parcel of Miss Moriarty's work for dance in Munster for fifty years: she had spent her life doing much of what he heralds as a new development. In the introduction to the section of his report on 'Dance in the Regions and Community Dance' he states:

> Only when local people and their children can participate, and feel that they are participating in local dance activity whether by attending a class at a village hall or by preparing costumes for a community dance production, will dance become really meaningful to them. Even fol-

lowing the progress of a local dance group in the newspaper contributes to an awareness and understanding of theatre dance. The Arts Council has realised the importance of localised arts activity for some time, and, over recent years have begun to provide a framework for regional arts development.[44]

Miss Moriarty had been aware of the importance of local participation ever since she began teaching and had been putting her insight into practice over a lifetime. She had not thought of coining the impressive term 'regional arts development', but that was precisely what she was involved in with her schools of dance all over Munster.

The dance officer said on a radio interview[45] that Irish National Ballet was 'out of sync (i.e. out of line) with the rest of the development in dance'. What is termed 'the' development in dance refers to the councils' particular focus of interest: community arts and art-in-education; the very different but vital role of a performing company is disregarded, indeed denied. One could understand that limited finances might force the council to choose between funding community-dance or the performing company, but not that it should deny the value of the latter.

Termination of funding to Irish National Ballet was contemplated by Brinson in 1985. In an article in the *Irish Times* of 11 March 1989 Carolyn Swift reports Peter Brinson's comments on the stopping of the Arts Council grant. He said:

First, this was a courageous decision with which I agree. Second, we would have made a similar root and branch recommendation in my report had it been politically possible at the time.

Having quoted his statement in full, Swift comments:

One cannot but wonder how this ties in with the declaration in the report that 'to lose Irish National Ballet would be to lose a creation of great value ... and throw away the work and expenditure of many years'.

Brinson's remark seemed to confirm Aloys Fleischmann's worst fears: he believed the board and Cork public had not been treated honourably by the council and its commissioned expert, whose word, on Brinson's own evidence, could not be trusted. He wrote perhaps the bitterest public letter of his life on the subject, but had to withdraw it before publication due to a threat of legal proceedings from the council.[46] He believed that the council had closed the Cork company down in order to set a Dublin company in its place. He was mistaken: the council did not want a classically-based company anywhere; nor did it want a national school of dance. He also believed the council had already made plans for the closure in 1985: in this he was partly mistaken.

We have seen that in 1984 the idea had surfaced among council executives of disbanding the company, and that it was rejected by the dance officer of the time. A memo of 1986 mentions the possibility of a 'final solution' but lists other options to be examined first.[47] What Peter Brinson stated publicly about having wanted to make a 'similar root and branch recommendation had it been politically possible' is elaborated in a personal letter to the dance officer:

> When I did my report for you I considered recommending dissolution as one of the options. In the event, with your advice and Adrian's, it seemed that reduced numbers and budget was about as far as we could go politically at that time.[48]

In February 1989 the council abolished professional dance in Ireland by also terminating without any notice whatsoever the grant to the Dublin Contemporary Dance Theatre, which had been highly praised in the Brinson Report and had received a bigger grant after the reduction of aid to the Cork company in 1985. What the council continued to promote was community dance, and dance-in-education, and the Limerick Thomond College projects whose dancers trained in Brinson's Laban Centre.

When Colm Ó Briain challenged the Arts Council to a public debate on the closure of the company, the dance officer wrote in a memo to the director of the council[49] that he personally thought it highly unlikely the council would agree to such a debate

> ... as it regarded its responsibilities in the area of public accountability to be adequately discharged by virtue of its relationship with government, through its formal annual reports, through *Art Matters* and through statements to the media.

The interests of clients and the public are not safeguarded by such a minimalist form of accountability. An Arts Council which claims to be 'the primary shaper of contemporary arts policy'[50] cannot legitimately refuse to participate in a public debate of its policies. It is ironic in view of the manner in which their organisation sometimes treated clients that one dance officer should have criticised Miss Moriarty for running her company like a Victorian headmistress, and the other have found the board to have been lacking a culture of self-criticism. The Irish Theatre Company and Dublin Contemporary Dance Theatre were told without any warning that their funding was to cease: it would be hard to imagine a Renaissance prince behaving in a more autocratic manner.[51]

From the inception of Irish National Ballet in 1973, Miss Moriarty received encouragement and very practical support from Ninette de Valois, the dancer and choreographer who, together with Marie Rambert, had made ballet a great British art in the early decades of the century. Herself Anglo-Irish, she had once tried at Yeats' behest to put ballet on a professional footing in Dublin and had failed. In 1973 she was given the Erasmus Prize by the Dutch government, and having attended unannounced the inaugural performance of the Irish Ballet Company, she decided to give it half of the considerable award so that it could finance special courses to be given on a regular basis by distinguished guest teachers. Miss Moriarty's former teacher Marie Rambert had given support and encouragement to the first professional company, Irish Theatre Ballet, also attending its first performance.[52] The third patron, Alicia Markova, had agreed to dance in a Cork Ballet Company performance for the Dublin Theatre Festival of 1961, but the whole festival had to be cancelled due to a theatre workers' strike.

In the summer of 1985 Miss Moriarty wrote to Dame Ninette to tell her she was resigning from Irish National Ballet; she received the following reply, together with a draft of an article Dame Ninette was planning to send to the *Irish Times*. For the first time, Dame Ninette addresses her informally:

12 July 1985

Dear Joan Denise,

I am distressed about the news. I very much want to pay a tribute to you in the *Irish Times* but did not like to do so without first speaking to you ... I am not getting myself in any way involved with Mr Brinson's report, in fact I have not heard anything about it. My idea is to pay a tribute to you on hearing that you are retiring from the directorship of the Irish National Ballet, which would not exist except for the work which you have done for it.

... I have the greatest admiration for the work you have done and would very much like to give the general public in Dublin an idea of how brilliantly I think you coped with the effort at the beginning.

The following letter from Dame Ninette was published on 10 October 1985 in the *Irish Times*:

Sir,

May I, through *The Irish Times*, express my deep appreciation of Miss Joan Denise Moriarty's efforts as founder and leader for so many years of the Irish National Ballet? ...

Miss Moriarty showed at the very beginning an intelligent approach to the formation of a small classical ballet company for Ireland. We were not embarrassed by a display of a small overcrowded duckpond with ducklings paddling away under the title of *Lac des Cygnes*. She showed taste and intelligence in her division of labour, turning to a brilliant young modern choreographer, Domy Reiter-Soffer – whose work, totally in keeping with the size of the company, produced two modern ballets that made a deep and lasting impression on me.

Again, Miss Moriarty's own very real knowledge of her country's lovely national dances resulted in their introduction into certain suitable short ballets in the repertoire. I have pleasant recollections of *West Cork Ballad*, and *The Devil to Pay*, as well as *The Playboy of the Western World* performed during the Irish National Ballet's very successful visit to Sadler's Well Theatre in London. When she came to her first presentation of the 'classics' for her very small group of young classical dancers, she turned to the great Danish School and gave us one of the most ravishing of their tiny yet famous classical ballets – *Konservatoriet*. It was beautifully danced because it was well within the range of the performers. I have always remembered it with much pleasure. She also had in her midst a young male virtuosity dancer, Babil Gandara, who I longed for London to see.

We have to remember, though, Miss Moriarty's background – a pupil of the Rambert School of Ballet in England, where she learnt the meaning of keeping things in perspective.

I speak only of the past and its beginning. Changes must come and, needless to say, are in the end all for the best; but this makes it all the more important that one woman's intelligent effort should not be forgotten or underwritten. – Yours, etc.

(Dame) Ninette de Valois, CH.,
Royal Opera House, Covent Garden, London.

Three years later, on 24 February 1988, Dame Ninette sent a message to the tribute for Miss Moriarty organised by the Cork Arts and Theatre Club *This Is Your Life*:

I am indeed sad not to be with you all tonight for this tribute to Miss Moriarty. I have been asked for a special story about her but there are so many incidents relative to her energy, her enterprise and her sense of adventure that I cannot think where to start. I hope that Ireland will never forget what she did for the ballet in her country. With my admiration and love.

Just two months after the tribute, Irish National Ballet was disbanded. The last letter from Dame Ninette among Miss Moriarty's papers was written on 15 April 1989:

> My dear Joan Denise,
> I have just received the sad news about the Arts Council grant. I am so very sorry for you all.
> I understand some sort of petition is being got up in this country which will, of course, when it reaches me have my signature.
> With all my very best wishes

For the second time, an attempt to establish professional ballet in Ireland had failed. Miss Moriarty may have been inspired by the memory of that first attempt to bring dance to the Abbey Theatre through Ninette de Valois when she chose a late poem by W. B. Yeats as the basis for her last ballet *Sweet Dancer*:

SWEET DANCER[53]

The girl goes dancing there
On the leaf-sown, new-mown, smooth
Grass plot of the garden;
Escaped from a bitter youth,
Escaped out of her crowd,
Or out of her black cloud.
Ah, dancer, ah, sweet dancer!

If strange men come from the house
To lead her away, do not say
That she is happy being crazy;
Lead them gently astray;
Let her finish her dance,
Let her finish her dance.
Ah, dancer, ah, sweet dancer!

To music by Sibelius the ballet was performed by the Cork Ballet Company in the Everyman Theatre Cork, in Crosshaven, in Skibbereen and Tralee in April 1991. Miss Moriarty had not been allowed to finish her dance in the larger domain: she had, however, continued with it in her immediate environment, travelling with her amateur company as far as was possible, encouraging these dancers to choreograph and having them perform their works.

Miss Moriarty created an enduring place for dance in Ireland. Had she been younger when Irish National Ballet was closed down, she would not have rested until it had been restored. May her work be completed.

2: The Cork Ballet Company
(1) *The Mallow School of Dance*

Sister Angela Bolster (Cork)

As a youngster, I learned Irish dancing, ballet, tap and ballroom dancing from Joan Denise Moriarty. My recollections of Joan go back to the mid-1930s, when she opened her first school of dancing in the Parochial Hall, Shortcastle, Mallow. I remained with Joan until I transferred to Cork in 1938 to attend St Aloysius School, commuting daily from Mallow to Cork until about 1941. Before she moved into her Patrick Street studio in 1940, Joan gave her first dance classes in Cork in a now demolished school, which stood in what today is known as Bishop Lucey Park. I attended this school for a short time also.

We, her pupils, loved Joan Denise. She was at once beautiful, gentle, refined, very respectful in her dealings with us, very patient when we were slow on the uptake, and I can honestly say I never once heard her say an angry word; nor did she ever lose her temper. That she was totally dedicated to her work was obvious and I believe that very fact brought out the best in each one of us – especially when the occasion came for Joan to stage her first 'dances' in the Mallow town hall.

For musical accompaniment at our lessons, Peter Meighan was violinist. He was as dedicated as Joan herself and I can still see him with his violin, patiently waiting as Joan dictated rhythm and poise to us as we struggled on the floor! It was great fun, but it was also hard work – and both Joan and Peter were perfectionists. Joan's great ambition was to have a dancing display in the town hall and in this she succeeded. All I can recall is that one item was to the music of *Moonlight and Roses* and Joan herself danced in this. There was also a Grecian scene in which Joan surpassed herself.

I entered the Convent of St Marie of the Isle in 1944. Looking back over the years of my early involvement with Joan Denise Moriarty, I can recall very clearly the ethos of courtesy and dedication she exuded at all times and conveyed to her pupils. Her courtesy and graceful carriage always impressed me. In fact, I like to transfer to her the words of King Lear as Cordelia lay dead in his arms: 'Her voice was ever sweet, gentle and low: an excellent thing in a woman.' This could be a fitting epitaph for one of the calibre and dedication of Joan Denise Moriarty.

(2) *The Cork Ballet Group – The early years in Cork*

ETHEL BEARE (SALFORD)

I attended Joan's school of dance until 1945, when I left Cork for England. I met her in 1940 when I joined her keep fit classes: she had recently moved to Cork from Mallow and also taught tap, ballroom, and Irish dancing. She chose six of us for her first ballet class, not because she thought we could become prima ballerinas but because she saw that she had imparted her enthusiasm for this unfamiliar form of dance to us, and she was determined to promote an understanding of it in Cork or even beyond. So we six can perhaps be called the pioneers of Irish ballet.

Joan had an attractive personality with a gentle humour and ready wit; she was versatile, gifted and a most talented and inspiring teacher. She attended singing classes with Tony Moffitt, who was musical director of the Cork Opera House, and she was an accomplished piper. Her colourful, original and artistic imagination made it fun to work with her. Eventually we were asked to appear on stage with the Aristocrats in a variety show: they were an amateur dramatic group and we had many engagements with them. We did all kinds of dance: I remember one based on *Rhapsody in Blue*, and one tap dance in which we danced on small imitation suitcases: that was quite spectacular and a great success with the audiences. I also recall Joan dancing a magnificent solo to Ravel's *Bolero*: she looked ravishing in a long black velvet dress with a border of green and white flowers around the hem – it was a creation made by her friend the designer Wendy O'Connor which dramatically set off her lovely colouring and glorious red hair.

But in the beginning Joan had a great struggle to survive, having used up her savings to equip the studio, and not having many pupils in the early years. She had a nervous break-down in 1941 and spent some time in hospital. Then she was brought to stay for several weeks with the O'Connor family of Clydaville in Mallow, where the charming Austrian mother and the five girls brought her back to health and 'saved her reason', as she said. In 1944 she had an accident on stage when we were in Queenstown appearing in pantomime: she caught her soft-toe ballet shoe on a loose floorboard, and broke her leg. She quietly had the curtain lowered, so that no one was aware of the injury. I went with her in the ambulance to Cork, and she was very concerned that she might never be able to dance again. But once she was allowed out of hospital, she managed with characteristic determination to teach until she could resume dancing.

The atmosphere in her classes was always relaxed and cheerful. Joan had infinite patience and good humour, and resolved our problems by repeating movements over and over again. I think she was such a good teacher because her work was a pleasure to her. She took people of all ages and backgrounds. When a show was coming up, she would rehearse far into the night being a perfectionist, and that often meant I missed my last bus. On such occasions Joan improvised a bed by joining a couch to her divan and I would spend the night at the studio flat. She was unconventional and good fun outside class too. We would go on interesting scenic walks, when time would stand still and it might be late in the afternoon before we realised we had not yet had lunch! A party in her studio remains in my memory, at which we were all invited to wear eastern dress; we sat on cushions on the floor, ate Chinese food, and it ended with a Chinese dance from the *Nutcracker Suite*.

It was with great pleasure that I accepted her invitation to attend the Sadler's Wells performance of her Irish ballet *Playboy of the Western World* and shared in the acclaim and appreciation of that enthusiastic audience. I was so glad she finally got the recognition she deserved.

ANN NEESON QUAIN (CORK)

I first heard of Miss Moriarty from my parents, Seán and Geraldine Neeson. They vividly remember her first visit to Cork in the mid 1930s with her mother, when she was a stunningly beautiful girl with 'flaming' gold hair and beautiful carriage. So when I asked to have dancing lessons some years later, they had no hesitation in picking a teacher. My first meeting was in the studio over Simcox's Store in Patrick Street where I was welcomed with a warmth that was to remain in our relationship for as long as she lived. In those days there were day and evening classes and Miss Moriarty gulped down her meal, often consisting of tea or milk and a bar of chocolate or a bun. Money was scarce and not to be used on food. This must surely have been the origin of her later stomach troubles.

We worked with the enthusiasm of completely captivated young dreamers. All forms of dance were included, but ballet was the main activity. We worked hard and soon created a troupe who performed in review and pantomime as the chorus line. But there was always one proviso: there had to be a ballet scene in each production or we would not take part. Now remember that ballet was little known in Ireland, seen only by those who travelled abroad. But Miss Moriarty was adamant. Her goal was a company to perform ballet in Cork first and then throughout the country. Can you imagine how it was to dance to an audience who heckled, jeered, laughed and generally gave us a hard time? All performers will know how we reacted – with a determination to prove we were right.

Our fees were, as I now know, just a pittance but Miss Moriarty included the time for classes and rehearsals without payment. She obviously had to get more paying students, so her work load increased. Life was hard for her then. However, this didn't stop her and she steadily increased the number of ballet performances. We even toured in County Cork. On one occasion the bus driver asked us where we were going and why (he seemed to think we were a sports team). 'A ballet performance – what's that?' He had never heard of it, but as he had to wait for us, he thought he might as well watch. To his surprise he liked it.

Cork was a buzzing city with lots of very dedicated people, all with ideas, and many needed dancers. Miss Moriarty choreographed and danced in many of the play productions by Rachel Burrows, for instance. Leslie Horne and Alec Day had mammoth productions including orchestra, chorus, singers, actors and dancers, and all were produced with the cooperation of Miss Moriarty. When I read contemporary reviews of modern plays with so much innovation, I must smile. There is nothing new there: we had done it all years go. For us there are two figures who stand out head and shoulders over everyone else – Professor Fleischmann with his orchestra and Miss Moriarty, our teacher, choreographer and motivator.

The professor appeared a slightly scary person – austere and so correct. He was the only grown-up who called me Miss Neeson, and it was the same for all the other girls and, when we married, he always got all the new names right. Miss Moriarty developed into a teacher of extraordinary control and ability, and yet she could join with us as one of us without damaging her authority. We had to have all our dances ready for the first orchestral rehearsal. This was a very strict rule and meant extra work, but Miss Moriarty would not lower her standards, and when we had worked till we dropped and knew that we'd never move again, she'd gently say 'Just one more time'. And we did it just one more time – and another, and another.

Though she had a very active committee, and growing numbers of dedicated dancers, Joan Denise Moriarty was the Cork Ballet Company. That her work was appreciated by most Cork people is indicated by the nickname she was accorded – Joan De Knees. In Cork only the special ones are granted such an honour. Like so many others, my mother also held her in affection and esteem. Geraldine Neeson was the drama and music critic for the *Irish Times* and *The Cork Examiner* (as it was then); in November 1980, though she was not at all well, she insisted on going to the Cork Ballet Company's performance because 'I promised I'd be there and do the review'. This was her last theatre review: it was written six days before she died.

It was the Cork Ballet Company which introduced live ballet performances to Ireland and encouraged a big following of this most demanding of the performing arts. There could have been no Cork Ballet Company without Joan Denise Moriarty: an achievement that will be remembered.

(3) Performing with the Cork Ballet Company

HILDA BUCKLEY (CORK)
Speech at This Is Your Life *tribute to JDM of 24 February 1988 put on by the Cork Arts and Theatre Club*

I was in the Cork Ballet Company from the start and have been in almost every performance. It was a new world to us: we had never seen ballet. I loved the music, the colour, the movement; and we were all captivated by Miss Moriarty: she was so beautiful. There were the stars in the company – I was one of the also-rans: whenever a weird creature was needed, there I was. For when Miss Moriarty asked you to do something, you did it – even if it meant wearing a beard!

Miss Moriarty had such a wide range in the various roles she danced: a fiery tinker in *Puck Fair*, then the sadness of *Valse triste*, and the inspiring *La Calinda*. Our withers were wrung – we were all intensely affected by her performances.

She has such marvellous courage: she's always a step ahead in what she has done; she knows instinctively when the time is ripe for something, and she does it. Her capacity for hard work is phenomenal. She gets up at six – though I wouldn't be surprised if it was more often five – and has her day so well organised that she can run her schools, run the Cork Ballet Company, run the professional company, and create. How she does it, we do not know. She is a hard taskmaster, though, I will say that: she does demand a lot. But you know that no matter how hard she asks you to work, she works ten times harder herself, so you don't begrudge it.

But it's a painful art, the art of ballet. Never ask a dancer how they are – there's always something wrong with them, so don't inquire. You do suffer a lot, but you get so much out of it, and we owe it all to Miss Moriarty. Strong bonds of friendship have been formed among us members of the company – many people have mentioned that this evening – and they mirror the bond between us and her and indeed stem from it. There's an umbilical cord attaching all of us to Miss Moriarty –we just can't get away from her, and we don't want to get away from her!

Miss Moriarty is a very private person; she doesn't talk about herself, but I know of lots of very kind deeds she has done that most people know nothing about. To me she's been a wonderful friend, and if I were ever in trouble again, she would be the first person I would go to.

Miss Moriarty, you are very, very dear to all of us.

A decade later
We always had problems finding enough boys. Jack Sheppard was our first and gradually, through blackmailing and browbeating brothers and friends, we managed to get about ten. The Cork Steam Packet and Dunlops were a great source of supply in the early days. Milo Lynch, who came from The Steam Packet, had his start as the back-end of a cow in *An Cóitín Dearg*; he did a lot of principal parts with us later. Then there was John Hickey, who was gorgeous looking. When we did Act Two of *Swan Lake* with Peter Darrell of Sadler's Wells, John danced as the Prince's friend Benno, and he was so handsome that a lot of people thought he was the guest artist.

Three of us who worked together for The Cork Steam Packet formed the first committee. If we were going away touring, as we did in the early days to Clonmel, Mallow, Limerick, we would go down the night before and try to set things up, unpack costumes, do ironing, etc. With permission from our boss, we would work on a Saturday afternoon in The Steam Packet typing the programme with all the names – quite a complicated task – and run off the necessary hundreds of programmes for various tours. We really sweated over it, but it was great fun. We brought ballet to Killarney, Clonmel, Waterford, Limerick. What an undertaking: a whole ballet company with costumes, etc., a full orchestra. Then there were the heady days of Dublin, in the 1970s, playing to packed houses in the Abbey and Gaiety with the full Cork Symphony Orchestra. What an experience!

Miss Moriarty would never tell anybody anything, especially not us dancers: we were the last to be told what show we were doing for the coming season. The orchestra always knew before we did, which was a great joke. Of course, we all had friends in the orchestra and so we'd find out. But Miss Moriarty didn't believe in unnecessary talk. When the time was right, she would tell us, and that was the way she did it. But, when she was creating her own works, she'd sit us all down after class and tell us what we were going to do; then she'd play a bit of the music and would tell us all about it, maybe dancing some of the parts. As in the early days all the ballets were her own creations, we never knew what they were going to be about until she told us. Then those of us like myself who weren't good dancers would be given our parts: I would hear that I was a mother, and I would groan because I hated doing mothers' parts, and I often got them. But it was terribly exciting. I think the success of the early ballets was due to her gift for spotting talent, and she built her ballets around us, around our personalities, around our talents – she brought out the best in everybody.

At one stage Miss Moriarty started a series of little lectures in the studio – she was always trying to better us, to educate us. She had Professor Fleischmann give us a talk on music, and I remember Dan Donovan speaking on the theatre in Cork. She also brought us over to the School of Art several times to see the paintings there. She was always broadening our horizons.

I think we've always felt that the word 'lady' described Miss Moriarty, from the very beginning in her young days right up to her last. She instilled discipline, hard work, loyalty and friendship. Thanks to her, we all made great friends: forty-seven years later, so many of us are still in touch. So many of her pupils have gone all over the world, and when she was alive, if they ever came to Cork, they always contacted her, which gave her great pleasure. When I retired, we started our Friday Club. In a moment of enthusiasm, I said one night 'Wouldn't it be great if we had a class for just us' – I meant for those of us who weren't up to the high standards of the present-day dancers, who are so good technically. She took me up on it. I think she really enjoyed that: it brought her back to the early days. We went out for lunch afterwards to the Grand Circle and she seemed to relax with us; we got to know her better as a person than we did over the years when she was only our teacher.

You must remember that when the company started first, it was not long after the war and life was pretty grey here. We didn't have many visiting theatrical companies and the world of ballet was just magic to us, pure magic. I can still remember the first wonderful, exhilarating night that we rehearsed with the Cork Symphony and the professor and the singers for the Polovtsian Dances. I don't think anybody could have been higher than I was that evening.

I know that I express the thoughts of all my friends from the old days when I say that we cannot thank Miss Moriarty enough for the enrichment she brought to our lives. And the professor played no small part in that: he was always there, was always a great friend to us, always great fun. They both made a deep impression on our lives: we will never forget them.

META O'MULLANE (CORK)

Miss Moriarty was a very strong, self-reliant person. One always felt that she knew exactly how things ought to be done. Always extremely punctual, she could never understand anybody being late for rehearsal. I shall always remember our thirtieth ballet birthday, which was celebrated with a dinner going on till 1.00am or so; however, we still had to be in the Opera House for 9.00am the following morning, as we were to have a stage rehearsal for our forthcoming ballet – we were there: on a Sunday morning!

Whenever we did a short two-act ballet, such as *Giselle* or *Nutcracker*, she always did one of her own Irish ballets, or a modern one, of about half an hour as a curtain raiser. Always innovative, these ballets were fun to be involved in because they were based on the talents of the members of the company. She had ingenious ideas about the technical side of the production: I recall the ballet she did on *William Tell*, dancing the title role herself. In the story, the rebel William Tell is forced by the tyrannical ruler to shoot an apple off his son's head. Obviously there could be no bungling, and no accidents. Her idea was to have a very thin piece of wire attached to the apple when it was placed on the boy's head; somebody in the wings pulled it off, while another person threw an apple with an arrow through it onto the stage. The audience was amazed at Tell's marksmanship! This is just one example of her stagecraft.

Another characteristic was her care and concern for anybody in the company in trouble; she would always waive fees if any of us got into financial difficulty. I will never forget how very generous she was to me when I was unemployed, giving me a small job travelling to Bandon, Mallow and Bishopstown with her teacher Breda Quinn. Another time, when I had helped with a children's show in the Firkin Crane, she said there was a profit and presented me with £50 at the end of the show – she was not only thoughtful, but always so tactful too.

We all loved Miss Moriarty. She deserves recognition and a

place in history for the extraordinary work she did, and for her selfless dedication to ballet in Ireland.

PAT O'GORMAN MCCARTHY (DUBLIN)
Being part of Miss Moriarty's ballet class, which I joined in 1942, gave me some of the happiest years of my life. From the beginning she was an enigmatic figure and my hero. She was the most dedicated person I have ever met. She committed herself to a task that was daunting, to say the least: to establishing a ballet company in Cork and Ireland, though her students in the 1940s had never even seen a ballet. To have undertaken it was astounding; to have achieved it is incredible. She was a marvellous teacher, and was one of the most decisive influences in my life. It is amazing how many people's lives she influenced.

Her great dictum was 'never say can't'. She certainly lived by it, as she overcame impossible obstacles to get the ballet week on stage every year. I remember the first night of ballet in 1947. We worked so hard rehearsing, often on Sunday afternoons in a very dusty hall on the quays belonging to the Ancient Order of Hibernians. We were very excited about what we were doing and Miss Moriarty insisted on the highest standards. The standards not only applied to the dancing; they also applied to our appearance, our punctuality and our behaviour in the studio and elsewhere during rehearsals. We called her 'Miss Moriarty', which was the normal practice in the 1940s and 1950s. Young people never addressed adults by their Christian name.

In 1947 we had our first big performance. Having attained the highest standards we could reach, we arrived at the Aula Maxima to rehearse with the Cork Symphony Orchestra. That was my first meeting with the illustrious professor of music. What struck me most about him was his gentleness. When the orchestra played badly he gently persuaded them to do better, always addressing them as 'Ladies and Gentlemen'. We thought they were so lucky. Miss Moriarty on the other hand would threaten to put us out of the ballet if we made unnecessary mistakes! We loved the fun and excitement of it all. With so many people involved, discipline was very strict and had to be. I have to say that in the eleven years I was associated with the ballet company, I never saw any unbecoming behaviour. What was there was dedication, commitment and hard work to bring to Cork an appreciation and love for ballet. For forty years Miss Moriarty and Professor Fleischmann gave Cork a Ballet Week and an International Choral Festival. I can never thank them enough for imparting their enthusiasm for ballet and music to us. Some of the most wonderful and happiest times of my life were spent in Miss Moriarty's studio, and those memories will never leave me.

PATRICIA MOYNIHAN DONOHOE (BELFAST)
I first danced with the Cork Ballet Company in 1948 and stayed with it until my parents died in 1955 when I moved to Dublin. I loved that first Ballet Week and to this day I relive the pleasure of dancing on stage with the company. Miss Moriarty was in some ways like a mother to me: I loved and admired her, and never lost contact. Any time I was in Cork we would spend some time together. I moved to Belfast in 1960 as my husband lectured at Queen's University; when Miss Moriarty came up here, we always had a great reunion.

I feel my training with the Ballet Company was the best preparation I could have had to help me face life. The discipline, hard work, accepting disappointment at not getting a part and, most of all, going on no matter what: public smiles and maybe private tears. We were like a family and the members have a bond which will always remain.

On being faced with the Troubles up here, I wondered what I could do to help. It seems to me that music and dance are great healers, so I tried to do what I had learnt in Cork, and to give some pleasure by giving a dancing class as a voluntary helper at our local Youth Club. I was invited to enter a team for the Northern Ireland Association of Youth Clubs competition 'Saturday Night Fever'. Doing the choreography and training of the team was hard work, but when we won an award at the Europa Hotel we knew it had been worth while. I do all sorts of dancing to all sorts of music. I then started giving an evening of dance at a club run by the Association of Mental Health. So Miss Moriarty is well known in Belfast, as I never stop boasting about the Cork Ballet Company, the first ballet company in Ireland. I always tried to get down to Cork for Ballet Week or on special occasions like the thirtieth anniversary. Miss Moriarty brought me backstage to introduce me to the cast. She told them all about me: she had that lovely gift of making a person feel special and important.

It was my work which kept me going in difficult times. My husband died in 1985; my mother-in-law only survived him by a month. In 1989 my eldest boy died of cancer on the first anniversary of his engagement – aged 27. He had graduated in Celtic Studies and English and was working in Queen's translating the Bible into Irish when he became ill. Though a bit of me died with him, the support and kindness I received and the work I was involved in kept me going. I owe so much to Miss Moriarty and Professor Fleischmann: they made a wonderful team, and those of us lucky enough to have known them had the privilege of learning from them. May they rest in peace.

TONY KENIRY (CARRIGALINE)
From Piping to Dancing

I started my dancing career when I was seven years old. I first learnt Irish step dancing from the great teacher Mr Jack Griffin in Carrigaline, himself a pupil of the famous Monty Riordan of Douglas. I danced at many concerts and shows; I joined the Carrigaline Pipe Band in 1943 and played the pipes for two or three years. Music and dance have played a big part in my life.

I first saw ballet in 1945 in the Palace Theatre. At that time, just after the war, movies were scarce and some of the cinemas put on Cine-Variety, which meant an hour and a half of films and an hour of variety on stage. It was in the Palace that I first saw Miss Moriarty and her dancers in several short ballets. They made such an impression on me that when I saw her advert in the *Echo* for new dancers some years later, I sent in my application to join. I received a letter asking me to come for an audition at the studio in Patrick Street.

That was the night I almost didn't join the Cork Ballet. I got as far as the door, but could not pluck up enough courage to knock, so I went off to The Long Valley for a glass of Beamish stout. But then I did knock, and met Miss Moriarty for the first time. I danced a reel and a hornpipe for her and she said the magic words 'Thursday night at 7.30'. So that was how I joined the Cork Ballet Company in 1949. I had been wondering whether a boy from the country would fit into this world of art, but I need not have worried as I was made feel very welcome. In less than six months I was doing leading parts – this was on account of my years of Irish dance training, which had given me a good foundation.

One evening during our break in rehearsal, Miss Moriarty commented on the coincidence that we had both came to ballet from piping. That was the first time I heard she played the war pipes, and that the Cork Ballet Company began after she made a bargain with Professor Fleischmann that if he would conduct his orchestra for her dancers, she would play the war pipes for his work *Clare's Dragoons*. She said that she'd love to visit the Carrigaline Pipe Band – this would have been in 1950. So I made arrangements with William Cogan, the pipe major, and he was delighted to have her come. I met her in the village off the bus and we went to the band hall, where the pipe band put on a very special rehearsal for her. Some even came in full dress uniform. Then William Cogan tuned in a set of pipes and she played a lovely solo selection. As she marched up and down some of the drums joined in. It was a very enjoyable evening and a most successful visit. The lone piper who played at her funeral forty years later was that Pipe Major William Cogan.

The first classical music I danced to was Schubert: I had my first part as the prince in *Rosamunde*. What I love about ballet is the combination of music, movement and mime: your body is like a musical instrument that you play in unison with the orchestra. At that time there were two ballet shows a year – one in November and the Ballet Week in May at the old Opera House. The following year we had the first Irish ballet: *The Children of Lír*. The next year I had a big part in *An Cóitín Dearg* (The Red Petticoat); then I danced the role of Pádraic Pearse in *The Singer*, which was a great success: Pearse's sister Máiréad Mac Piarais came to Cork for the opening night. After Ballet Week in Cork we took the ballet on tour – we helped to introduce ballet to the south. I danced leading parts in many ballets until 1956. After my mother died, I went to London for five or six years.

Another exciting milestone in the Ballet Company history was the visit to Cork in 1951 of the Ballet Rambert. Madame Marie Rambert was a patron of the Cork Company. We were the welcoming party and entertained them to high tea at the Savoy. On the opening night we had a block booking at the Opera House, where we gave them a great reception.

During those years Miss Moriarty had a romance with Charles MacDonald, the son of Colonel MacDonald of Brickfieldstown House, Robert's Cove. She lived at that time with his sister and her husband, George Collins, so he often called at the studio to take her home after class. This romance went on for five or six years; they were a lovely couple to see when they walked out: both tall and stately. As he lived near Robert's Cove, he often stopped at my home in Carrigaline to give me a lift to class. At that time, I was running two local dancing schools plus my day-job and was always rushing, so I was very glad of the lift. I remember one evening I had to be up for a stage rehearsal at 7.30. On our way in we got held up on the road behind a herd of cattle and so I was a half hour late that night. How would I face Miss Moriarty and the rest of the class? But I had to, and I remember saying to her 'We got held up by a herd of cows, me and you know who.' She blushed and I got away with it. But she often had her own back on me afterwards. If I was late for class she said 'I suppose you were held up by a herd of cattle!'

One evening Miss Moriarty asked me to stay on after class. She said 'Charles has asked me to marry him. As he is selling the home and moving to England, it means that I will have to give up all my work here with the ballet'. It took her several weeks to make up her mind: she decided to stay with the Ballet Company and make it her life's work. For that she gave up the hope of marriage, home and family. It was a pity, as they were both lovely people. It was a very big sacrifice on her part, for which we should be very grateful.

My special friend and benefactor was Frau Tilly Fleischmann, who took me under her wing and to whose encouragement I owe most of my success. She kept up my confidence all over the years as I was a rather shy person. She was one of Cork's leading musicians, and I attended many of her wonderful piano recitals in the Imperial Hotel, especially appreciating her Chopin evenings.

In the Ballet Company we were like a big family, spending many evenings a week together; before Christmas we had the ballet dinner in the Metropole Hotel, and in the summer we had an outing with a picnic lunch and dancing on the beach. During my years with Miss Moriarty, besides dancing and music, I learnt much about the art of stagecraft: the arts of production, choreography, stage make-up, stage lighting and decor. I have produced many variety shows and pantomimes, and have been in cabaret in London.

Thank you Miss Moriarty for all the time and inspiration you gave to us over all the years!

Betty Long O'Connor (Newbridge)

I started my ballet classes with Miss Moriarty around 1944, and loved every minute of them. As she believed that the purpose of ballet classes was performance, I quickly found myself on stage in the Father Mathew Hall, the Cork Opera House, and also in subsequent years in Limerick, Clonmel, Mallow and Killarney. My abiding young memories are of spending most of my evenings and weekend afternoons at practice and rehearsals at Miss Moriarty's studio coming up to the May Ballet Week. For us dancers this was the most special event of the year: it was all we wanted to do at the time. I also remember being afraid of my life ever to get my hair cut; running to catch the last bus to Dillon's Cross after rehearsals, frequently missing it and having to walk the two miles home.

The first rehearsal with the Cork Symphony Orchestra at the Aula Maxima of the university was an exhilarating experience. It was so different dancing to the music being played by the big orchestra, having only heard it played on the piano in the studio up to this. We would hold Professor Fleischmann in some awe, but he was always gentle and softly spoken, even though at times he must have found it difficult, to say the least, getting the dancers in harmony with the orchestra and sometimes adapting the tempi to our needs. Hearing the music he composed for the ballet such as *The Golden Bell of Ko* or *An Cóitín Dearg* always gave us a special feeling of privilege. We teenagers were introduced through the ballet to a wide range of classical and modern music, and this has left us with an abiding appreciation and love of good music. Part of our musical training was supplied by our pianist Miss Stenson, who had extraordinary patience with us. She matched our interest and enthusiasm as she cheerfully played the music over and over again late into the evenings until we knew every note, had mastered every step, and could thus bring our general performance to the high standard Miss Moriarty expected of us.

Being part of the ballet in Cork meant much more than just dancing – Miss Moriarty organised outings to the sea during the summer holidays. We would have a picnic, dance on the beach and she would give impromptu classes. I still cherish photos of those happy times. She would keep a certain but always friendly aloofness on those occasions, which was expected and accepted by young dancers used to the discipline that distinguishes ballet everywhere.

After I got married and left Cork to live in Co. Kildare I lost touch with ballet affairs in Cork. However in 1965 I was asked to give ballet classes in a private school in Newbridge. I accepted the offer after some serious consideration: ballet is a difficult discipline to resume. I attended courses in Dublin organised by the Irish Region of the London Royal Academy of Dancing. But however good these courses were, I could not have undertaken regular teaching of the various grades or entered into the world of Royal Academy exams without the sound technique I had been taught by Miss Moriarty. These foundations and the discipline of dance learned long ago from her formed the basis of all my teaching, and my classes have enjoyed a hundred percent success in examination results down the years. We also have a ballet performance every second year with proper stage facilities – lighting, costumes, make-up, scenery, and music – though alas only on tape. I learned from Miss Moriarty that the end purpose of dance is, after all, performance, a fact which is sometimes overlooked if too much emphasis is put on passing grade examinations.

The great days of the Cork Ballet Company were unique in Ireland: no such development took place in the dance scene in Dublin or anywhere else in the country. It was an extraordinary combination in Cork at the time: a dedicated choreographer/ballet mistress and keen dancers; an eminent conductor and an available symphony orchestra, all encouraged by an enthusiastic circle of friends and supporters. Remarkable standards were achieved with dancers drawn from a comparatively small population pool. The performances of the Cork Ballet, season after season, received praise from recognised critics, and widespread admiration and indeed envy from the larger metropolis. And all this was created from scratch in a city and a country without any previous ballet tradition whatever.

A very special 'Thank you' to Miss Moriarty for having given us the opportunity to experience, appreciate and practise dance!

MARY CONRAN MARTIN (DUBLIN)

We recently organised a get-together of those now very senior citizens: the original aspiring ballerinas of the Cork Ballet Group and later Company now resident in Dublin and neighbouring counties, and one and all agreed that Miss Moriarty and 'the professor' had been a major influence in our lives. Their total dedication and determination had made us very willing slaves roped into their cause of introducing ballet to Ireland.

Five nights a week and Sunday afternoons we spent rehearsing in the studio and in dirty halls in hot June weather coming up to the performances, but when the Cork Symphony Orchestra struck up the national anthem our dreams were realised – our moments of glory had come!

I retired for the first time, with much weeping and gnashing of teeth, at the end of the 1956 Ballet Week, as I was getting married. When my first baby was born the following year, Miss Moriarty visited me in the nursing home bringing a tiny pair of ballet shoes for my new daughter, and she enquired whether I would be back for the show two months later. I think my gynaecologist thought I was having hallucinations on his next rounds and I was not amused when he said I would have to wait for six weeks before returning! I didn't and scandalised the gossip faction of Cork – 'a mother up on the stage in a tutu'. Famous or infamous??!! I retired again for baby number two and again and again and again. Perhaps moving to Dublin in 1967 was a relief all round or they would have had to shoot this 'Dying Swan'.

I was born into a ballet-family. My mother, Madeline Gordon, was involved in dance ever since she herself was a little girl. At one stage my two sisters, my mother and I all danced together in the same production. There were one or two occasions when I was a young teenager that stand out very much in my mind. Once during a rehearsal for Shakespeare's *Winter Tale* in the Cork School of Music when Miss Moriarty was teaching us, I was very tense and eager. When I could not get the steps immediately I found my eyes filling with tears. She just smiled and reassured me that this happened to all dancers, that it was normal. On another occasion I was dancing in the 'garland dance' in *Sleeping Princess*. At the dress rehearsal I had received no prop garlands and was devastated. I will never forget Miss Moriarty putting her arm around me, walking me back stage to get my prop, reassuring quietly and gently.

But it was very different when I joined the Cork Ballet Company the following year. I was soon given solo parts, but no matter what experience I gained, she never showed outwardly that she had confidence in me. I never got any praise or encouragement until the very last year in 1991 when she called me over to her wheelchair and said: 'You are dancing very well – keep it up.'

The best part of my mother's experience was the Cork Ballet Company and their relationship with Miss Moriarty. They had a great social life – they went to parties and even picnics by the sea. Miss Moriarty was very different with them – she praised and encouraged without stint. But when she started the professional Irish National Ballet, she subjected her amateur company to all the professional ideas she was putting in place. Ballet for us became very serious and some of the enjoyment went from it; especially the social side, which in my time was practically non-existent. Also the technical standards rose and it became difficult to keep up. We danced with professional male dancers from the Irish National Ballet and were expected to match their technique. That was very difficult, given the amateur nature of the company, and Miss Moriarty got very frustrated with us especially during rehearsals. However, it was very challenging and exciting as well. What an opportunity: to dance with professional dancers in full-scale ballets produced by international ballet directors to a live orchestra!

Ballet week in the Opera House will always remain for me a memory of mixed pain and pleasure. The excitement of performance is one which must be experienced to be understood. I had a leaden feeling in the pit of my stomach on entering the Opera House backstage door to go up to the dressing-room. But once I was standing at the side of the stage on opening night, all the hassle, tears, torn toes and short tempers of rehearsal seemed worth it. I can still see Professor Fleischmann in his tuxedo waiting for the call to start the national anthem; the dancers warming up on stage; the professional guest artists with their full make up on and their bathrobes on over costumes. It was a feeling like nothing on earth, waiting for my piece of music and going out on stage: it was nerve-wracking and exciting and stupendous.

We had many happy and joyful moments with Miss Moriarty. Her company classes were fun: we used to laugh with her and get so excited that she would have to ask us to stop. Rehearsals were different: they were more serious. We worked very hard, until we knew every step automatically. When we went on stage, the whole thing just flowed. When it came to smaller productions or 'dance-ins' as they were called, rehearsals and performances were more relaxed and we really had a great time. Miss Moriarty would travel with us to various towns such as Clonmel and Tralee; we tried to get to know her as a person, but never succeeded. The only people in the company who remained close to her throughout the years were the older members, on whom she relied for support. While we always had tremendous respect for Miss Moriarty, we were from a different world than she and the veterans; we questioned more, we did not accept things so easily, and thinking back now, I imagine she found this difficult to deal with. She was always a disciplinarian first and foremost.

Yet when some of us called to her home around the time when the Arts Council's report on dance was published, we realised perhaps for the first time that she too could need support and reassurance. We had always seen her strong, sure and confident, never weak. Though she had often suffered injuries – once a broken sternum and another time a broken foot – this had never stopped her teaching and working. She was indomitable. And she expected the same from us. When the curtain came down in the Opera House at the beginning of Act II *Swan Lake* because of a bomb scare, we all went outside in the freezing November air in our thin white costumes. We thought nothing of putting on another performance on the Sunday to make up for the disrupted evening, even though Cork Ballet had to bear the costs. We danced on injuries – 'the show must go on'. Of course this was dangerous, but we did it because we had to. She was constant and we also had to be: this taught us strength. Those dancers who survived and went on to enjoy many performances and classes with Miss Moriarty were given a rare gift – the fulfilment of dreams built on hard work and dedication.

When Miss Moriarty died, everything that was the Cork Ballet Company and school for me died with her. I could not bear to go into the studio, its offices, dressing-rooms and classroom as I would have been waiting for her to appear. I could not bear to see her painting, which had looked down on me for the best part of 20 years. There was no company without her strength and perseverance. She was the company: she did it; she was Cork Ballet. It was the end of performing in ballet for me, that last performance she was alive to see in 1991.

CARMEL AUDLEY (KINSALE)
At the age of twelve I joined the Cork Ballet Company for the production of *Giselle* and from that time the studio was my second home, and for my friends and me a safe and happy place on which I think back with much pleasure and of which I have fond memories. The discipline of those days is still with me, and I am grateful for such training.

When I was about sixteen I had a disagreement with Miss Moriarty; I was taken to her flat above the studio which was such a magic place filled with paintings, books, music and of course the studio cat. We had a chat, and resolved our differences, then returned to the studio, and it was never mentioned again. Once she gave me advice on a major step in my life (not a dance step!), which I did not take; sadly she was right, but at twenty-one I thought I knew better. My twenty-first birthday present from Miss Moriarty was a painting of a ballerina taking a curtsey: she said it was like me taking a curtain call for life. This painting has a special place in my home. I also treasure the ballet shoes she brought to the hospital on the birth of my son – never worn!!

Miss Moriarty, as she was always called (except when we would be very brave and call her 'Moriar' in the dressing-room!), was never at fault. I worked for her for three years, and on a teaching trip to Limerick we once ran out of petrol. It was her car and she was doing the driving, but the fact that we ran out of petrol was my fault – as she put it: 'You were talking too much!' Did I disagree? Never! We had to hitch and when successful with a lorry, I was very polite and allowed her to enter the cab first, so she was quite close to the driver. She saw the funny side of the event when I teased her. She did have a light side which very few people saw.

I realise how privileged I was in my formative years to have been so influenced by the arts and a great lady. Even though she never married and had her own children, she gave so much to so many children. I do hope she realised how much I loved and respected her. I am now in my 51st year and still teaching ballet with great pride and joy. Miss Moriarty will always be with me as she was such a part of my life, like an extension of my parents. This great lady gave so much to so many: the love of ballet, music, art – and most of all of *life*. Always so elegant, and at all times a lady.

Geri O'Kelly (Dublin)

Some years ago I was working on a production of *The Merchant of Venice* in the Abbey Theatre. During a coffee break I was chatting with some of the company in the corridor outside the rehearsal room when the lift doors opened and out walked Joan Denise Moriarty. Instinctively I jumped to my feet, curtsied to her and greeted her as 'Miss Moriarty'. My reverent greeting was a cause of great hilarity among the company and I found it difficult to explain the awe which she inspired in me even as an adult.

'Inspiration' is the only word I know of that in any way describes the profound effect Miss Joan Denise Moriarty has had on my life and that of countless others. She has given us the gift of dance; some have gone on to be part of the dancing profession, others are quite simply an educated audience, but all of us are inheritors of her great passion for the ballet.

It all comes flooding back as I write this; pushing open the door of her studio at No. 1 Emmet Place, the smell peculiar to the building, the anticipation of the class, scraping the hair into a bun and getting the hair-band on correctly, waiting to hear the piano play the 'curtsy' music of the previous class so we could get going. And the joy of being summoned to the inner sanctum of her office to be fitted with that first pair of *pointe* shoes; the austere self-portrait she had hanging on the studio wall; the unspoken recognition that no matter how awkwardly an exercise was being performed there was a dancer's soul in there somewhere trying to get out; her telling us that what was in front of us was not just the studio wall but the packed auditorium of the Opera House.

And then the shock at seeing her photograph on the front page of the Sunday newspaper announcing her death, and the tears at her funeral which were as much tears of gratitude for her life and what she had given us, as grief at her passing on.

Thank you Miss Moriarty.

My memories of the ballet studio in Emmet Place are very clear – the narrow stairs leading up to the dark small changing-room where we put on our soft black ballet shoes with the elastic across the arch – white ankle socks (mine were usually a shade of grey) and green tunics, the pocket embroidered with the letters JDM. I used to feel very important when I put on that tunic. Then we'd go down into that distinctive studio, its maple floor flooded with light from the three long windows looking across to the School of Art, the huge mirrors floor to ceiling and the barre that stretched all around the reflective walls, with the ancient piano in the corner.

Class always started promptly; Miss Moriarty greeted us in her dark polo-neck top and trousers, scarf knotted behind her head, the black, silver-topped cane in hand, austere and regal as always. For the next hour we would do our best to achieve the best fifth position, *pas-du-chat* or *ronde-de-jambe* that we could possibly manage. She made us feel that only the best was good enough, and when she dropped a pearl of praise in our direction (which was not very often!) I felt as if I was really important and meant something special to her just then. She was not at all demonstrative, not given to coaxing or praising much, but she seemed to be totally dedicated to getting across the art of graceful movement and ballet, things she herself seemed to do effortlessly.

Sometimes she used to say with a slight hint of mock exasperation in her voice: 'Why is it that Irish girls walk so badly, as if they are ashamed of their bodies? Walk tall, girls!' she would insist, 'walk as if you are being pulled up by a piece of string attached to the very top of your heads!' This admonition made a big impression on me, and JDM still wants me to 'walk tall' some forty years later.

Miss Stenson the pianist sat in her black velvet hat, which she appeared never to remove, playing the same bars over and over and over again, never seeming to get impatient with the constant interruptions as Miss Moriarty would stop to tap an errant ankle with her cane, or press a knee into the desired position. Tinkerbell, Miss Moriarty's cat, would sometimes deign to grace us with a visit. She was such a supercilious cat – a black and white fluffy Persian – that would walk along the barre with her tail in the air and that expression which always seemed to say: 'How very boring!' I got the feeling that Miss Moriarty was pleased to see her come into the studio though she pretended not to be at all pleased at the intrusion.

I just loved that studio, taking my place very proudly at the barre. I felt really special then: very different to my situation in the world outside. I always had the feeling that Miss Moriarty was nurturing me, and that she was interested, perhaps even fascinated by the movements that this young body of mine was trying to make. Never once did I ever experience a sense of humiliation, of having been denigrated, something that was often with me outside of Miss Moriarty's, but rather I felt her benign interest in me as a unique individual. At the end of every class we as a group would all curtsey to her, and she would always thank us graciously as in some kind of mystic ritual.

When *Giselle* was put on in the City Hall with Domini Callaghan and Michel de Lutry in the principal parts, I was very disappointed not to have been chosen for the *corps-de-ballet*. Miss Moriarty gave me and a friend the job of usherettes instead. Our task was to parade around the hall banging gongs in order to let people know that the curtain was to rise in five minutes time and that they should now take their seats. She had dressed us in green costumes with special hats, and we felt as important as if we had been the stars on the stage that night. And of course we saw *Giselle* seven times from beginning to end. What a spectacle that was: the glow of the music-stand lights from the orchestral pit shining on the burgundy coloured curtain, the hush of expectation from the audience awaiting the appearance of the conductor, Aloys Fleischmann, and then the beginning of the music. Afterwards there was the thunderous applause and the many curtain calls at the end. It was another world for me. In the rather dreary repressive atmosphere of Cork in the 1950s, being a part of JDM's ballet school was as close to real magic as I could ever have been. She had opened a door to a world I might never have known existed, a world of colour, of music, of dance and, most of all, of lightness.

But this world nearly came to an end for me when my mother stopped me from going to classes because she could not afford the fees. For her it must have seemed like a luxury and there were other more pressing needs to be catered for, like food on the table for instance. Then one morning a letter arrived and I knew it had to be from JDM because of the characteristic green ink she used. She wrote to my mother to say that she had missed me at class recently and wondered why I was not coming any more as I had seemed to enjoy the dancing and had even showed some talent. When my mother replied and said that she could no longer afford it, JDM wrote that she would halve the fee to 7/6. I used to feel very self-conscious bringing in my envelope of rattling coins instead of the customary ten-shilling note and two half-crown coins. JDM never made any comment on the fact that my envelope was any different to the others. She was so tactful.

I think of Miss Moriarty today as a very positive influence on me as a teenager growing up in 1950s Cork, at that exquisitely sensitive time of life.

(4) In the Gods of the Old Opera House

COLONEL SHANE O'CONNOR (NEWBRIDGE)
As an engineering student of University College Cork (1950–1953) it was a matter of principle for me and fellow engineering and science undergraduates to show that we also were interested in literature, music, art, etc. Some arts students tended to be rather patronising toward us alleged philistines. The Opera House was a cultural mecca for all of us in an Ireland not exactly overendowed with cultural opportunity in the 1950s. We flocked en masse every season to the gods. As a flock we were not always on our best behaviour and mild unruliness reared its head from time to time, on one or two occasions necessitating a visit from the manager Mr Bill Twomey at the interval. Needless to say I stood aloof from any uncouth behaviour!

My favourite performances were the seasons of the Cork Ballet Company. I still have the programmes as evidence. I thought it most natural and appropriate that a ballet be accompanied by no less than a symphony orchestra. To this day I cast an anxious eye at the pit whenever we go to the ballet. Dance was an entirely new experience, and it was necessary to educate oneself in its traditions and conventions and to develop an appreciation of a strange but enchanting new art form hitherto unknown to a raw young man up from Kerry. Arnold Haskell's *Ballet* in Pelican proved an excellent introduction. I still have my copy, and what began as a student infatuation at the Cork Opera House over forty years ago has remained a lifelong interest.

Time will never dim the enchantment of those early Cork Ballet performances, so beautifully danced by a group of dedicated young amateur dancers who captivated their audiences by performances that belied their amateur status. Those audiences were proud that Cork had its own ballet company and its own symphony orchestra, conscious that the southern city was uniquely blessed in Ireland. I have clear recollections of my impressions of both Miss Moriarty as dance mistress and of Professor Fleischmann as conductor, both surrounded by an aura of rather remote but confident authority and an austerity born of the demands of their art.

The leading dancers in the Cork Ballet in the early 1950s were two charming and talented young girls, Patricia O'Gorman and Betty Long. With clever casting, Miss Moriarty ordained that they each be given the chance to dance main roles on alternate evenings each season. I never thought I would ever meet one of those ethereal beings, and stage door Johnnyism never entered my mind. However, fate took a hand. In 1956 I attended a military ball in the officers' mess at Sarsfield Barracks, Limerick (where I was on temporary duty. My home station was Collins Barracks, Cork). I immediately recognised the charming and beautiful young lady sitting opposite me at supper: none other than that same Betty Long. Later as we danced, Miss Long admitted to being rather impressed by the idea of a military person being knowledgeable not only on ballet but Cork Ballet at that. For my part I was glad to graduate from distant admirer to, at least, acquaintance. And what a charming coincidence that Betty's home at White's Cross, Cork was only a mile away from my military station on Military Hill. The rest, as they say in the time honoured cliché, is history.

(5) Backstage and Behind the Scenes

FRANCES BARRY (CORK)
Making the Costumes

I was dressmaking nearly forty years ago when Ms Moriarty came to me and asked me to make the costumes for her ballet. We continued this arrangement down the years for her Cork Ballet Company and her National Ballet Company.

I always found Ms Moriarty a lovely gentle lady, who worked extremely hard at her dancing schools and anyone who worked for her was inspired to do the same. Some of her young pupils, who started their dancing careers in her schools, are still voluntarily maintaining all her costumes and everything else associated with her schools because they held Ms Moriarty in such high regard. She was such a great lady she could make you so enthusiastic about the ballet; indeed you would get carried away with it.

From a work perspective she was a perfectionist. There was one occasion where some costumes had to be dyed, but did not turn out as they should have, so we had to wash and dye them a couple of times until eventually she was satisfied. She would often ask how long a specific job was going to take; we wouldn't know at the time, but as her friends, we would do whatever was necessary to complete the work on time. We would not dare disappoint her. Ms Moriarty had a lot of great friends besides myself who would all help decorate the costumes, tutus, etc., for her: they would put on the sequins or do whatever she asked them to do.

Ms Moriarty's ballet meant everything to her and you were also expected to have the same passion, which for the most part I did. Joan Denise Moriarty was a very lovely lady and is sadly missed by all her ballet friends and associates.

CHERRY HUTSON O'KEEFFE (DUBLIN)
Costumes and Set Design

My mother and father Clare and Marshall Hutson were both graduates of the School of Art, where he worked all his life and she up to her marriage. They were designer and costume-maker to the Cork Ballet Company for over ten years in an honorary capacity. He designed most of the scenery for the company. Frank Sanquest also did some, and Frank would 'execute', i.e., work from my father's drawings and designs painting the stage sets. My father made lovely models, and also little model stages, all constructed accurately to scale. I would have liked as a child to have kept them myself, for example the cradle, the throne, and lovely graceful stools he made for *The Sleeping Princess*. It was amazing what he could do with a bit of stiff card, paper and glue; the finished products – shields, helmets, headdresses for *Macha Ruadh* and other productions – looked wonderful on stage, forming part of the great illusion created for the audience in that marvellous theatre, the old Cork Opera House.

My mother did fine paintings and drawings, but she was overshadowed in that respect by my father's great talent. However, in her role as costume designer and maker she was out on her own. She often made every single costume for the entire show. She had an unerring eye for colour and design, and her results were professional. The *Vltava* 'stream' costumes, for example, were most imaginative. The very small streams were pale blue where the water came bubbling from the spring at the source; then they gradually changed to pale green and deeper green and then to brown for the rapids. They were a simple sleeveless bodice with straps, and material attached to the waist. She also designed the lovely peasant costumes which were the pride of the Folk Dance Group, and were also used in *Playboy*: the red petticoats, black tops and white crochet shawls for the girls.

Being wardrobe mistress, she was backstage for all performances: she is remembered as having been quietly supportive of everyone, a rock of serenity in an ocean of stress. She never got into a flap and calmed anyone who did; she was very watchful and carefully checked that everyone's costume was as it should be before they went on stage. She also did trojan work with her team organising the Orchestral Society receptions after the concerts.

When my mother became president of the Irish Countrywomen's Association, as well as teaching art in two schools, my father felt the ballet was too much for her, and she, being the obedient wife she was, did what he suggested and retired. But she told me later that she would have liked to continue, and she always said that she had some of her happiest and most satisfying times doing the costumes. All the girls were very fond of her and she of them. When she left she was given a presentation and everyone was very sorry to see her go. My father then detached himself, and Pat Murray, who is a pupil of his, took over doing the scenery in 1958. Maeve Coakley took on the costumes and also made a marvellous job of it.

I came to Dublin in 1964, and when I told people I'd danced in the full length *Sleeping Princess*, in *Swan Lake*, *Coppélia*, *Petrouchka*, etc., they didn't believe me – thinking that maybe if you lived in London you could claim that. It was Miss Moriarty's extraordinary achievement to have accomplished this – nobody else could have done what she did.

Professor Fleischmann always had incredible energy and enthusiasm, even in the most adverse circumstances. He had players who were not all so talented, yet he always had enormous patience with them. The orchestra played miraculously for us, or so it seemed when we heard and compared the early rehearsals with the performances. He was always cheerful, though some of those sounds produced must have been painful to his ears.

We dancers became acquainted through the ballets with an enormous range of splendid music which we would otherwise never have encountered. We did *Petrouchka* for example – never in those days would I have dreamed of listening to Stravinsky, yet we came to love the music. I now help to manage one of the Dublin Youth Orchestras, and this year our exchange orchestra from Bavaria is playing Smetana's symphonic poem *Vltava*, which Miss Moriarty choreographed for the Cork Ballet Company's first performance in 1947, and in which I danced. These are wonderful memories – which the people of Cork must have too – of a *most* remarkable achievement lasting over forty years.

(6) The Folk Dance Group

MONICA GAVIN (CORK)

From the very beginning of her career, Miss Moriarty had a close association with the Gaelic folk culture. She was a champion Irish stepdancer in her youth; she worked with traditional Irish musicians such as Seán Ó Riada and Ceóltóirí Cualainn, and with equally happy results also with The Chieftains and Na Filí. Fr Pat Ahern consulted her when he was planning the programme for his folk group 'Siamsa Tíre'.

It was her expertise in the traditional field which brought her into contact with academic musicians using traditional Irish material: in 1945 she performed the war pipe solo in Professor Fleischmann's *Clare's Dragoons*. She was to use both types of Irish music in the eleven original Irish works she created for her companies. These were based on myths and legends, folk tales and customs, using traditional Irish dance steps and rhythms and incorporating classical movements to give them a dramatic quality. Suitable music was found in works by Irish composers.

In 1957 the Irish Folk Dance Group of the Cork Ballet Company was formed to take part in the Choral Festival, as our contribution to the new national festival 'An Tostal'. At that time, Ballet Week was also part of 'An Tostal' festivities. Folk dancing was fun and proved a great way of getting boys into the company. Mind you, it did not always work: one such gentleman, when told by Miss Moriarty that some exercise would be good for his legs, pulled himself up to his full height, said 'There is nothing wrong with my legs, Miss Moriarty!' and exited.

The group was invited to a Youth Festival at Wewelsburg Castle, Germany in 1958, where our leader was secretly referred to as the sergeant major. She was given a tremendous ovation for her Doodlesack solo at a celebrity concert in the town hall, where all visiting groups performed. For those who don't know, Doodlesack is German for war pipes.

In 1961 we visited the Dijon International Folk Dance and Wine Festival. This was a highly organised gathering of top folk dance groups from all over the world to celebrate the new season's Burgundy wine. Apart from concert performances, a major part of the competition for the Gold Collar was a huge parade of all groups and bands through the main streets of Dijon. This area was cordoned off and thousands of spectators paid to stand on the footpaths and watch the dances and hear the wide variety of music. It was a marvellous thrill to march behind the Irish flag and our striking leader, who in her dark green kilt and jacket played our signature tune 'The Men of the West' or 'The Boys of Kilmichael' on the war pipes. Our accordionist was a very young Michael Casey, now manager of Music Services in Radio Teleifís Éireann. He was so excited by the variety of music, particularly the swinging Glenn Miller sounds of a terrific American Army brass band, that he developed a chronic nosebleed and someone had to sit on him to keep him quiet. We won the Bronze Collar for International Groups for our dancing, production and parade.

As prize-winners in 1961, the Folk Dance Group was invited back to Dijon in September, 1965 with nineteen other prize-winning groups to celebrate their twentieth anniversary. Yugoslavia won the Gold Collar. It was a great achievement that our group took second place for promenades, behind Hungary, and third place for production, against almost professional competition, especially from eastern Europe. Once again, Miss Moriarty was the outstanding figure leading dancers and musicians, who included Matt Cranitch and the late Ned Meagher, and we got a great reception from the crowd. The women were fascinated with our red tweed skirts and the boys' tweed suits and commiserated with us in the very warm weather. We did learn to appreciate German beer and Burgundy wine!

The group travelled to Germany again in 1966, this time to Berlin; we were specially invited to a big rally at the Arena, where the chief address was made by Herr Willy Brandt. Then we went to Folk Dance and Wine Festivals at Deidesheim and Dillenburg where, once again, the presentation, production and the enthusiasm of the dancers and musicians won the group a major prize.

In October 1966, Ciaran MacMathúna introduced the first of thirteen Irish Dance Programmes given by the Cork Ballet Company on Radio Teleifís Éireann. The half-hourly television series commenced with *Rinnce Mór* or the Big Dance, *Yellow Beggar*, etc., went on to *North Road*, *Planting Stick* (Fleischmann), *Straw Boys*, *Gathering Duileasc*, *West Cork Ballad* (Ó Riada) and *Devil to Pay*, which had been choreographed by Miss Moriarty for Irish Theatre Ballet. Domy Reiter-Soffer danced in *West Cork Ballad*. The final production was *Seal Woman* with music by Hamilton Harty, which was full ballet on points. The series was a triumph for Miss Moriarty, who devised and choreographed all the works, and was a marathon for those involved in every production. Every second Saturday we travelled by train to Dublin, spent from 10am on Sunday in RTE rehearsing, they filmed the programme at 5pm and taxies took us to the station for the train at 6.15pm. On Monday night we rehearsed the next programme and started a new work. Adrian Cronin directed the series and it was a great tribute to the company and its director that the original series of seven programmes was extended to thirteen. Unfortunately, the tapes were re-used for other broadcasts, so there is now no record of the *An Damhsa* television series. The same thing happened to the TV programmes made around that time by Jimmy O'Dea, Seán Ó Riada and others.

LAVINIA ANDERSON (CORK)
Almost forty years ago Miss Moriarty spoke to us of Cork Ballet Company of her love of the folk idiom and how she wished us to learn Irish dancing. We knew, of course, that she was an excellent Irish dancer and that she took a great interest in all things relating to Irish culture. Her skills at the war pipes were known and admired. She had already created several works which, although strictly in a balletic mode, were based on Irish folklore and legend, and bore witness to her love of Ireland, its myths and music.

We were dismayed – all the time we had spent at learning the rudiments of ballet and now we were to become Irish dancers! She explained that we would not be learning Irish dancing but folk dancing. We had no idea what this was. So one fine summer in 1958 we gathered in the studio for the new venture. She taught us jigs and reels, but of a special quality all her own. There was a story or a theme running through each dance. We used our hands, our heads, indeed every part of our bodies: not for Miss Moriarty the stereotype blank faces and hands glued to our sides. She taught us to appreciate the brilliance and richness of our Irish music and legend. The dancing wasn't easy. We had to learn completely different techniques, to use completely different muscles; then there was the timing, the batters – for some it was almost a nightmare. And to crown it all: we, proponents of the most silent of the arts, had to sing! However, fired by her enthusiasm we persevered on the hot summer nights. Night after night we battered and reeled and sang. We sweated and swore but we stuck at it. We knocked our ankles, pulled our calf muscles and listened to her weave her magic about our history and capture our imaginations and our hearts.

Then one night she told us we had been invited to a Folk Festival in Germany to represent Ireland. While we would be accommodated free in Germany, we would have to pay for the travel ourselves. This was in 1958 when perhaps the furthest any of us had ever been in our lives was Dublin; now we would be travelling by liner, visiting Paris, going on to Germany for a week, and then flying back to Cork. We were bowled over. We would have begged, borrowed or stolen the money to go. Our costumes were like nothing we had ever seen before: magnificent red handwoven petticoats worn with black tops, Aran shawls and black tights, or pretty blue woven dresses again worn with the black tights. However, we were inclined to laugh at the boys in their thick woollen trousers with Aran sweaters and berets. She told us that our skirts were the traditional wear of the Aran islanders and we felt proud to be wearing them. She herself would be wearing her green kilt and would be leading us playing the pipes.

The weather got hotter and we got better. Some of us even found we could sing. So, early one morning off we went on our great adventure. The liner, Paris, our new-found freedom: it was heady stuff. Then two days after we had left the safety of our 1950s homes, we found ourselves standing outside our bus in a small German village where, like refugees, our names were called out and our hosts stepped forward and we were told to go with them and be sure to be in the square at 9am the next morning. And so for a week, led by this vision, or more exactly, by this visionary, we danced our way through villages, castles, town halls and schools, bringing our culture, our music and our dance to people who hardly even knew where Ireland was. Crowds would gather everywhere we went, to see us, yes – but principally to see this living embodiment of what was Ireland, with her tall thin dancer's body and flaming red hair leading us through the streets to the music of her pipes. She was proud of us but more proud of her Irishness and that she was able to show to others what it was to be Irish, what Ireland was for her.

Many times after that she was to lead her dancers in their native costumes, dancing to their native music abroad and at home, despite the criticism of those who wanted everything to remain the same, who were averse to progress and to development of the culture. She was never dismayed or disheartened. She knew there was something there, something that had to be developed. She continued with her folk dancing and gradually incorporated it into her folk ballets. Hers were the first of their kind in this country. Recognition has come to the wealth of tradition which is ours, culminating in *Riverdance*. Every time I see it, I see a tall beautiful woman accompanying them, playing her pipes, and taking such pride in the fact that at long last the folk dancing of Ireland has finally found its place in the world.

(7) The Schools of Ballet

BERNIE FLEMING (CLONMEL)
Barbara Essame, Eleanor Carroll and the Clonmel School of Ballet
The Joan Denise Moriarty School of Ballet commenced in Clonmel in 1959. This came about at the request of Mrs Barbara Essame, who wished to have ballet classes available for her daughter and friends. By a coincidence at approximately the same time Mrs Eleanor Carroll also wrote to Miss Moriarty suggesting that a school was required in the Clonmel area. It was agreed with both of them that should they secure a viable number of pupils, Miss Moriarty would begin a school. The number recommended was 30, but the ladies secured 60 pupils and so the school began.

This school for girls and boys has continued successfully for 37 years and now has third generation pupils on its roll. Its success can be attributed to the work of the two founders, and to the dedicated voluntary support given by a group of parents for more than 27 years: they were Breed Brown, Lily Carew, and Teresa Kent. I did not become involved until much later, when my daughter took up ballet. Miss Moriarty became a personal friend of Barbara Essame's and her late husband Michael, continuing contact with them until her death.

During all these years Miss Moriarty taught in the school. Her presence in the class was magic for her pupils. At the displays for parents and friends, she made a powerful impression. Her handling of the programme was serene and controlled. When she appeared on stage regal as a queen to address the audience, her grace and smile captivated all. She gave the message to parents that her pupils were given a training and a discipline that was unequalled. She was respected and admired by her pupils, one reason being her extreme fairness. She was distant but kind and never showed any bias except perhaps, we sometimes felt, to pupils with red hair!!

Miss Moriarty brought both the Cork Ballet Company and National Ballet to Clonmel: they were received with great enthusiasm. In the beginning dancers stayed with parents of pupils of the Clonmel School of Ballet. For the twenty-fifth anniversary of our school, we celebrated the occasion with a supper in our hall and many from the professional company attended. The dancers were always invited to the home of Barbara and Michael Essame after the performances; we were glad to meet so many different nationalities and we think they enjoyed the hospitality.

There have always been children from all backgrounds in the

school. From the beginning the fees were affordable and one or two scholarships were offered each year, where the school felt there was a reason and a need. In one case, a mother died leaving six children, one of whom was a keen dancer; she was offered a scholarship and continued in the school until she reached third level education, and then she went on to study dance at a college where she also won a scholarship. The school also gave scholarships to the first of the second generation to attend the school. Money was never the aim; on the contrary, the policy was to be forever conscious of keeping fees and expenses at a level that did not prevent anyone from enrolling.

We are so pleased that Miss Moriarty's tradition is being carried on by her successor, Breda Quinn, and the other teachers.

Breda Quinn (Cork)

Maybe you would think that somebody trained to be agile on her feet would also have some skills with her hands, or rather with the pen. But if there is anything I would do all the tiresome jobs in the world to get out of, it is writing – especially when the task is an impossible one: to give a sketch of somebody as complex, as splendid and as important to me as Miss Moriarty. It can't be done, and it has to be done.

I first met Miss Moriarty when I joined her Folk Dance Group, and was soon encouraged to join 'the ballet', as she maintained every dancer should have ballet training. Through the folk dancing I got my first trip outside Ireland – I could never have done this on my own, as money was not plentiful and without the group travel concessions and free accommodation with families we could not have afforded it, nor would we ever even have thought of heading off for France or Germany. With that she taught me something I have never forgotten: that much can be done with little if you only have the idea. Mostly it's not the lack of means which is the problem, but the lack of a clear mind about what is needed and possible – maybe having that clear mind is what they call vision.

When I became one of her ballet teachers, I taught in some of the schools outside Cork. I had a very good working relationship with her: it was her self-control and calm that I admired most of all. I had seen that in operation during chaotic rehearsals before shows, of course, where everything you could possibly imagine went wrong, and yet she remained imperturbable. But somehow I had always taken that for granted until I saw her keep her composure in every-day situations. For example when she came to visit the outside schools, I would sometimes take her in my car. Once it broke down, and we had to thumb a lift to Clonmel – an unknown to Miss Moriarty needless to say. There was not a word of annoyance out of her, and she stood there regally beside me while I flagged down cars, as if this was the most normal way to travel. We didn't have to wait long for a lift! Another time on a return trip from Clonmel, the engine blew up, and we had to thumb a lift to Fermoy and wait for a car to come from Cork to collect us. Again there wasn't a trace of exasperation or impatience: she took it all in her stride, whereas I was fuming and fussing and of course wasting my energy. It struck me then that you can only stay calm and overcome the big crises if you have trained yourself to do it through the small ones. I found that as an employer she was kindness personified. I lived with my aunt, who died suddenly one Christmas. Miss Moriarty not only came to the funeral, but visited me on that Christmas morning as she was worried about me being on my own. I will never forget that.

I read recently about the huge amount of money the IDA invests to establish new jobs through foreign firms. Miss Moriarty created a lot of employment at a fraction of that cost. She had us teachers in work; she had her dancers, administrators and theatre staff; she gave work to musicians, dressmakers, carpenters, printers and advertisers. As well as the employment she gave to some of us, we all learnt lessons from her of the greatest importance for life. She gave us confidence, she gave us ideals, she taught us to look for and bring out the best in everyone. As long as I live I want to continue in that sense to be her pupil.

3: THE MUSIC FOR THE DANCE

(1) *Miss Moriarty the Piper*

WILLIAM COGAN, PIPE-MAJOR OF THE CARRIGALINE PIPE BAND
I started piping in 1941. My tutor was Tadhg Crowley, who was a famous piper and traditional musician. At that time he had a music shop on Merchants' Quay which his son Michael now runs in Mac-Curtain Street. I remember Tadhg telling me he had given Joan Denise some tuition in piping.

Some time during the early war years I can recall cycling to Cork with some friends to hear Joan play the pipes at a variety concert in the Savoy Cinema. She was dressed in traditional Irish costume – saffron kilt, etc. – and as she marched to and fro on stage, her carriage and deportment was something greatly admired by all. The piping, to me, was excellent: splendid tone, and even though we were seated high up and very far away from the stage in this huge auditorium, every note could be heard crystal clear.

Unfortunately I never met Joan Denise until many years had passed. She had long since put aside the pipes in the interests of the Ballet, but her interest and love of the pipes remained.

TADHG Ó CRUADHLAOIGH OF CUMANN PÍOBAIRÍ NA HÉIREANN (THE IRISH PIPERS SOCIETY)

16 October 1945

Dear Miss Moriarty,
Congratulations on your excellent performance with Professor Fleischmann's orchestra. The pipes came over grand! You put over the show in superb style. I thought I would have the pleasure of congratulating you in person, but, as time is slipping by, I thought it better to drop you a line.

Hoping you are keeping well and with best wishes,
I remain yours respectfully
Tadhg Ó Cruadhlaoigh

(2) *The Music for the Folk Dance Group*

CLEMENT GARVEY (SHANNON, CO. CLARE)

I came to Cork in the early 1950s to study music with Professor Fleischmann. From this came my acquaintance with the Cork Ballet Company and Joan Denise Moriarty, and the experience of playing in the old Opera House before it burned down. These were years when money was scarce, especially for the arts. I was well aware of the personal effort and self-sacrifice that was needed to make anything worthwhile happen, like keeping the Symphony Orchestra and the Ballet Company going, getting the Opera House rebuilt, getting the Choral Festival off the ground, and the campaign to have at least a professional string quartet for Cork.

My closest association with the Ballet Company and Joan Denise was in 1958 when a folk dance group from the company was invited to an International Festival at Wewelsburg in Westphalia. I was privileged to be the fiddler for the group. We left Cobh on the liner *Mauretania* for Le Havre, stopped off in Paris, and went by train through Aachen to Salzkotten. The festival was started by refugees who had been resettled in this area, and had kept their culture alive and active. It was also part of the post-war reconstruction effort, and sacrifices were made by many to accommodate us. I was hosted by a war-widow and her son who were very confined in their accommodation, but I was made most welcome. We had a visit to war-graves – a salutary experience – and lectures, folk dances and singing each day at what had been Himmler's castle in Wewelsburg. The diverse cultures of Europe were being reconvened in harmony. We were taken to see the great cathedral of Paderborn, which has a wonderful Romanesque doorway something like that of Cormac's chapel in Cashel. I was only later to find out about the important role played by Irish missionaries such as Killian, Conleth and Totnan in Würzburg, and many others in other parts of Germany and the continent.

I was indebted to Joan Denise and the company for my first experiences of Germany. To me she was a person of great dignity and character who, in giving an example of dedication, discipline and hard work, inspired others with these virtues.

TOMÁS Ó CANAINN (CORK)

I first met Joan Denise when I came to Cork in the early 1960s. She was completely dedicated to dance: it was her life. My daughter Nuala took ballet lessons from her in the late 1960s and early 1970s and found her a strict and inspiring teacher, as did so many from Cork and its surrounds.

My only personal musical connection with her occurred at the Cork Choral Festival in the 1970s when, as a member of our group, Na Filí, I played for her dancers in the City Hall. She was familiar with Irish dance music, of course, and was well qualified to specify the type of music she wanted us to play. We enjoyed the occasion, as did her dancers.

MICHAEL CASEY, MUSIC DEPARTMENT RTE (DUBLIN)

Although they were both very well known to me by reputation, it was not until 1961 that I first met Aloys Fleischmann and Joan Denise Moriarty. The 'Prof.'asked me if I would play the accordion with the Cork Folk Dance Group for the Dijon Folk Dance Festival in September of that year. I told him that I did not play the accordion, but such were his considerable powers of persuasion and encouragement that I went straight out and bought myself a Paoli Sporani 120-bass piano accordion and, with the aid of a hastily purchased tutor, taught myself to play in the space of a few weeks. I still remember the instrument's distinctive red colouring and slightly musty smell. It was hard work playing it, much harder than playing the piano, as the arms quickly got tired from pushing that large bellows in and out. It was even more difficult to carry its case for anything but a short distance as it really was a very heavy instrument: and all of this for an unpaid gig!

That excursion to the festival in Dijon happened at a seminal time for me, not least because it was my first trip to the continent. I went there as a tee-totaller and came back a part-time alcoholic! I quickly got to know a little more about those people who had so impressed me by the old-world courtesy and charm they both extended to this rather excitable newcomer. During that trip I made many friends in the Folk Group, which have extended to this day.

There are many things that stand out in my mind from that time. I developed a rather spectacular nose-bleed on stage during one of our performances at the Palais d'Exposition in Dijon. The blood ran from my nose on to the red-coloured accordion and then dripped into the floor. I just about finished the performance and was carried off to hospital immediately afterwards. Both JDM and the Prof. were very solicitous towards me and they often spoke of it to me during the ensuing years. I remember going with the Prof. and a number of others from the Folk Dance Group to the museum in Dijon where there is quite a large exhibition of material pertaining to the French composer Jean-Philippe Rameau.

I also remember his kindly advice when we were in a recording studio there. I had just learned to play the accordion and here I was making my first commercial recording! When I listen to it today, I cringe. Fleischmann at the time told me gently and politely that what I was playing of course was not really in the traditional style and he made some helpful suggestions. It was a start, if not a very good one, to a recording career that has continued to this very day. He was right to make these suggestions of course: but this was in the days before the music revolution of Seán Ó Riada – another student of his. Later that same year, I attended University College Cork to follow the B. Mus. course and there I got to know Professor Fleischmann very well and spent a lot of time in his company. I was flattered to think that he considered me to be one of his brighter pupils. He generously organised scholarships and a studentship for me.

Shortly after our return from France, Miss Moriarty asked me to play the piano to accompany her various ballet classes, and this I did on a regular basis up to 1965, thus spending about 16 hours a week in her presence. We had many a chat about her trials and tribulations in setting up her ballet operation. She told me of one incident where, having advertised for ballet dancers in the local press, she was astonished to find that one young man turned up with a banjo looking for ballad singing lessons! This gives one some idea of the difficulties that she was up against at the time.

She did have some minor shortcomings. For example she had an unfortunate habit of saying *develuplé* instead of *developé*. But she was held in very high regard by her pupils and staff alike, and she had a very good way with people, especially when it came to motivating them. What limitations she possessed seemed not to matter at all to those around her: what really mattered was her inspirational goading of people to do things that perhaps they felt they were not truly capable of. She was a very private person who had a soft spot for those in difficulty. I know of a couple of cases where she reduced or even waived the fees completely for committed pupils who were short of money. She would never tell anyone about it, such was her sense of humility and her thoughtfulness.

The city of Cork mourned the passing of JDM and the Prof. much in the way they would honour a national hero and there are few I'm sure who would disagree with such treatment. Together they brought music and ballet to a city that, without their total commitment and tenacity in getting things done, would probably not have had anything near the amount of activity and standards of these arts that Cork possesses today.

Thank you both for all you have given to me.

MICHEÁL Ó LOCHLAINN OF COMHALTAS CEOLTÓIRÍ ÉIREANN (ASSOCIATION OF IRISH MUSICIANS)
Message to JDM at This is Your Life *of 24 February 1988*
We admire your artistic vision and inventive qualities, which pioneered the wedding of ballet and traditional Irish music, giving each an exciting new dimension. Our Cork musicians were proud to tour with you in Munster for your Irish folk dance programmes and some travelled with you to France. We enjoyed your stately lead and kilted dress, your playing martial airs on the war pipes at each venue that we visited. Our partnership may have been shortlived, but we made many new friends. The background to the success you now celebrate lies, we believe, in your ability to motivate others, to be friendly with all involved, demanding in detail, and always a model of professionalism.

Gura fada buan í.

(3) Playing for the Ballet

PADDY MOLONEY, THE CHIEFTAINS
I was so glad to hear that a book was being written about my dear friend Joan Denise Moriarty. I have many warm memories of the time The Chieftains and I spent working with Joan on *The Playboy of the Western World*.

I have been associated with film and stage productions of the play itself, but none compare with Joan's wonderful production, in which she adapted The Chieftains' music and brought the play alive with dance.

I have great memories of playing live each night. The first performance was during the Dublin Theatre Festival in 1978; after this Noel Pearson brought it to the City Center New York for two weeks; then one week at Sadler's Wells in London for the Sense of Ireland Festival, and then there were several performances in Cork, Belfast, and Brittany in France.

I was fortunate enough to have been asked by my good friend Aloys Fleischmann to play at her funeral, and remember standing alongside the coffin outside the church joking and feeling she was there among us joining in the fun.

My one regret was not having had Joan play the bagpipes with The Chieftains, because by all accounts she was a fine player.

She will not be forgotten.

ANNETTE ROHU DE FOUBERT (CORK)
The Cork Symphony Orchestra
The Cork Symphony Orchestra has the distinction of being the first orchestra, amateur or professional, formed in the Republic of Ireland and of being in the *Guinness Book of Records* for playing under the same founder-conductor for longer than any other orchestra. Founded in 1934 as the Cork University Orchestra, it included only a small number of university students and graduates, the majority of the players being amateur or professional from Cork city and county, supplemented by the Army Band of the Southern Command. The orchestra functioned under the auspices of the University Arts Society and gave two or three performances each year in the Aula Maxima of University College Cork. The other function of the orchestra was to perform the music of students' orchestrated works. This gave students experience in conducting and also a platform for new compositions. Here musicians such as Seán Ó Riada, Pilib Ó Laoghaire, Séamas de Barra, John Murphy, Patrick Zuk, Micheál Ó Súilleabháin and many more were able to conduct and hear their own compositions for the first time.

Being one of these students, I found the experience fulfilling and memorable. Even during the war these performances continued, and in 1939 the Cork Orchestral Society was founded and the orchestra renamed the Cork Symphony Orchestra. It gave its first Symphony Concert in the City Hall in March of that year, followed by a series of performances in the Cork Opera House. Then in 1947 the cooperation between the Cork Symphony Orchestra with the Cork Ballet Company came into being – a partnership which lasted for nearly half a century, the forty-fifth performance taking place in 1992 in the presence of the President of Ireland, Dr Mary Robinson, after the deaths the same year of the two founders. This was a memorial production of *Giselle*, a most fitting tribute to their life-long inspiration and dedication.

As a founder member of the Cork Ballet Company I can vividly remember the evening Professor Fleischmann came to the small dance studio over Simcox's store in Patrick Street, Cork. He put this proposition to us dancers: 'If you give up every other form of dance discipline for ballet I will support you with my Symphony Orchestra'. (Our programmes hitherto had been varied and included

94

several dance forms.) We accepted. The following year in May, 1948 for the first time in the history of the Cork theatre, a local company gave a series of ballet performances at the Opera House with full symphony orchestra and Aeolian choir, lavishly costumed and staged. No similar venture had ever been undertaken in the country.

I was both dancer and player in *The Golden Bell of Ko*. Cast as a Chinese mandarin, I sat cross-legged playing a series of steel blocks measuring from six to twelve inches long. Professor Fleischmann had each one tuned to a different pitch, and they sounded rather like a glockenspiel orchestral part. Then I would run to the ornate box at the front of the auditorium where the large bell was situated, and, swinging from a strong rope attached to this bell, I had to sound the knell – I could only hope in the right bar and on the correct beat – making the great tolling bell peal out.

Sadly, my dancing days were soon to be over. However, I had been a timpanist and percussion player from the age of twelve and I now became an orchestral player. This posed some problems, as I was female and hitherto this section of the orchestra had always been in the hands of the male army players. I remember a performance in the Savoy Cinema, Limerick where in transit my sticks were mislaid. The army drummer was loath to lend me his. The interval was far longer than any interval ever was, while the other players negotiated with him. Having finally agreed to give them to me, he placed the sticks on the cash desk of the cinema – they rolled in, and the desk was locked! Panic reigned until the manager was located to retrieve the controversial sticks and, at long last, the curtain could rise and the ballet proceed.

The Cork Ballet Company with the Cork Symphony Orchestra contributed to the colour and pageantry of the opening and closing ceremonies of the Cork International Choral Festival, when the Cork Corporation in their red robes walked in procession through City Hall led by the dancers carrying the flags of the different countries of the choirs, to the music – often composed for the occasion by the conductor – and sung by massed choirs. There is one opening ceremony I shall always remember. I had just received a new set of tubular bells, and the professor had written a work for the occasion with an introductory solo for these chimes for the processional march. All went well at rehearsal. However, when I started to play, each bell proceeded to descend to the platform with a resounding thud, until I was finally left with one bell. What a calamity during the first performance of a new work! I will never forget the startled look of the conductor – this must have been the most embarrassing moment of my life.

I also remember the occasion when Professor Fleischmann took two players and my timpani in his car to perform in Limerick. On the way his car overturned, the two players ended up in hospital, but the professor arrived unharmed to take the rehearsal – the remaining members of the orchestra having travelled by coach. I was told that my timpani were quite safe, as he had left someone on guard duty with them on the road, and they would be transported in time for the performance. This was so. The criterion was that 'the show must go on'.

The Cork Ballet Company and Cork Symphony Orchestra brought tremendous pride and joy to the people of Cork and further afield. I feel privileged to have performed in the inaugural production of 1947 with the Ballet Company, and to have played with the Symphony Orchestra up to the final tribute performance of *Giselle* in 1992 after the death of the founders.

ANGELA O'KEEFFE (GALWAY)

When I joined the Cork Symphony Orchestra with my sister, Professor Fleischmann's name was already familiar to us, as he had studied music at UCC with our mother, Ena Hendrick – she had been the only music student until his arrival in her third year. For me as a teenager, it felt so grown-up to be addressed by the conductor as 'Miss Hendrick', and indeed I never heard him address any member of the orchestra otherwise than in this formal fashion. He was always the essence of courtesy. However much provoked by the inadequacies of his amateur musicians – and in retrospect, I think these must have been considerable – he never embarrassed anyone, always conveying his message with the utmost tact. In fact I now realise he must often have simply refrained from criticising where he knew it couldn't achieve anything. Nonetheless, one was very much aware of his high standards and his perseverance in getting the best possible performance from his orchestra.

I felt immensely grateful to him for making it possible for me as an amateur cellist to play in a symphony orchestra and become familiar with an extensive orchestral repertoire. I have appreciated all he did even more over the past five years, having been myself involved in the organisation of an amateur orchestra in Galway. I know my sister feels the same sense of gratitude. The time spent in the Cork Symphony Orchestra as well as being a highlight of our youth, greatly enhanced our enjoyment of orchestral music in the ensuing years. It was a gift we could never repay.

My association with Miss Moriarty began in the early 1950s when, at the invitation of Professor Fleischmann, I joined the Cork Symphony Orchestra as a young cellist. Two of my sisters were already involved in Ballet Week.

We always did a full scale symphony concert in the City Hall, but the highlight of the year for me was the annual ballet production at the Cork Opera House. Orchestral rehearsals began about two months before the production date: this was necessary as we only rehearsed once a week. About three weeks before the opening night, the orchestra and the company joined forces and rehearsals became more frequent. We approached this night with a mixture of excitement and trepidation – had we rehearsed enough? – would there be any major calamities? Professor Fleischmann welcomed Miss Moriarty, the soloists and the company and the rehearsal commenced. Miss Moriarty always sat with the musical score on her lap. She directed the rehearsal from this and was obviously completely *au fait* with the musical side of things. Of course, there were problems. The tempi had to be co-ordinated. Often the solo instrumentalists were unable to attend rehearsals until the week before the ballet commenced, which made things difficult for the dancers. The professor sometimes got so rapt with the music that he forgot to watch the dancers and Miss Moriarty would have to shout 'professor' to let him know that they had stopped.

It was obvious that everyone – both dancers and musicians – had the utmost respect for the professionalism of the professor and Miss Moriarty. Their absolute dedication and determination to overcome all obstacles was a source of constant amazement to us. I believe Miss Moriarty's contribution to ballet in Cork and in Ireland in general was only possible because of her complete and utter dedication to her art, which took a heavy toll on her health. She is greatly missed and I will always remember her with gratitude and admiration.

I want to take this opportunity to say how much I cared for and respected Professor Fleischmann. To me he was quite unique. I was, and still am, fiercely loyal to him and would never countenance a word of criticism against him. I know that I would have given up playing the cello a long time ago, were it not for the Cork Symphony Orchestra and his constant encouragement and unfailing good humour and kindness. I feel greatly privileged to have known him.

(4) Kindred Spirits

MARY HORAN (CAMBRIDGE)
Harpist, Cork Symphony Orchestra 1980–86
Ballet, perhaps more than most of the performing arts, demands inspired collaboration. As Stravinsky has vividly portrayed in *Apollon Musagète*, it springs from the offerings of many muses. It takes nothing less than a meeting of minds to bring them into accord. History bears witness to a profound complicity in this regard. Without Diaghilev, for example, would Stravinsky have produced *Firebird* and the subsequent balletic masterpieces of the twentieth century, *Petrushka* and *The Rite of Spring*? And without Balanchine would these and his later creations have attained true realisation and acclaim? Such indeed was the depth of communion and the close spiritual bond between the latter, that when an acquaintance commiserated with Balanchine on the recent death of his friend, he waved it aside with the words 'Ah, but he's still here'.

It seemed to me that a similar sublime unanimity characterised the long collaboration between Dr Joan Denise Moriarty, founder and artistic director of Irish National Ballet and Professor Aloys Fleischmann, composer, and conductor of the Cork Symphony Orchestra. Year after year their combined efforts produced marvels on the stage of the Cork Opera House which in terms of consistent artistic excellence, scale and innovation were unrivalled by any comparable venture within the country, even within the walls of the capital. One of the glories of these productions was that they largely involved native Irish artists, most in fact being culled from the city and its environs. At a time when the arts in Ireland were still comparatively undeveloped, this ability to make the most of home-grown talent provided a welcome boost in morale. It also fostered a salutary civic spirit.

It is one of the sadnesses of life that we tend to take for granted the stable and familiar things which by their constancy blend into the background like the landscape that surrounds us, and which we only begin to look at objectively and gauge their true worth when they are gone. Now that these two venerable personages have passed into eternity we might ponder on their achievement. What was the nature of their shared vision and what were the forces that propelled them, against the odds, to genuine artistic achievement? How to describe the felicities of character and circumstance that enabled this valuable association to prosper over the decades?

First on a purely aesthetic level, one might venture to suggest that they shared a similar poetic orientation to their arts – a poetry which derived its source and substance from Celtic mysticism and which ramified outwards to embrace classical mythology. In this respect they perpetuated a particularly Irish form of artistic expression, a mainstream conjunction of the Hibernian and the universal/ archetypal which carries within its flux figures such as Yeats, Russell (AE) and Pearse, and which in the realm of music had hitherto yielded the richest dividends in the works of non-natives such as Arnold Bax. In his ballet, the *Táin*, based on the legend of the *Táin Bó Cuailnge*, Aloys Fleischmann celebrated on a large scale a style of elevated lyrical composition, cultivated over the years, which drew on the mythical Irish past.[1] This same world in all its enchantment and ferocity was conjured up by Miss Moriarty in her choreography of legends such as *Lugh of the Golden Arm*,[2] based on the music of Ó Riada and de Buitléar. In contrast to this mythical vein, her dance version of Synge's *Playboy of the Western World* and her miniature ballets such as *Puck Fair* (music by A. Potter) captured the earthiness of the peasant world with realism, wit and poignancy.

Like Bax, both had an outside perspective on the Irish cultural heritage. Their respective experiences of other cultures, at a time when life in Ireland for the majority was still very parochial, fostered a salubrious detachment, and enabled them to bring to their own heritage, enriching features, both practical and artistic, from abroad. Miss Moriarty's childhood in England, where her family participated in the Gaelic Athletic Association and Gaelic League and where she was instructed in bagpipe playing and Irish step-dancing, had instilled the immigrant's love of homeland. Her classical dance training led to contact with figureheads such as Madame Marie Rambert and Dame Ninette de Valois, who supported her endeavours to propagate ballet in Ireland. Aloys Fleischmann's German parentage and studies in that country had imbued him with a love of the late Romantic idiom, particularly as manifested in Wagnerian opera. This relish for the expressive late nineteenth-century musical language was the legacy of his mother in particular, who had studied at the Royal Academy in Munich with Kellermann and Stavenhagen, students of Liszt. In her book, *Aspects of the Liszt Tradition*[3] which records what she learnt from her teachers, she reveals a rare capacity to combine an intensely vivid poetical explication of the piano compositions of Liszt and Chopin with a down-to-earth description of the technical means by which this high flown Romantic repertoire is best realised. The same respect for technical prowess –

applied in this case to conducting – allied to a genuine poetical response to the music was endemic in the musical nature of her son, qualities which were invaluable when it came to the realisation of the musical dimension of the ballet repertoire.

Fitting tribute will no doubt be paid to Miss Moriarty's pioneering spirit and vision – and account taken of her collaborative gifts, choreographic ingenuity, and unique contribution to ballet in Ireland – in the fullness of time. The present writer can only offer a few observations based on productions witnessed at first hand while performing as harpist with the Cork Symphony Orchestra. I first encountered the *corps de ballet* of the Irish Ballet Company (as it was then known) at the final rehearsals for their winter production at the Opera House in February 1980. The programme was richly varied and as such representative of the lively eclecticism which characterised all their work: a suite of dances from Glazunov's *Raymonda* (originally choreographed by Petipa and reproduced here by Kathleen Smith), *Lugh of the Golden Arm* (choreography by Joan Denise Moriarty), Bach's *Brandenburg No. 2* (choreography by Czarny), and a bracing minimalist interpretation of the Orpheus myth devised by Domy Reiter-Soffer. As I was only involved in the Glazunov I had time to survey the phenomenon of a symphony orchestra and full *corps de ballet* all on one level, with dancers pirouetting and spinning in close proximity to the players, conductor and choreographers, principals and ballet master all striving valiantly to get the act together in the final few hours' rehearsal prior to the opening night. Positioned at the still centre of this ferment was Miss Moriarty. One was immediately struck by her air of quiet authority, as well as by her grace of movement and imperturbable manner. Decisions regarding tempi, repeats and other details of performance were made quickly and efficiently, a prerequisite given the limited rehearsal time. Professor Fleischmann's courtesy and willingness to marshal the orchestra to produce exactly what was required in terms of interpretive nuance was an invaluable asset. Discipline, patience and humour prevailed, and so the task of synchronising music and dance was achieved with ease and civility.

In the years that followed a series of equally compelling productions ensued. Highlights of the 1981 season were Miss Moriarty's choreography of the 'Dance of the Hours' from Ponchielli's *La Gioconda; Paradise Gained* – a portrait of the life of the Parisian author, Colette – choreographed by Domy Reiter-Sofer to music by Milhaud; and Mahler's *Adagietto No. 5*, as choreographed to much acclaim by Royston Maldoom. Once again, being involved only in the

Adagietto, I observed the final rehearsals at close range, noting the strengths of the collaboration: discipline, vigorous repartee between conductor and ballet master (David Gordon) in close consultation with Miss Moriarty, decisive strategies, gracious compromise. The tempo was a slight bone of contention in the *Adagietto*, Professor Fleischmann favouring a more nuanced and protracted reading than the dancers were accustomed to, but a consensus was reached after some experimentation.

The November 1983 production of *Swan Lake* (reproduced by Richard Collins) provided an opportunity to view the Cork Ballet Company and the orchestra working together. Here was a more sustained work, placing greater demands on both. One of the principals was Patricia Crosbie (Odile/Odette) – the other Frederik Jahn Werner of London Festival Ballet (Siegfried). The dynamic Richard Collins was the producer: brimming with energy and charisma, he mobilised the dancers to deliver their best. This highly-charged direction placed greater strain on the orchestra, and it was with the greatest of aplomb, humility, wit and with equal reserves of energy that Professor Fleischmann met the challenge. Miss Moriarty acted as mediator, occasionally voicing a gentle but judicious opinion to visible effect. It all came together magnificently and judging from the volume of applause on the first night, and indeed throughout the week, must surely have been one the most successful productions to date.

Tchaikovsky – this time *Nutcracker* – was the choice for the 1984 season. The production once again was by Richard Collins who attended the final rehearsals, and the cast included Patricia Crosbie (Snow Queen/Sugar Plum Fairy), together with Nigel Burgoine of London Festival Ballet (Nutcracker) and Simon Klepper (Rat King). Viewing the rehearsals again from my position in the orchestra in the long stretches where the harp is silent, it struck me that this production built on the momentum established in *Swan Lake*. The orchestra was keen and responded to the atmospheric tonal palette of the score, vividly realising the dark-hued wind sonorities in particular. Professor Fleischmann's spirited direction drew out the best in the players – a vitality that is sometimes lacking in the routine performances of professional orchestras and which more than compensated for any rough edges – and the combined efforts of Miss Moriarty and Richard Collins exerted a similar influence on the dancers. Rapport was at an optimum. There was a buoyancy about this production which seemed to proclaim that a plateau had been reached after the cumulative toil of so many years. As the curtain fell to rapturous applause on the first of December, the last night of a week of full houses, it seemed inconceivable that major cuts in Arts Council funding in 1985 would severely curtail future ballet productions.

Because of the single-minded commitment of both Miss Moriarty and Professor Fleischmann to maintaining the tradition of presenting ballet to Cork audiences, the reduction in funding had less of an impact than might otherwise have been the case. Adjustments were made and work with the Cork Ballet Company continued as before. If one were to summarise their philosophy – the key to their resilience – it might well be 'joy in the striving'. The spectacular staging of ballet with all the effects of lighting, design, décor and costume, while a delight for the general public, was not their priority. Altruists both, their aims were primarily didactic. They were concerned above all with improving the quality of life, of using their respective arts to enrich the cultural and spiritual life of the individual and, by extension, of the community. Both had devoted a lifetime to furthering this ideal. The Cork Symphony Orchestra, founded in 1934, grew from a small university orchestra to become a major feature of city cultural life. Similarly, Irish National Ballet had rapidly established a touring programme which incorporated many of the towns across the country, bringing ballet to people who would never otherwise have had a chance to experience it. Both had endured the privations which promoting the arts in a largely philistine environment entailed.

On a personal level, too, the sacrifices which they made in order to channel all their energies into their arts were clear for all to see. In the tradition of the ballerinas of the old Russian school of dance, Miss Moriarty remained single. She was noted for her total dedication to teaching, for the long hours which she sustained and for the austerity of her professional and domestic regime. Her thin, fragile frame, demure mien and impeccable deportment bore testimony to the discipline and frugality of her daily life. Nothing other than a missionary zeal engendered by the recognition of a need – that of bringing the art of dance, and all that it implied in terms of aesthetic awareness and cultural refinement, to a country emerging out of centuries of deprivation – could have warranted such renunciation. She bore the burden of her vocation stoically, devoting all her energies to cultivating the talents of others.

Professor Fleischmann's zealousness was equally remarkable. After a long day at the university he would arrive almost an hour before rehearsals and arrange the hall for the orchestra. Chairs and music stands would be unstacked, unfolded and positioned in place, often with the help of only one or two volunteers. He dashed about collecting instruments and players and at the end of rehearsals supervised the clearance of the hall while attending to the musical queries of every last person. Sometimes when the hour was getting late he would be rescued from this work by his wife and ferried away to rest.

Without such total involvement and personal sacrifice on the part of Professor Fleischmann, the task of running an orchestra without significant funding would not have been possible. Cork city, like the other provincial cities in those days – Limerick, Galway, Waterford – would simply not have had a symphony orchestra. For a city which long took pride in its cultural richness (and is, after all, the home of the renowned writers Ó Faoláin, O'Connor and Corkery) this would have been a sorry loss. That the person best qualified to do so (and who might just as easily have made a name as a conductor, composer or scholar in the international arena) should have had the resources of character to endure the hardships of building up and maintaining an orchestra with next to no funding, was serendipitous indeed. Others who founded or maintained orchestras in similar circumstances in the first half of the century – such as Thomas Beecham with the Hallé – had considerable private funds or, as in Germany, municipal financial backing. Few would have been willing to attempt such a feat, equipped with little more than abundant enthusiasm and fierce social zeal. That it was all done so graciously and unobtrusively added to the nobility of his achievement.

Public recognition came in the form of the Freedom of the City for Professor Fleischmann, an Honorary Doctorate from the National University of Ireland for Miss Moriarty. Apart from the pride which they must have felt at receiving such acknowledgement of their work from city and country, such accolades for people as simple and devoid of pretensions as Miss Moriarty and Professor Fleischmann can hardly have been valued to the extent which they sometimes are by the more worldly. What they did value was respect and human dignity; not just for the privileged and renowned but for every individual in themselves. During their lifetimes their superior gifts and the exemplary way in which they conducted their lives commanded this respect, and it was unconsciously given. This possibly was the reward they cherished most. They were regarded as paragons of all that was highminded and noble: beacons of hope in a world growing ever spiritually more depleted. The virtues of self-denial, dedication, respect for one's fellow creatures, love of city and country, and the ability to work for ends that are devoid of self-interest, were theirs in abundance. If any memorial is to be created in their honour, it is one which would proclaim these values – enunciating its message across the nation – which would be most appropriate and would repay, in part, the debt which all of us owe them.

(5) Aloys Fleischmann's Ballet Music

SÉAMAS DE BARRA (CORK)

From the outset Aloys Fleischmann's ambition as a composer was to find an authentic voice for aspects of the Irish experience which had never before been articulated in music. Strongly critical however of the narrow parochialism that bedevilled so much of Irish life, including Irish musical life, in the years following independence, he was also concerned to compose out of an understanding of what it meant to be an Irish composer in a larger European context. He reconciled these aims in a deeply imaginative musical response to the country's manifold literary heritage and, initially, in the successful evolution of an idiom which, allowing the accent of traditional music to sound naturally, is yet sophisticated enough to sustain complex structures. His early works, with their unforced and spacious accommodation of dignified nationalist sentiment, were certainly of sufficient resonance and persuasiveness to bring him to national prominence as a composer of serious intent and significant achievement. Fleischmann was, consequently, a natural choice to receive in 1944 a commission for a work to celebrate the Thomas Davis centenary, and in response he produced what is arguably one of his finest compositions. It was also the occasion of his first collaboration with Joan Denise Moriarty.

The commissioned work, a setting of Thomas Davis' patriotic poem *Clare's Dragoons*, and based on the vigorous martial air traditionally associated with it, was written for baritone solo, chorus, orchestra and, curiously, war pipes. This unusual and original addition to otherwise standard performing forces is due to his having seen Joan Denise Moriarty, a champion piper, hold her audience in thrall by a display of virtuosity at a concert of Gaelic music held at University College Cork in July 1939. Fleischmann was sufficiently impressed that now, six years later, he invited Miss Moriarty to perform his new work which had developed around the idea of an integral part for her instrument. In agreeing, so the story goes, she seized the opportunity to overcome one of her greatest handicaps –

the difficulty of providing adequate music for the ballet group she had been training. There and then she struck a bargain: 'I will,' she told him, 'if your orchestra will play for my ballets'.[4]

The first performance of *Clare's Dragoons* in Dublin in September 1945 took place before an invited audience consisting of the president, taoiseach, cabinet, senate, dáil, judiciary and civil service. Fleischmann described it as being 'probably the most Philistine audience ever assembled in Dublin, most of whom had never been at an orchestral concert before, so that a less receptive audience could hardly be imagined'.[5] The performance in Cork shortly afterwards however was a triumphant success, the march of the piper through the auditorium to the platform to join the other performers at the climactic final restatement of the tune being a genuine *coup de theatre*. In due course the Cork Ballet Group, as it was now called, presented its first production with the assistance of the Cork Symphony Orchestra under Aloys Fleischmann. This was in June 1947, for one night only, but it was the beginning of an association that was to last for almost fifty years. For Aloys Fleischmann the collaboration with Joan Denise Moriarty, both in establishing amateur ballet in Cork and subsequently in setting up the professional companies, was unquestionably a major creative stimulus and the works he wrote for the Cork company were to occupy his principal compositional energies for the next decade.

For a composer whose declared aim was 'to delve into the hidden Ireland, and to create an idiom which would express in music some of the essence of this rich untapped literary tradition',[6] this collaboration presented a unique opportunity to bring music into direct contact with the root of things Irish, as embodied in the country's myths, legends and folk tales, by presenting them in ballet form. For nationalist composers the immediate appeal of the theatre had always been very attractive, and opera was the great vehicle for nationalism in music in the nineteenth century. In this country, however, where the chances of having an opera produced were remote, even if a composer was foolhardy enough to write one, the chances of having a ballet produced were, up to now, virtually non-existent. But, unlikely as it must have seemed, the scarcely imaginable possibility of Cork having a ballet company of its own had become a reality due to the presence in the city of this remarkable woman.

Fleischmann wrote five ballets for Joan Denise Moriarty, and the direct exploration of various aspects of the Irish experience in three of the four he composed for the Cork company culminated in his final ballet score, the *Táin*, written for the Irish Ballet Company in

1981. Based on the *Táin Bó Cuailnge* (The Cattle Raid of Cooley), the twelfth century account of the exploits of Cuchulainn and Queen Medb, it was in many ways the climax of his composing career. Not only was it his most ambitious score in terms of length and organisation, but the opportunity to engage the greatest of the ancient sagas in this way enabled him to produce a late triumphant example of his personal response to the problem of shaping a distinctly Irish utterance.

Apart from compositional considerations, Fleischmann's involvement with the emergent ballet group was completely consonant with his decision to put his energies at the service of the cultural life of Cork on returning to the city in 1934 to fill the vacant chair of music at UCC. This was the local focus of his concern for the musical and cultural well-being of the country as a whole, and it had his unreserved commitment. That the standard of performance and production by the Cork Symphony Orchestra and the Cork Ballet Group might be variable he accepted as inevitable in any such amateur enterprise. If, in his support for and defence of these and other provincial cultural activities, he sometimes appeared vulnerable to the charge of being insufficiently discriminating it is because for him and for his committed contemporaries, in attempting to overcome the country's pervasive cultural inertia, any enterprise, no matter how tentative, was clearly better than nothing. 'No people who are trying to do anything *at all* should meet with mere discouragement in this land of ruin and weed', wrote Micheál Mac Liammóir in his diary for 1955.[7] Fleischmann would have agreed, and realising fully the fragility of such endeavours, he was fiercely protective. Dependant on local talent and local resources, both he and Joan Denise Moriarty were prepared to acknowledge the necessity of small beginnings. Nevertheless, with the Cork Symphony Orchestra in its second decade, the Cork Orchestral Society only slightly younger, a vital and expanding music department at UCC and now the Cork Ballet Group, all locally rooted but outward looking, it must have seemed in 1947 that the prospects for the musical life of the city were good.

It was a sweet irony too that Cork, whose philistine attitude to the ballet had been affectionately satirised by Seán Ó Faoláin in his play *She Had to Do Something*, should now, of all things, boast a ballet company of its own. Ó Faoláin's play, produced at the Abbey Theatre in 1939 and based on a visit of the Anna Pavlova Ballet Company to the city in 1931 'which resulted in denunciations from several pulpits, empty houses, and the frustration of a small minority who hailed this sudden bonanza in an otherwise barren season',[8] may have held Cork up to gentle ridicule for the amusement of Dublin audiences, but it now appeared as if Cork would have the last laugh.

The response to the first production was so enthusiastic that Moriarty and Fleischmann were encouraged to present a full week of ballet the following summer. The advance publicity sounds a distinct note of justifiable pride: 'For the first time in the history of Cork Theatre a local company will give a series of ballet performances with full symphony orchestra and choir, lavishly dressed and staged', and goes on roundly to assert that 'no similar ambitious venture has ever been staged in this country'. As well as a revival of Elizabeth Maconchy's *Puck Fair*, first performed in Dublin in 1941 and now re-choreographed by Joan Denise Moriarty, the programme also included a new ballet specially written for this production by Fleischmann himself. *The Golden Bell of Ko*, the first of the Fleischmann ballet scores, is also curiously one of the very few works of his not in some way related to specifically Irish subject matter, based as it is on a Chinese legend.

It is clear from this score that Fleischmann had a natural flair for the ballet: the music shows a talent for the vivid and colourful depiction of character and incident, and a precise, well focused response to the demands of the scenario, from quirky humour to tender pathos. He made no concessions to the amateur status of either the dancers or the orchestra, and it is a difficult score both in the elusive irregularities of its phrase structure and in the technical demands of its orchestration. Nor did he make any concessions to what would undoubtedly have been an inexperienced audience still unfamiliar with Bartok and Stravinsky. The often angular melodic lines, the pungent harmonies and ambivalent tonality, while tame today, must have sounded startling in Cork in 1948. It proved to be Fleischmann's most popular ballet however, and was twice revived by the company, first in 1953 and subsequently in 1973 when it was also presented in Dublin.

Fleischmann composed his second ballet score, *An Cóitín Dearg* (The Red Petticoat), in 1950–51 to a scenario by Mícheál Mac Liammóir, who also designed the décor and the costumes for the first production. The initial idea for this ballet goes back at least to 1942 when Mac Liammóir published the greater part of the scenario – the conclusion was teasingly omitted – in the September issue of *The Bell* for that year. Under the title 'Design for a Ballet' it was presented as work in progress, together with a commentary, in the form of letters to Mac Liammóir, from Cepta Cullen who was to choreograph it, and from Michael Bowles who was to compose the music.[9] But this particular version never appears to have been written. Fleischmann, who subscribed to *The Bell* and was an occasional contributor, had obviously read and liked the scenario and corresponded with Mac Liammóir as early as 1946 with a view to composing a score himself. The ballet had already been produced: Mac Liammóir refers to an existing score by Tyrell Pine, although he makes no allusion at all to any music by Michael Bowles. Nevertheless, he tells Fleischmann to 'please go ahead', and adds 'I look forward so much to hearing your music and am very proud to think that an idea of mine should make you want to write it'.[10] Although Mac Liammóir evidently had no objection to two versions, Fleischmann shelved the project for the time being.

Mac Liammóir, who clearly held Fleischmann's abilities as a composer in high esteem, not only welcomed the idea of their collaboration but saw no reason why it should necessarily be restricted to the ballet. Fleischmann recounted to the present writer how Mac Liammóir and Hilton Edwards invited him to dinner around this time and how, as the climax of the evening, Mac Liammóir produced a copy of his play *Diarmuid agus Gráinne* with the suggestion that Fleischmann consider it as the basis for an opera. The fly-leaf was ceremoniously inscribed: 'Dom' charaid Aloys Fleischmann le dóchas! Micheál Mac Liammóir, Baile Atha Cliatha, 1946, '(to my friend Aloys Fleischmann, with hope! Micheál Mac Liammóir, Dublin, 1946), and the book duly presented. But Fleischmann demurred and the opera was never written. In fact there is no evidence that he ever seriously entertained the idea. It is true that the legend of Diarmuid and Gráinne may be too uncomfortably close to that of Tristan and Isolde to encourage the attentions of a prospective composer, but the very poor chances of production were, in all likelihood, the real deterrent. The ballet however was written, a production being guaranteed, and was presented as part of the programme for the Cork Ballet Group's fourth season in May 1951.

The fact that the first and third acts are set in Connemara and the second in New York gave Fleischmann the rare opportunity pointedly to contrast a popular style, sophisticated and cosmopolitan, with a style based on the idioms of folk music. Briefly, Colm and Nora, the hero and heroine, are frustrated in the tentative beginnings for their love for one another. Lacking the courage to confront their circumstances, Nora leaves for New York and Colm, dejected, follows her. Although enjoying material success in this shallow and affluent milieu they are however unhappy, and they return home. Clothed in their elegant finery, they meet again and, significantly, fail to recognise one another; but Colm changes back into his báinín, Nora into her red petticoat, and as Mac Liammóir puts it: 'nuair a fhilleas siad ar an tsimplíoch is dual dóibh annsin aithníonn siad a chéile agus an grá atá eatorra arís'[11] (when they return to the simplicity that is natural to them they then recognise one another again and the love that is between them). The old story, in the other words, of gaining the world and losing your soul.

Apart from the many splendid opportunities it afforded the composer, this scenario must have been particularly resonant for Fleischmann whose entire philosophy of the value, indeed the necessity, of native rootedness it reflects. This intense sense of personal rootedness shaped the evolution of his distinctive style, and it informs the outer acts of *An Cóitín Dearg* in their confident depiction of the imaginative and intellectual conditions necessary, not to be sure for an idyllic but, for an authentic, life. Jazz, on the other hand, as many of his students could testify, represented decadence, and in the central act of the ballet he unabashedly employs popular idioms to convey the empty lives of those for whom there is 'nothing in the world but their money and their pleasures'.[12] Over-simple equations perhaps and if, together with others made in this work, they appear today to be in some respects questionable, there is no doubt that for Fleischmann, as his career demonstrates, they were fundamentally valid.

The *Irish Independent*, writing that 'the most successful feature of the ballet was Aloys Fleischmann's attractive score', nevertheless thought the popular idiom a little stiffly handled and suggested that 'perhaps his jazz might be described as academic ragtime.' Reading this unlikely reference to jazz from the austere pen of Aloys Fleischmann evidently startled some people, among them Alfred O'Rahilly, president of UCC, who, not having seen the ballet, was unaware of the ironic context. His assistant, conveying his congratulations on the success of the production, adds: 'The president says that he is delighted that, according to the *Irish Independent*, you are coming more close to the level of his musical appreciation. He says, however, that he does not believe it.'[13]

It is a measure of the confidence that Fleischmann and Moriarty had in the standards attained by the Cork Ballet Company (as it had become in 1954), and in the role it now played in Irish cultural life, that they felt it appropriate to issue an invitation to the president of Ireland to attend the 1955 season. The invitation was accepted and

Seán T. O'Kelly and his wife travelled to Cork for a gala performance. The main attraction was undoubtedly the first complete staging in Cork of *Coppélia*, but the most significant was the premier of Fleischmann's new ballet *Macha Ruadh* (Red[-haired] Macha).

In the opinion of the press this was the most memorable ballet season to date, and *Macha Ruadh* was singled out as the most successful new work yet presented. Fleischmann's score, with its brash, clashing sounds, as of ancient weaponry, is particularly evocative of the legendary past in which the ballet is set, and is a splendid example of the noble, heroic mode he excelled in, even if he later allowed himself to view the work as a sort of preliminary sketch for the *Táin*.[14]

The story of the warrior queen who vanquished her enemies and established Eamain Macha, seat of the high kings and ancient capital of Ireland for six hundred years, is a fascinating choice of subject. Considering the focus of national attention presidential patronage would bring and the timely opportunity this offered for a significant public statement, one is increasingly persuaded that the subtext of *Macha Ruadh* amounts to something like a manifesto. Authorship of the scenario is uncredited but it was probably written by Fleischmann and Moriarty in collaboration and the fact that they decided on and adapted this particular tale, relatively obscure, indeed unmentioned in the more popular surveys of Gaelic literature and generally omitted from the anthologies of Gaelic legends,[15] is surely not fortuitous. A courageous woman, striving against the odds, who, ultimately victorious through sheer force of personality, establishes a great tradition! Even if one cannot say with certainty that this was deliberate and conscious self-mythologising it is unlikely that a discerning audience could have failed to draw the parallel, especially as Joan Denise Moriarty herself danced the title role. At the end of the ballet as Cimbáeth, Macha's triumphant adversary, approaches to slay her, he suddenly grows irresolute and falters, quelled by her beauty and noble bearing. Kneeling, he submits completely and pays homage to her as his queen. On one level at least, I suggest, this is a confident symbolic projection beyond present struggles to the eventual recognition of the value of Fleischmann and Moriarty's work, and the acceptance of the ballet as a vital and intrinsic part of the cultural life of the country.

Acknowledging the cynics, the preface to the programme booklet for the gala performance offers a summing up of this moment of confident stock-taking: 'Any nation working with its heritage of music and dance forms can make a contribution to the art of ballet, and while it may be easy to dismiss with a smile Ireland's chances of ever influencing this art, let us realise at least that in this production of *Macha Ruadh*, music and movement, costuming and decor have been conceived and wedded together to tell a story that is taken from the traditional history of our country, and that those responsible for the creation and execution of this ballet and its music are all men and women of Ireland.'[16]

Fleischmann, now also director of the Cork International Choral Festival which had been founded in 1954, had the idea of introducing the folk dances of different countries to vary the festival's otherwise choral programmes. Experimenting with this attractive juxtaposition, which proved very popular with audiences, he composed a short choral dance suite in 1956 to unite Irish traditional dancing with choral singing. Based on the rhythms of jig, reel and hornpipe, *Na Tri Captaeni Loinge* (The Three Sea Captains) for unaccompanied choir was sung at that year's festival by Cór Cois Laoi, conducted by Pilib Ó Laoighre, and danced by the Lehane sisters. In his final score for the Cork Ballet Company he developed this idea further. *Bata na bPlanndála* (The Planting Stick]), also described as a choral dance suite, and scored for mixed-voice choir and chamber ensemble of flute, harp, percussion and string quartet, was written for the Folk Dance Group, a division of the Cork Ballet Company which specialised in the steps and patterns of Irish dancing. It is an imaginative recreation of one of the occupational mime dances common in Ireland in the sixteenth and seventeenth centuries, and is based on the rhythmic movements used while planting potatoes with a special stick. There is no narrative structure: *Bata na bPlanndála* simply presents scenes of the work in the fields and the return home at the end of the day.

The new work was given at the 1957 Festival, again by Cór Cois Laoi, and this time conducted by Fleischmann himself. Although slight, it is an attractive score in which there is a direct, uncomplicated and wholly appropriate return to folk music as a source of inspiration. Fleischmann discovered and uses one authentic planting-stick tune, and while the rest of the melodic material is original it is modelled on the patterns of folk song. He handles and develops this material with great skill, especially in constructing transitions and shaping the climaxes, and the manner in which he avoids the pitfalls of over-sophistication and maintains the work's essential simplicity, without sacrificing interest, is remarkably ingenious.

There is a gap of more than twenty years between *Bata na bPlanndála* and Fleischmann's next, and final, ballet score. In the meantime, after one unsuccessful attempt at establishing a professional company, the Irish Ballet Company had been formed, for which Joan Denise Moriarty had created the enormously successful *Playboy of the Western World* in 1978. While this was playing to great acclaim in London and New York she was planning the company's next big venture: a ballet version of the *Táin Bó Cuailnge*, for which Aloys Fleischmann was to compose the music.

Like many of his contemporaries Fleischmann, a composer of an essentially conservative cast of mind, experienced a sort of crisis of artistic conscience around the middle decades of the century. Unsympathetic to the more outlandish developments of the avant garde, he nevertheless became increasingly defensive about his own music, about his early works in particular, and it is not unlikely that the change in his style evident from the 1970s onward is due, partly at least, to intimidation together with a feeling that he was behind the times. After all, criticism and commentary was almost entirely and favourably preoccupied with serialism, integral-serialism, aleatoricism, electronic music, and so on. Greater figures than Fleischmann, Copland comes to mind, began to question themselves under this intellectual barrage. Nevertheless the holding centre of his artistic personality was secure, occasionally self-deprecating though he might be, and there was a clear limit to how much recent technical innovation it could, or needed to, accommodate.

Before the premier of the *Táin* however he took the unprecedented step of publishing an apologia of sorts, as if to forestall the kind of criticism he expected the score to provoke. 'Over the past few years it has become clear that there is one kind of music which is almost certain to evoke an enthusiastic response, namely music written in an idiom which is at first hearing virtually incomprehensible. Though idiom is important, one would have thought that the more vital factors, factors needing examination and assessment, would be the range, variety and depth of the ideas, the validity of the structures, and above all, whatever the idiom, whether the music speaks with a distinctive voice'.[17] This is at once a plea for relevant appraisal and a tacit acknowledgement that he is unlikely to get it. Yet one of the most remarkable features of the *Táin*, which accommodates his expanded idiom yet astonishingly allows the seamless incorporation of much of the earlier *Macha Ruadh*, is its demonstration of the consistency of Fleischmann's distinctive voice, and in this it mirrors the consistency of purpose underlying his entire career.

The *Táin* was staged at the Dublin Theatre Festival in October 1981 and was an outstanding success. It is not that the reviewers considered it flawless, but the achievement was generously acknowledged and it was regretted that there were no immediate plans to stage the work outside the country. In the light of subsequent developments the opinion of the *Daily Telegraph* that 'the ballet has already established itself as the finest achievement of the Irish Ballet Company', and that 'it should take its place permanently in the repertoire'[18] sounds a little hollow, but it was unquestionably a fitting climax to the long collaboration between composer and choreographer.

Unfortunately circumstances prevented Joan Denise Moriarty from bequeathing the tradition of dance she strove to create and struggled hard to maintain. The victory of *Macha Ruadh* was not, alas, to be hers, whatever triumphs there were in the course of the battle. In Fleischmann's case most of the institutions he founded and fostered still exist and, above all of course, he left the enduring legacy of his compositions. It is a sobering thought however that forty years and more ago Cork could see the creation and production of a series of ballets that could not now be staged anywhere in the country. Apart from anything else, this means that, there being no chance of experiencing the music in the context for which it was written, a final assessment of the effectiveness of Fleischmann's contribution to the ballet is impossible, at least for the time being. It is sad to think that of so much work so little should endure. Something of great value has been lost, and one concludes this survey realising, if one did not realise it before, just what an impoverishment were the deaths of Joan Denise Moriarty and Aloys Fleischmann.

4: FAMILY, ASSOCIATES AND FRIENDS

(1) The Moriarty Family

BEDA BROPHY
Out of the Mists of Memory

Joan Denise Moriarty's grandmother, Hannah O'Mahony, later McCarthy, and my grandfather, Denis O'Mahony, were sister and brother. My mother, Brigid Amelia O'Mahony (Bea for short), and Marion McCarthy, afterwards Mrs Moriarty, were not only just cousins but good friends in their teens and early twenties.

I recall some reminiscences of my mother's from those days. Marion had an older sister, Hannah McCarthy, and a brother Denis Florence, who died in early manhood. The two girls were very gently reared. Chicken featured largely in their diet as suitably delicate for young ladies. Ironing was out of the question as it would 'spread' and spoil the shape of their hands. A teacher from Cork (I think his name was Mr May) came to give them music lessons. Marion also showed artistic talent in watercolours, mainly still life, and she was an accomplished needlewoman. She crocheted and knitted beautiful little jackets for my two older sisters and made elegant hairbands for them in black velvet embroidered with pink rosebuds and foliage. My sisters were eight years and six years my senior, so I have only the vaguest of memories of that time. But I do remember lovely embroidered cushions that Mrs Moriarty had given my family as gifts. I also remember a very beautiful picture of Mrs Moriarty in a very formal evening gown and little circlet head-dress which had an upturned brush or feather ornament on the side. I have been told this was a formal head-dress for untitled people instead of the tiara worn by the titled. She was a very elegant, beautiful woman with large, dark expressive eyes.

I remember also gifts from Mrs Moriarty, who must have been living in England at that time, of oilskin coats and sou'wester rain hats; I used to think they were so bright that it didn't matter that the day was wet and gloomy. Mrs Moriarty had three sons: Jack, who looked like his mother and had lovely dark eyes, Denis (called Syd) and Gus (called Bon), were older than me and made little impression on me. They would have been friends with my sisters, who were nearer to them in age. I do remember being taken out to tea by Denis, when I was about fifteen years old and at boarding school in

Eccles Street Dominican College in Dublin. He was in his twenties then.

My first memory of Joan Denise is when she visited us with her mother; I think they had just returned from England on a visit. She would have been about eight or nine years old at the time and brought her doll; I, at the superior age of ten, condescended to play with her! She was a lively happy little girl with bright red-gold hair. It would have been about 1922. I remember another visit when Joan Denise brought her war pipes and played for us. She walked up and down the garden as she played and looked very spectacular indeed. The music was strident and challenging, but it was a very compelling performance. We were told she had injured her arm and it was suggested she take up the playing of the pipes to strengthen her arm. It must have been quite successful, as she never had trouble afterwards.

We met occasionally but more rarely as the years went on, as our interests were so different. But my family were glad and happy when Joan made such a wonderful success of her dance school in Cork. She dedicated herself utterly to her art; it was her life-work. We met for the last time in my sister's home in Dublin where Joan was staying on a visit. I feel now that she must have suffered from deep personal loneliness.

MADELEINE O'CONNOR (MALLOW)

My two younger sisters Bobbie and Lana were among Joan's first pupils in Mallow – they started taking lessons in 1934. But they had only just begun when Bobbie got scarlet fever. Naturally, the parents of the other children were not very keen to have her sister amongst the pupils. So Joan gave Lana private lessons in her own house. Lana says that Joan's home was a beautiful and happy place to be in, that she loved going there, and used to visit Joan's mother regularly after that until Mrs Moriarty's death in 1940.

Joan soon became a friend to the whole family: we were eight children. Our mother was Austrian; she came from a family in Montafon who have been artists and painters for generations. My father Richard was an engineer and county surveyor, a man of the widest interests ranging from the arts to aviation. I often think he and Joan had a lot in common. He had an imagination that you would not be surprised to find in an artist, and developed ideas that nobody had dreamed up before him. Let me give you two examples. He had charge of all the roads in County Cork and loved every inch of them, particularly West Cork. Driving over there once, he saw small children trudging over rocks to school. He said to us at supper that evening: 'They must have a proper road.' That was what inspired him to build the Healy Pass, which was opened in 1931. He was fascinated by the prospects which flying introduced, and drew up plans and costings for an airport near Cork; he formed a company which he called Aer Lingus. Unfortunately the authorities could not be persuaded to take action. Joan much admired his vision and his energy, and his death, coming just after her mother's, was a sad blow to her.

Early in 1942 she came to stay with us for two months. She had moved to Cork after her mother's death, had a hard time making ends meet, and about a year later became ill and was in hospital for a long time. My mother and Lana went to visit her one sunny afternoon and found her in bed crying. So my mother packed up her things and took her off home to Clydaville. There she took long walks, chopped wood and generally helped in the big family, becoming one of us.

My sister Wendy trained in London as a dress-designer, and worked in the early years from home, but she used Joan's Cork studio to take orders and do fittings. She made a lovely black velvet gown for Joan – happy the designer that can create for such a model! Joan was a most loyal friend and never forgot us no matter how busy she was. She came to see us whenever she could, and always invited us to her shows. I will never forget the opening performance of her first professional ballet company in 1959. You would imagine she would have had other things on her mind on such an occasion, but not only were we invited to Cork – she actually dispatched the chairman of the new company, Mr James O'Donovan, in his car to drive us up! We were taken to the City Hall for a reception, where she met us with the Lord Mayor, Senator Jennie Dowdall, and my mother was presented with a huge bouquet of flowers.

The last time I saw Joan was in Shanakiel Hospital in Cork shortly before Christmas of 1991, about a month before she died. The nurse told me that she had just been given an injection as she was in great pain, and could see no visitors. So I sent in the baby Christmas tree I had brought from the garden and a card. Before I was down the stairs the nurse came running after me: I was to please come back. Poor Joan was clearly suffering terribly. She cried when she saw me, and told me she envied me our large family, she having nobody. I reminded her of all those times in Clydaville, how she called my parents Mummy and Daddy, and was like a sister to us. We did indeed feel she belonged to us, though also to so many

116

others to whom she gave so much.

My family will always remember her as a beautiful, lively girl, as an enthusiastic teacher, as a faithful friend, and as a brave woman who had to struggle with many hard rocks to achieve her Healy Pass. My father did not live to see his airport in Cork; she lived to see her vision, the professional ballet company, created and destroyed. There is now a flourishing airport in Cork, though for a long time the authorities said the plan for one was a mad idea. I am sure that there will sometime again be a professional ballet company in Ireland, and that Joan Denise Moriarty will be remembered as the lady who showed that it can be done.

(2) Joan Moriarty's Early Years

AIDEEN RYNNE (ATHENRY, CO. GALWAY)
Joan was not only related through the maternal line to my mother, Catherine Lucas *née* Herbert, but was also a close friend of hers. It gave the family immense pleasure that Joan and my father, Anthony T. Lucas, were awarded honorary doctorates on the same occasion: he for his continuing academic work and services as director of the National Museum; she for her valiant work to establish ballet in Ireland on a professional basis.

Our documented knowledge of Joan's life up to the 1930s is scant: it begins with her performing career in Liverpool. Her mother, Marion Moriarty, was born in Mallow on 21 December 1876, the youngest child of Denis McCarthy and his wife Hannah *née* Mahony. Marion's father was a leading vintner in Mallow, his very successful business having been established in 1854. Having lost both her parents by the time she was twelve, Marion was sent to boarding school in Fermoy where her love of music and art was nurtured. Marion's husband, Michael Augustus Moriarty, was the youngest son of John Moriarty and his wife Ellen *née* O'Connell. His family were a Mallow legal family, and he worked there as a solicitor in the early years of the century. Michael Augustus' brother, John Francis Moriarty, had a distinguished career at the bar, becoming a Lord Justice of Appeal in 1914 – he is described entertainingly though none too charitably (nor always accurately) in Maurice Healy's *Munster Circuit*. Michael Augustus and John Francis had been educated at the famous Jesuit College, Stonyhurst. Their period there coincided with that of Arthur Conan Doyle and reference to their brilliant abilities is made by Owen Dudley Edwards in his biography of Doyle.[1]

Michael Augustus' family is entered in the Mallow Census of 1901; there were two male infants: the elder was not yet two years old and the younger eight months. We have no knowledge of when, or where, Joan was born but her birth is not recorded in Mallow. The first we learn of her is when Marion brought her on a visit to Mallow at the age of 18 months. Family members who knew Joan as a child believe that she would have been born in 1912 or 1913; the estimates of neighbours in Mallow who knew the family well vary between 1910 and 1913.

By 1907 the Moriartys were no longer residing in Mallow – there is no entry for them in Thom's Directory of that year,[2] but it is believed that the family may have spent a short period in Dublin. We have a record, in the Grant of Probate in 1949 to Marion Moriarty's will, of the death of Michael Augustus in New Brighton, Cheshire on 27 May 1913. He left no assets. My aunt Beda Brophy remembers hearing how the boys, who had been in a private boarding school in England, had to change schools for financial reasons. However, when Denis, the second son, wished to study law he was enabled to do so with the help of Marion's sister Hannah and her husband Frank Barry. (Marion's brother Denis had also studied law and had married Celeste Nunan, the sister of James, a solicitor whose office was at the Clock House in Mallow.) Denis qualified in 1927 and, having completed his traineeship with the O'Meara solicitors in Mallow, set up practice there. Jack, the eldest son, and the youngest, Gus, became mechanics; I am told by Mr John Coulter of Mallow, who became an apprentice to Gus, that Jack was particularly gifted at his work.[3] He was a keen sportsman, fishing and shooting being his passions. Gus was renowned for his prowess on the hurling field both in England and Ireland. He was a magnificent handball player and hurler and I'm told he had a glorious singing voice.[4]

In 1936 an advertisement for their Mallow garage states that they had 22 years of practical experience in London, Birmingham, Liverpool and Coventry. The family may have moved around with them: in a letter from Joan to my parents, written when she was in hospital in the winter of 1941, she says she had great conversations with one of the night nurses about the different parts of England which they both knew.

We know from Joan (and from Dame Ninette de Valois) that she studied ballet with Marie Rambert. Any documentation there was – bills, etc. – would probably have been among Marion Moriarty's papers, none of which have survived. The archivist of the Rambert

Dance Company tells us[5] that no records were kept of Rambert School pupils, only of performers. Joan often told the story of how her studies with Rambert came to an end. She got scarlet fever at the age of 14 and was in bed for some months. During that time she grew to her great height of nearly six feet. She described graphically to Robert O'Donoghue how, on her return to class, Madame noticed how tall she had become and in her temperamental fashion shouted that Joan was to leave as there was far too much of her there.[6] In those days no girl of such height could become a professional classical dancer. But Madame comforted her afterwards, and gave her the idea of taking up teaching. She was to become an approved teacher of ballet, registered with the Royal Academy of Dancing.

Our first source of biographical documentation is a personal scrapbook of Joan's, found among her papers, in which she kept newspaper cuttings about her public activities during the 1930s. At that time she was living with the family in Liverpool. All the children had pet names – Joan's was Mollie, and she was, according to an old family friend, Mr Tom Redmond, the princess of the family. Relatives (two sisters) had schools of dance near Liverpool. Emily Moriarty had a ballroom dance academy in Rock Ferry and was a fully qualified member of the Imperial Society of Teachers of Dance;[7] Muriel Moriarty-Elliot was a member of the Royal Academy of Dancing who ran a school of ballet in Mosley Hill, a suburb of Liverpool. I managed to find a former pupil,[8] who told me that she was an excellent teacher who helped to train her for the Royal Academy Solo Seal examination – the highest there is. She recognised Joan from old photos, and said she used to call from time to time. She was much younger than Joan, however, encountered her briefly in 1938–39, but knew nothing about the earlier years. One of the cuttings in Joan's book said she went to Broughton Hall School. This was a private Liverpool day-school run from 1928 by Mercy nuns; it no longer exists as a private school and there are no records of pupils in the convent.

During their time in Liverpool the Moriartys kept up close links with their Irish home, and were Gaelic enthusiasts. At their fine house 'Avondhu' in 29 Upper Parliament Street[9] they hosted the Cork hurling team whenever it played in the city. I understand from a family friend residing in Liverpool that the family were active in many different ways. The boys were members of the Gaelic Athletic Association,[10] the family read the *Cork Weekly Examiner* and the Republican journal *An Phoblacht*. Joan was a member of the Liverpool Gaelic League and the Liverpool Scots Society.[11] She is remembered by Liverpool people a little younger than herself who saw her dance as being a 'beautiful and graceful dancer.' Others remember her attending ceilidhes in Liverpool. She spent holidays in Scotland with cousins where she learnt to play the bagpipes and wore the family tartan.[12] She became the champion Irish stepdancer of Britain on 24 April 1931, also winning a swimming championship.[13] On 2 July 1932 she was the only woman to enter the solo war pipes competition at the Tailteann Games in Croke Park in Dublin, and she won a silver medal, playing before a huge crowd.[14] The following year she came from Liverpool to Killarney for the Munster Open Piping Championship, winning against 22 competitors. In July 1933 she was the first woman to enter for the solo pipes contest at the Scots Highland Gathering at Morecambe and Heysham in Lancashire: an audience of several thousand watched 200 competitors perform.[15] In Liverpool in 1932 and 1933 she was invited to play the pipes and dance at many Irish functions, including the official Patrick's Day banquet.

In the autumn of 1933 the Moriartys returned to Mallow: Marion had inherited six small houses from her sister Hannah. Initially, on their return to Mallow the family lived in the town in a flat over Denis' office. They later moved out of town to Ballygarret House for a short period where many a happy musical evening's entertainment was hosted by Marion. They later moved into one of the houses Marion had inherited.

In December 1934 Joan advertised the opening of a school of dance; she gave her first display the following year. She also took part in musicals, operettas, pantomime and Gaelic concerts of all sorts – playing the pipes, dancing and singing – and was an enthusiastic badminton player and swimmer. We know from letters addressed to her there that she was in London and in Dorset in the summers of 1938 and 1939; she may have been thinking of staying there, but returned when the war broke out. From 1938 she went to Cork once a week to give dance classes in the Gregg Hall and in Winsor School, continuing however to live at home in Mallow. In February 1940 her mother died at the age of 64 after a short illness during which the children minded her at home. Joan spent a fortnight in Dublin with my parents that April, and three weeks in the summer.

On 11 November 1940 her brothers helped her move into the Cork studio in Patrick Street. She wrote in her diary: 'Please God I'm doing right.' She gave keep-fit classes, taught tap-dancing, Irish step-dancing, ballroom, and ballet, and gave classes once a week in Mallow. It was not a good time to start out on such a venture. The war made transport very difficult; it ruined the family business in Mallow – there were no cars on the road any more, the Moriarty garage closed and Jack and Gus had to go to England for work. They were not in a position to help Joan, who was in financial difficulties. Denis could not help either: he died after a long illness in 1947; probate had not yet been granted to his mother's will – she had died intestate. The rent books from 1945 to 1952 were found among Joan's papers and show serious arrears from the beginning of 1945 to the end of 1949. We know from a letter that she was having financial problems in 1944;[16] it is unlikely that her first three years in Cork will have been any easier. She became ill in November 1941 due to worry and lack of proper food and spent many weeks in the Bons Secours hospital. She spoke of this later as a nervous breakdown.[17] The O'Leary family, whose children she had taught in Mallow and who may have been related through her mother, looked after the hospital bill and her rent during this time, as well as sending her to convalesce in Glengarriff. Then Joan was taken to Clydaville in Mallow by the O'Connor family. She had another long bout of illness at Easter 1944, after she fell during a performance in Cobh and broke her leg. She thought her dancing days were over,[18] and suffered a spell of depression.

However, she danced again in Cobh the following year; she took part in numerous variety shows in Cork during the 1940s; she won prizes in the Feis for piping, Irish dancing and singing; she gave broadcasts of bagpipe music on the radio. With her piping solo in Aloys Fleischmann's *Clare's Dragoons* of 1945 that artistic cooperation began which was to produce such exceptional results. Just as fate linked one of the great occasions of the latter half of Joan's life with our family when she and my father received honorary doctorates together, so too was this early event also shared with my family: my father's diary records that Joan stayed with us in Dublin during that week, bringing the family to the Thomas Davis centenary concert to hear her play.

Joan and my parents shared many happy times together during these early years and I have a particularly fond memory of a holiday shared in West Cork in the early 1950s. My own daughter too has had the joy of knowing Joan and experienced her kindness to her as a little girl full of enthusiasm for ballet. She has been conscious too of Joan's advice to her: 'Work hard every day'.

(3) Associates and Friends

BERNADETTE GREEVY (DUBLIN)
I first made the acquaintance of the late Joan Denise Moriarty during rehearsals of the important ballet interludes in the three great operatic works *Samson and Delilah, La Gioconda* and *Orfeo* in the Dublin Grand Opera Society during the late 1970s and early 1980s.

Her deep insight into the contrasting styles of dance and movement essential in these diverse works, her gift for improvisation, her infinite grace of movement and gift of imparting her knowledge to the dancers, left an indelible impression upon me.

These talents, coupled with gentleness of manner, infinite courtesy and a truly civilised approach to life made the friendship which grew between us a gift which has been transformed, since her death, into an enduring happy memory.

ANNE COUNTESS OF ROSSE (BIRR CASTLE, CO. OFFALY)

29 April (1976?)

Dear Miss Moriarty,
You wrote me a charming letter last year, when you heard how enraptured we were with the wonderful performance of the Cork Ballet Company when they came to Birr – and I told Mr Tom Donnelly too – had I only known before I should have tried to work on another visit to let people know in advance. There are many people in the Midlands to whom it would have given such joy.

Now I am writing to ask you if it would be at all possible to come earlier this year – and be one of the main features of our 'Vintage Week', which is in fact a 10-day festival covering every interest, and arts and crafts.

You must be so proud of a Ballet Company of such high calibre and I long to have the joy of seeing a performance again. With best wishes to you all and Mr Donnelly and the dancers who came here.
Best luck – Yours sincerely,
Anne Rosse

(P.S.) Tell them I'll see that the hall is spicker and spanner this time! – even if I have to take bucket, pail and brush myself.

Birr Castle Ireland   17 August 1977

Dear Miss Moriarty,
What an honour we all felt it – that you should have come to Birr
yourself last night and be part of that really wonderful evening. It
was something that we shall long remember. I hope that the company realised what enormous joy it gave to Birr – it was an especially fascinating programme too. There is something so dear and
charming about all the personnel of our Irish Ballet Company – they
bring with them a very special outflow – from you yourself, if I may
say so, to dear kind Tom Donnelly right down to the nice electrician
who did so much to help me tog up the room!

    As you know, ballet has played a very real part in my mother's
and my life from the earliest days. So it was immensely exciting to
me to be able to see such a performance as last night's right here in
Birr. Thank you one and all just a thousand times for giving us all
such joy. We all send our love and thanks for the pride we feel in
having had such an evening.
    Most gratefully yours –
    Anne Rosse

THE EARL OF ROSSE (BIRR, CO. OFFALY)

                                                    25 August 1985

Dear Professor Fleischmann,
Many thanks for your kind letter of the 10th. The let-down has certainly caused the greatest sadness to all of us in Birr, most of all to
my mother, who did so much to build up the annual performance
of the ballet company as the cultural highlight of Birr Vintage Week
and indeed of our whole year in this part of the Midlands.

    I appreciate the company may have had few options in the light
of the savage slashes in the grant aid received and really wonder
how much our rulers reflect on the consequences of their action. No
one certainly can reconcile such action with the vain boasts of maintaining the 'quality of life' so laboriously attained.
    Yours sincerely, and very sadly
    Rosse

MICHAEL TWOMEY (CORK)
I've had a lifetime of experience in all aspects of theatre from Shakespeare to pantomime – but alas, not in ballet. I cannot therefore give

a professional opinion on the work of Joan Denise Moriarty, but I do know how highly she was regarded by all those who were competent to judge. I knew her personally and had many a discussion with her on theatrical matters. To me, she was a lady of the utmost dignity, of immense culture, a professional to her fingertips, and totally immersed in her profession. I know that she lived for the ballet. Her unbounded enthusiasm and unending search for perfection affected all who came in contact with her and was reflected in her pupils – many of whom I know well. But she also maintained a strong interest in all other facets of theatre.

I had the privilege of researching and presenting her *This is Your Life* in the Cork Arts and Theatre Club some ten years ago. This is an honour conferred only on those who have earned the very highest esteem for their work in some aspect of theatre. During the course of my research I learned much about her, as a person and as a professional, and it served to heighten even further my regard for her. Many prominent persons travelled from London, Dublin, and other places to pay her tribute on that memorable night. Congratulatory messages were received from some of the greatest international names in ballet. But perhaps most impressive was the depth of affection she could inspire in those who had worked with her down the years.

COLUM Ó CLEIRIGH (DUBLIN)
In 1950 I was appointed substitute teacher in Dromahane Boys' National School. This was a charming village three miles from the town of Mallow, Co. Cork. The town boasted of two cinemas, locally known as 'above' and 'below'. I preferred 'below' because they always played Tchaikovsky's music, which included the 'waltz of the flowers'. This was illustrated by a short ballet on the screen before the big film. I had never seen live ballet on the stage. One day it was announced that Miss Moriarty was coming up from Cork City with her ballet company. I can still see in my mind's eye a spotlit rose-bud in the corner of the stage. As the music developed, the rose petals began to open. To the delight of the astonished audience, out stepped a minute little girl, who pirouetted around with skill and grace. She could not have been more than seven or eight. Nor can I ever forget the great lady herself, Joan Denise, floating sylph and nymph-like on her points across the stage. I was suddenly choked up with tears at the magic of it all, and terrified that someone in the audience would see how moved I was.

I read everything about ballet I could lay my hands on at the local library, and listened to lots of ballet music. The following year a friend of mine who worked in London got tickets for me to see Tchaikovsky's *Swan Lake* at Covent Garden with Frederick Ashton and Margot Fonteyn. This confirmed my belief that there was a need to promote what Joan Denise was doing for our country. In 1952 I visited the old Opera House in Cork to see *Coppélia*. It seemed to me to have all the charm of Covent Garden. The sets, costumes, the precision and discipline of the dancing was a visual feast that kept me spellbound. I was sitting beside a young schoolboy called David Goldberg who told me that his mum Sheila was a friend of Miss Moriarty's and that JDM was a very approachable person. I took him at his word and when the performance ended, off with me as bold as brass backstage to meet the great Madame of ballet. She was encouraging when I said I wanted her to bring her troupe to Clonmel, where I was teaching in the Christian Brothers School.

Clonmel had a thriving dramatic society, the Vocational Education School had for years organised lectures on various musical topics, there was a choral society, so it was not too difficult to get a committee together to bring the ballet company to the town. When the great night came, the Regal Theatre was packed to capacity. The pope himself was there, not the Roman one, of course, but the famous barrister and genealogist Pope O'Mahony, whose niece was one of the dancers. Clonmel audiences had been well used to seeing operas brought by the Boyer family; the Gate Theatre had come with Mac Liammóir and Edwards and many other companies, but this was a first for ballet. Professor Fleischmann was there with his full orchestra; there was a huge corps de ballet, including many able-bodied men who put down the notion that ballet was just frills for silly girls. The evening was a huge success. Every member of the cast had been given accommodation with families, and the following day I invited the entire cast and crew to lunch at Hearn's Hotel. I still cherish the gracious letter in green ink from JDM to acknowledge the hard work and expense. This may have been one of the factors preparing the ground for the Clonmel School of Ballet. A similar story could be told of many towns throughout Ireland.

At the official reception the Mayor of Clonmel said Miss Moriarty would change the face of the nation with 'her ballerinas flittering across the stage', that she would improve many minds with her example of skill and dedication. How right he was. That she would manage to establish a national ballet company in Ireland, which was often to delight audiences in Clonmel, we could not then have imagined. May those that killed it hang their heads in shame.

My first sight of Joan Denise Moriarty remains extraordinarily vivid. It dates back to October 1945, to a performance of Aloys Fleischmann's setting of *Clare's Dragoons* in the Aula Maxima of University College Cork at which she played the war pipes solo with stunning effect, not only aurally but visually, as she marched down the central passage of the hall towards the platform where the composer conducted the Cork Symphony Orchestra, with the Aeolian Choir and the baritone soloist Myles McSweeney. The striking scene had a strong theatrical impact as her height, her auburn-red hair, costume, movement and playing fixed her with the force of an icon on my mind's eye. I was standing just inside the entrance door of the crowded Aula and had a perfect view of her total concentration on the work and got a clear impression of the aura she generated in embodying music, movement and interpretation in a way that so many of us in Cork would come to know so well in subsequent decades. The effect was not quite so concentrated in the City Hall performance on 10 October 1945 to commemorate the Thomas Davis centenary, as the larger spaces somewhat diffused the effect, but it was still a splendid occasion of a type that subsequently we were to become used to as the young Professor Fleischmann began to develop the various resources that would make such ambitious musical occasions and festivals a regular part of the cultural life of the city.

I entered University College Cork as a freshman in 1944 and selected the Dramatic Society (then moribund), the Arts Society and the 'Philosoph' Debating Society as my spheres of interest. I quickly became involved with Professor Fleischmann's work in the Arts Society, which presented chamber music recitals at regular intervals in the university. With my friend Der Breen, I had already while at school in the Presentation College taken to all forms of theatrical work like a duck to water. I soon found myself on the committee of the Arts Society and subsequently became its secretary and auditor, and over a period of about seven years was a kind of chief cook and bottle washer, doing everything from announcing the broadcasts of recitals from the Council Room to collecting funds when we were 'in extremis' for cash – a not infrequent condition. The Arts Society worked closely with the expanding Cork Orchestral Society, which organised an annual programme of musical events as part of the cultural life of the city. This expansive phase was stimulated by the end of 'the emergency' and the opening up of the narrow insular world to fresh post-war possibilities. One of the positive features of those war-time years had been the development of skills and talents on a kind of DIY basis that was to prove so effective in the future. The Music Department in UCC steadily developed and prospered; the Orchestral and other societies were looking for interesting and challenging repertory. Joan Denise settled in Cork and undertook an exhausting schedule of dance teaching, not only in the city but throughout Munster. She looked for opportunities to display the skills she was developing so successfully with her pupils and move her senior group in a direction that would achieve a serious professional role in the future.

From 1947 on I became heavily involved with a number of these ambitious projects. In December 1947, the Orchestral Society and Cork Ballet Group collaborated with Alec Day and S. L. Horne in presenting Milton's masque *Comus* at the Father Mathew Hall. This began my rather limited 'ballet' career, as I took the speaking part of Comus, the evil enchanter, while Joan Denise as Cotytto led the wicked rout of my followers, in addition to doing all the choreography. Her energy and enthusiasm amazed me and, while I as a lover of poetry and verse-speaking revelled in Milton's lines, I have to confess the dance sequences into which I had occasionally to be integrated often terrified me. I had to partner Joan in a couple of her spectacular balletic leaps for which I was often just out of position and a fraction late. She had been constantly lecturing me about the need for learning movement and kept encouraging me to join her company on a more permanent basis. I really had little skill in that department. A few terrifying near-misses as I rushed to prevent her from crashing heavily to the stage must have convinced her, too, that my dance possibilities were nil. In three subsequent productions she faced reality and safety by blending me into the choreography without making dangerous demands on my inadequate dance skills. She remained, however, a constant and persuasive advocate for her vocation and lost no opportunity of lecturing those around her with a kind of fanatical concentration that occasionally struck me as a sign of insecurity and some inner uncertainty. I was more laid back and intrigued by everything from sport to a wide range of cultural and literary interests that I suppose must have led me at times to dissipate my concentration and scatter my efforts. Nevertheless I marvelled at her devoted but seemingly narrow concentration. But how were we to know that she would in time achieve her ambition to run a full-time Irish professional ballet company from Cork!

Comus was followed in 1948 by the first of two productions of *The Fairy Queen*, Purcell's operatic entertainment based on Shakespeare's *Midsummer's Night Dream*. The same forces were involved in the production with a cast of hundreds: solo singers, choir, orchestra and full ballet company, 'down to the tiniest tots, all perfectly trained' (*Cork Examiner* review). I played King Oberon opposite my dear friend Lorna Daly, sadly recently deceased. The problematic logistics of staging a show of this size in the awkward and confined conditions backstage in the City Hall were successfully overcome, even though I felt it was almost impossible to create or sustain atmosphere. When it was revived in 1964 I undertook the rigours of directing, and on this occasion found myself in the role of Bully Bottom the weaver, one of the 'rude mechanicals' – a sad fall from the glory days of Oberon!

In May 1949 I had my most enjoyable outing in this sequence of productions when a potted version of Ibsen's *Peer Gynt* was presented in the old Opera house, with a lovely performance of Grieg's glorious incidental music, and splendidly danced, especially by the senior dancers who by this time under Joan's direction had become a fine ensemble. Lorna Daly played very movingly in the death scene. One of the hazards of productions on this scale were the occasional crises that were always a possibility. A practical problem involving a scene and costume change emerged at the dress rehearsal and I had to learn a long Ibsen soliloquy over the weekend. Somehow we got through. I was very happy that Daniel Corkery, my English professor at UCC, saw *Peer Gynt* and spoke very well of me and the production – not something you could always be sure of!

I collaborated with Joan as choreographer in several shows for the Cork Operatic Society, whose productions I directed between 1955 and 1971. Particularly effective was her contribution to the first Cork production of Harbury and Lane's *Finian's Rainbow*. I think the general success of all the well-drilled dancing culminated in an adorable and touching mime and dance performance of the deaf girl Susan Mahoney by Cherry Hutson. This was a poetic, delicate and moving performance that stands out as one of my finest theatrical memories. My recollections of *White Horse Inn* are not quite so positive. When it became clear that our imported guest stars were not ideally cast, I felt I had to tighten and cut the production. Joan had already rehearsed her dancers and fixed her choreography, and she refused point blank to make any changes or cuts. This showed the firm and rigid side to her character and I admired her loyalty to her dancers, even if it left me out on a limb. I came to the end of that show with feelings of relief.

'All the ranks of Tuscany' in Cork cheered when Jack Lynch allotted the funds to establish the first fully professional Irish Ballet

Joan Denise Moriarty

Cork Ballet Company, Swan Lake, *act 2, 1956, Peter Darrell, Domini Callaghan, John Hickey*

Cork Ballet Company, Les Sylphides, *1959*

Cork Ballet Company brings Nutcracker *to the Gaiety Theatre, Dublin, 1973, Hilda Buckley, JDM, Lavinia Anderson, Aloys Fleischmann, Helen Starr, Andrea Weinberger, Michael Glendinning, Michel Breuil*

Reception in City Hall, Cork, for Coppelia, *1970, [back l/r] Sean Cunningham, J. W. O'Donovan, Hilda Buckley, Pat Leonard, Domy Reiter-Soffer; [front l/r] Lavinia Anderson, JDM, Lord Mayor Peter Barry, Julia Cotter*

Cork Symphony Orchestra, conductor Aloys Fleischmann, leader Mary Bollard

Sleeping Princess, *1958, Domini Callaghan,*
Michel de Lutry

Marina Svetlova in Les Sylphides, *1959*

Wayne Aspinall and Patricia Crosbie in Cinderella, *1980*

Charles Czarny

Stanley Judson

Domy Reiter-Soffer

Peter Darrell

Hans Brenaa

Toni Beck

Joan Denise teaching in the studio, rehearsing Swan Lake, *1987 (Regina O'Sullivan, Teresa Dart-O'Flynn)*

Honorary Doctorate for Joan Denise – with Chancellor Whitaker

Folk Dance Group of Cork Ballet Company at the International Folk Dance Festival, Dijon, France, September 1961 – they won the Bronze Collar

An Damhsa *television series, 1966*

Marshall Hutson's design for Irish Theatre Ballet's Macha Ruadh – designer for Cork Ballet Company for many years

Marshall Hutson's portrait of JDM

The first professional company, Irish Theatre Ballet, Les Sylphides, *1960*

A blending of Irish and Classical traditions, Lugh of the Golden Arm, *1977 – Richard Collins, Babil Gandara*

The mourners – Patricia Crosbie, Eileen Barry, Margaret Goodner

Cork Ballet Company's thirtieth anniversary, 1977, Mairin Lynch, Aloys Fleischmann, An Taoiseach Jack Lynch, Sheila Goldberg, JDM, Lord Mayor G. Y. Goldberg, Anne Fleischmann

JDM and Dame Ninette de Valois, Abbey Theatre, 1978

Offering, *Irish Theatre Ballet, 1978*

Offering, *Irish Theatre Ballet, 1978*

The Playboy of the Western World, *Dublin 1978, Patricia Crosbie and Sean Cunningham as The Widda Quin and Christie Mahon*

Táin Bo Cuailgne *by JDM; music by Aloys Fleischmann 1981; Roger Wade and Carol Bryans*

The Chieftains

Ballet Master David Gordon *Designer Patrick Murray*

The professional companies have gone. Cork Ballet Company dances on. **Cinderella 1991:** *Hilda Buckley with Anne-Marie (Gordon) Murray, Colette McNamee, Alison Collins and JoAnn Durnin*

JDM's funeral procession led by Pipe Major William Cogan, 28 January 1992

The 'family' at JDM's newly erected headstone, November 1997

Company in Cork. All of us approved the recognition given to her and through her to everyone else who had shared in some way the toils of the day. We were all bathed in the reflected glory and looked forward to further expansion and artistic progress. This joy was to be short-lived. The extra burdens imposed on her increasingly affected her energy and general health. Professional work inevitably arouses critical sniping and surreptitious back-stabbing that gradually becomes more open. Furthermore all national funding causes problems. Arts Councils everywhere are responsible for distributing state largesse for which there is always intense competition and the cake is never big enough. As bureaucracies they use rather strict regulative criteria that show little concern for the truth of a historical process which has led to certain practical arrangements suiting the needs of particular times and places. In some ways I think that, however necessary subsidy has become to support ambitious local effort, there is a heavy price to pay. In the development we have been discussing, there were undoubtedly Cork answers to Cork problems. What other answers do we expect? Looking back, we find that the kind of leadership we had in the past is gone. Today there is a lot going on, with more facilities, more good teaching, but the scale seems more bitty. I wonder could the spirit of co-operation flourish again as it once used to do? Not only did Joan's dancers perform in the theatre, learn in the studio and demonstrate in schools, but they would carry the flags of the nations at the opening and closing of the International Choral Festival. It was all part of an overview that gave purpose and point to everything that could be deemed necessary for the rich life of the city and region. Looking back from today's perspective at the challenges of the post-war expansion and the responses to them, I think that the achievements of Joan Denise Moriarty and her likes must never be forgotten.

PETER BARRY (CORK)
Ballet was unknown in Cork in the mid-1940s except to a very small group of people. Television was still fifteen years away into the future; Radio Éireann, though reasonably widely available, was still less than twenty years old; and because of the war, travel to London had not been possible for ten years. Anyway, travel was for those with money – ordinary people went to Youghal, Crosshaven or Inchydoney on their holidays. Into this almost-desert, as far as ballet was concerned, stepped Joan Denise Moriarty with her plans to establish ballet schools and the Cork Ballet Company.

It is hard now to appreciate how this dedicated single-minded woman could have been so successful. But successful she was, with the help of a board of equally dedicated friends to back her. Foremost of these was Professor Aloys Fleischmann. For over a thirty-year period she dominated classical dance in Ireland – her detractors claimed that this was done to the financial disadvantage of Dublin. But who in Dublin, at that time, had the energy, drive, dedication and the army of helpers that Miss Moriarty had? If there had been anyone there even remotely of her stature, then ballet would also have thrived there, Dublin being the capital.

Joan Denise Moriarty's passion for music and dance, her selfless devotion to her students and her boundless enthusiasm has meant that the beauty of ballet and its music have come to be known, to be appreciated and loved by generations of Irish people, but particularly by the people of Cork.

FATHER JOHN LONG (LAKE OZARK, MISSOURI)
As a very young boy in Cork, during the 1940s, I discovered the Cork Opera House and every opportunity I got I attended something there. On a Sunday evening very early on in my theatrical love-affair, I attended the first evening of the Cork Ballet Company. And there was that lady with the glowing red hair and, as I was assured by the programme, the man waving the stick was a professor with a strange un-Cork name. At the age of twelve I was now hooked on ballet and being exposed to my first symphony. To me that is their legacy: they brought to Cork art forms that most Cork children and indeed adults would never have experienced. I for one am extremely grateful to them.

For many years I had been a witness to their work, the ballet, the symphony concerts, the Choral Festival. However, it was after I had left Cork and moved to the States that we became friends. I started bringing some amateur theatre from Missouri to Cork in the early 1970s. It was then, through Pat Murray, that I met the Professor and Joan Denise. On all my subsequent visits to home, I met them. Joan Denise and I frequently had lunch together and on several occasions I attended parties or dinner in her home in Montenotte. We had many long, long conversations about her work and her efforts on behalf of ballet in Cork and Ireland.

She did not see herself as a world-class choreographer; her main contribution was her vision for dance in Ireland. She felt passionate about that. And even if we allow for a little exaggeration in her recollections about her early days in Cork, she certainly paid her dues. She was a very disciplined woman and she had practices in her daily life that she saw as a personal expression of discipline. I remember being surprised when she told me that she usually attended 8am Mass on Sundays as she saw it as a discipline. On one Sunday morning she paid dearly for her commitment to Mass – she sat in SS Peter and Paul church to hear herself and her 'foreign art form' being accused of helping to destroy the 'morals of Ireland'!

When the National Ballet was formed, she and Muriel Large came to the States to audition dancers. They stayed with me for a week. During that time I drove them to various centres of dance in the Mid-West. I heard her discuss dance with many of the professionals at these venues and it was obvious to me that she was respected for her knowledge of dance and was seen by them as a pioneer. On the other hand, she was depressed when she witnessed the wonderful facilities these people had to work in, the warm well-lit studios with state-of-the-art equipment and spacious dressing-rooms. She of course had none of that in Ireland. Her practice-rooms by the railway station were, to say the least, not conducive to keeping dancers who had grown up in far better conditions. I worked with her there during the *Táin* and remember it being cold, dreary and dim.

Getting dancers of quality to Ireland and having gotten them there, keeping them, was an on-going struggle. The resources Irish National Ballet worked with were very minimal compared to even regional companies in the States. One wonders whether had she given in and moved to Dublin it would have improved. But she felt that its roots were in Cork and that it could serve the whole country just as well from there as from Dublin if it was given real funding and a really firm commitment from both public and private sectors. I remember being depressed during its final years when the Dublin venue was the Peacock and not the Abbey. I attended the Bolshoi performance of *Swan Lake* with her in Dublin and again was very pleased and impressed by the reception that was given her both by the company and the members of the audience. Not everyone was blind to her vision.

The *Táin* was a major effort on the part of Joan Denise and Aloys. I was in Ireland for that year and they were good enough to let me work on the crew. The company was too small for the epic piece it should have been and so I found myself in charge of supernumeraries. I remember eventually we had football players and hockey players among the group I eventually got together. With these she had to cover her stage and give the impression of great battles and pageants. It almost succeeded. Again it was only performed at the

Dublin Theatre Festival and was never given a chance to be re-worked. Nowhere else are artists under such constraints. But both of them were unfailingly gracious in spite of the conditions imposed on them by circumstances and personnel.

My last collaboration with her was a production of *Camelot* at the Opera House which I directed and she choreographed. She was presented with dancers of very little training and she knew exactly how to move them so that the piece had the exact look it should have.

I think a great injustice is done to her if people carp about her 'limited dance vocabulary' or that she was not a world class dancer. That was not her essence, nor is it her legacy. She was a patriotic Irish woman with a vision for Ireland and she worked on imple-menting that vision. She may not have always been easy to deal with, but she was a woman of her word and a woman who was not afraid of hard work to bring about her dream for Ireland and espe-cially its children.

The Professor likewise has left an extraordinary legacy to Cork. How many generations of Cork people has he touched and im-proved their experience of life. A generation after me three of my nephews were drawn to him in the Cork Symphony. The conditions he worked under were not great either, yet he had a sense of what he was contributing. All involvement in the arts does not have to be on a world class level, in fact that would be redundant to its very nature. Civilised people are involved in the arts. Both the Professor and Joan Denise Moriarty understood that. It was not that they were not perfectionists and did not long for better: but they were Irish and they knew the score. And more than anything else they were willing to pay the price.

They have left us more than memories; they taught us, they gave us experiences and took us to places poor children of Cork would never have dreamt of going. The people of Ireland owe them much and their memory should always be held high. It is my honour that they called me 'friend'.

Tony O'Reilly (Dublin/USA)

Joan Denise Moriarty was an icon of the ballet world when I first went to live in Cork in 1960. Jim McCarthy claims I dropped in to his house for afternoon tea and stayed for two years. But it was his won-derful wife Pat McCarthy (*née* O'Gorman), who as 'the sugar plum fairy' danced her way into the heart of all who watched her, told me of Joan Denise's long love affair with the ballet and with excellence.

Cork always wants to be the best at everything – and often is – and in the days when ballet in Ireland was Joan Denise, she led, sometimes sternly and always with dedication, from the front. Ballet requires poise and strength and athleticism. It also requires interpretive skills and musicality and a sense of teamwork. When you think about it, it requires all the skills of all the games and music we have ever played. Joan Denise was the apotheosis of all this, and I am honoured to be but one of her admirers.

MARY COLLEY (DUBLIN)
I think it was in 1970 that I first met Joan Denise Moriarty through my husband, George Colley, who was Minister for Finance. She had made a representation to him seeking backing for a professional ballet company and he agreed to give it. He had been a patron of the Irish National Opera and of the touring company of the Abbey Theatre, so he was very much in tune with her aim of bringing dance to the people of Ireland.

When I think of her I think of people all over Ireland – in Tralee and Derry as well as in Cork and Dublin who had the chance to see live ballet in their own place. She made that possible, and so enriched their lives – all our lives. I thought she was heroic in this – and also in her pursuit of excellence.

Afterwards I was part of a small committee in Dublin who raised funds and promoted *Oscar*. We were all very disappointed and sad when the Arts Council withdrew support, in spite of much lobbying.

8 October 1985
Dear Miss Moriarty,
I write to tell you how much I enjoyed the National Ballet at the St Francis Xavier Centre last week and to convey to you my congratulations. The occasion was tinged with sadness for me because you were not there – and because of the graceless treatment you received at the hands of officialdom.

You will be missed, but you have the satisfaction of having done a 'mighty deed', which has placed us, your fellow Irish, forever in your debt. What you have achieved in your work for dance has delighted us all and enriched the cultural life of Ireland. You have helped in no small way to convince us that we are capable of great things. Every good wish in the future
Yours very sincerely
Mary Colley

JAMES A. CORR (CORK)

I was chairman of the Cork International Choral Festival during the concluding five or six years of Professor Fleischmann's directorship of that festival. My memories of him are of a totally dedicated man with tremendous energy and commitment to the festival, which he directed for about thirty years, and never during that period did he receive any payment for his work. I worked very closely with him in fund-raising for the festival and attending the meetings of the various sub-committees of the festival. He was utterly committed to promoting music, song and dance in the city of Cork. I found him to be a real gentleman, proud of the arts in Cork, and always willing to cross swords with any organisation or person who was hindering the development of the artistic life of Cork city.

I did not know Dr Moriarty to the same extent that I knew Professor Fleischmann, but I found her a sincere person committed to promoting the art of dance in Ireland. She approached me on a few occasions as a member of the Cork corporation to obtain funding so that the Old Butter Market in Shandon could be refurbished and become the home of the National Ballet Company. That work is now completed and is today called the Firkin Crane Centre. We were glad to have been able to help save this part of our city's heritage.

RICHIE AND MAIREAD RYAN (DUBLIN)

We always were delighted with any ballet productions we saw by Miss Moriarty and invariably made special efforts to witness those performances, which was not always easy due to my busy public life. When I became Minister for Finance I was pleased to have the opportunity to provide the necessary financial assistance to the Irish National Ballet Company. Of course, my predecessor in office had already made certain commitments to provide finance, thus showing that the splendid work being done for ballet by Miss Moriarty was appreciated on both sides of the political divide.

My wife and I were good friends of Colonel Bill O'Kelly, chairman of the Dublin Grand Opera Society of which we are patrons. We were critical of the poor standard of dancers in some of Dublin Opera productions and kept at him to engage dancers from Cork. The society was not at all opposed to the idea but was naturally worried about the cost. As Finance Minister I was also able to provide them with finance to overcome their indebtedness. Ultimately, whether it was due to the persuasion of ourselves and others I do not know, but the society engaged dancers from Miss Moriarty's company and the Dublin Opera productions achieved new levels of excellence.

We can testify to the exacting standards which Miss Moriarty always demanded and the herculean work done by Professor Fleischmann in the music world together with the encouragement he gave to the ballet at a time when it was an art form insufficiently understood and appreciated throughout Ireland.

My wife, Mairead, joins me in the writing of this tribute. We both feel a sense of loss at their departure to a better place where we feel sure their contributions to the arts are being rewarded.

T. K. WHITAKER (DUBLIN)

I greatly admire the contribution Aloys Fleischmann and Joan Denise Moriarty made to Irish cultural life.

When Miss Moriarty received in 1979 an honorary doctorate from the National University of Ireland, of which I was Chancellor from 1976 to 1996, it was the wish of the Senate of the University, in the words of the citation, 'to pay tribute to her art, to the magnitude of her achievement in establishing a professional ballet company in a country which, up to recently, had no tradition whatsoever in that art, and, above all ... to her own creative output, which has enriched the ballet repertoire in our time'.

JACK LYNCH

Roinn an Taoisig/Department of the Taoiseach, Dublin

10 October 1978

Dear Joan,

I did not write to you earlier because, following the great success of *The Playboy* and the acclaim it received ever since the memorable first night last Monday week, I thought I would wait until you and the company had arrived back to the more tranquil atmosphere of home.

Máirín and I were delighted to have had the pleasure and privilege of being present on the first night. The combination of your beautiful choreography, the excellent dancing of the company and the fine playing of The Chieftains has produced a classic of which you especially and all the others concerned in the production – not to exclude Pat Murray – can feel proud. Máirín and I share in that pride and we wish you continued and further success.

Your ballet version of *The Playboy of the Western World* is a unique achievement and a milestone in Irish theatre and the visual arts. It will be enjoyed by generations to come.

Again our congratulations and our thanks.

Yours sincerely

Jack Lynch

SISTER ROSARIO ALLEN (CORK)

I first became acquainted with Miss Moriarty when, as a music student in University College, Cork (1957–60), I attended rehearsals for her ballet productions with the Cork Symphony Orchestra. Later, when on a few occasions I was asked to provide a choir for some ballets, I got to know her better, especially once, when we had an echo choir backstage. That was for *Hansel and Gretel*, if I remember aright. I never ceased to marvel at her great dedication to her work, and to her obvious love for it. She was very kind to me and to my pupils and she never failed to show her appreciation of our little contribution to the great work.

For many years I accompanied groups of pupils to the ballets in the Cork Opera House, where the great lady rarely appeared to take her bow at the end of the performance. On a few occasions we were fortunate enough to have her and some of her dancers visit our school. The girls were always enthralled with her talks and with the illustrations by the dancers.

It was typical of her that she left her hospital bed to be present at her company's performance of *Cinderella*. It was with sadness that we heard of her death not long afterwards.

SISTER MARGARET QUIRKE, PRINCIPAL, LORETO CONVENT (FERMOY)

I think I was a teenager in school in Clonmel when Joan Denise started her ballet school in the town, so I considered myself too old to enrol! About four weeks before my Leaving Certificate exam, my dad decided I needed a break. What was his treat? – a trip to Cork to an evening of ballet with Aloys Fleischmann's Cork Symphony Orchestra. Whenever I pass the spot on the road where we had our picnic, I always think of that magical evening. When I went on to UCC (1961–1965), I never missed any concerts or ballet performances.

I joined the teaching staff of Loreto in Clonmel in 1968; then I became principal of the school, and always received an invitation to the end-of-year concert of her school of dance – so many of our pupils attended ballet classes. Joan Denise opened the door to so many and gave them an appreciation of dance and music. I admired her and Professor Fleischmann so much for the effort, dedication and enthusiasm they both had for the arts: they did so much to give people pleasure. We are all deeply indebted to them.

SISTER MARY IMELDA CONNOLLY, CONVENT OF MERCY (CALLAN)

Sister Marie Thérèse Saunders was principal of St Brigid's Secondary School for 40 years. She was responsible for bringing the Irish

Ballet Company to the school when the company went on tour during the 1970s and 1980s.

It was a very happy occasion for the staff and students when the annual visit was announced. Some weeks prior to the performance a public relations young lady – who since masterminded the 'Cork 800' Festival – visited the school and introduced the repertoire to the students, which helped them to follow the theme of the dances and appreciate the works. The electricians and the stage crew usually arrived the day before the performance to prepare the stage. When the performance was over, usually at 10.30pm or 11.00pm, they set to work dismantling the set and loading the truck until 3.00am.

The dancers practised for several hours before the performance. Meanwhile, we provided them with tea or coffee. I remember the ballet master, Mr David Gordon, who sat in the audience making notes of each performance. The dancers were often sent backstage after a performance to perfect their dance. They put on a matinée for the students and had a wonderful relationship with them. Other secondary schools in the area and some primary school pupils occasionally attended the matinées. One of our pupils has since gone on to study ballet in London; she now has her own school of ballet and modern dance. Joan Denise Moriarty attended the performances regularly. These were very special occasions both for the Irish National Ballet Company and for the school. We remember her as an elegant lady who commanded the respect of all the dancers, and was totally devoted to her art and to the welfare of the dancers. As we watch *Riverdance* and *Lord of the Dance* we recall how Joan Denise had combined ballet with traditional Irish dance at the time.

We considered it a privilege to prepare a supper for the company. Each one was so appreciative of a hot meal that it made it all worthwhile and, at the end of each visit, they presented us with a token of their appreciation, flowers, shrubs, books, etc. We have very happy memories of managers, dancers, crew and wardrobe mistress.

Callan was the venue for their performance in the Kilkenny area, as we had the largest stage. Consequently, supporters came from Kilkenny city and surrounding areas as well as from Callan. Over the years we found a growing appreciation of ballet among the students, parents and general public, and so the attendances grew. The dances by Joan Denise Moriarty, especially *Devil to Pay* and the *Playboy of the Western World*, were very well received. We sincerely regret the demise of the company and feel the cultural life of the school has suffered. At the time, we wrote to the Arts Council protesting at the withdrawal of their financial support to the company.

By way of introduction: I was rector in Lisnaskea when Joan Denise came with her beautiful Irish Ballet Company to perform in the High School. I am now in Longford, but have Cork connections: my son is Dean of Cork and St Finbarre's is his cathedral there; my daughter Claire is a barrister in Cork and lives with her husband Canon Michael Burrows and family in Bandon.

To come back to Joan Denise. Her tour was arranged by Tom Donnelly (from Carrigaline) with the headmaster of Lisnaskea High School under the auspices of the Arts Council for Northern Ireland. Each occasion was a one night performance by her ballet company as part of their tour. A great burst of Irish culture was presented to us (e.g., *West Cork Ballad*) on each visit, as well as classical ballet. We looked forward to her visits and were all the richer for her coming. She always had a large audience in Lisnaskea. Afterwards, of course, we met her and the cast for supper, prepared by the ladies.

One of her performers at the time was a son of the late Canon Collins of Westminster Abbey, London. Another was a lovely girl by the name of Joanna Banks, who always attended Evensong in Holy Trinity Church, Lisnaskea. Joan Denise, I remember, sent us an invitation to a ballet performance in Dublin where, among many other guests at the reception afterwards, were the former Taoiseach, Mr Jack Lynch and his wife Máirín, both ardent supporters.

The ballet came at a troubled time in Lisnaskea and brought all traditions together for an evening of sheer delight – no mean achievement at the time. To socialise over supper with Joan was an enriching, searching experience. She expressed herself to me always with deep feeling and a degree of intensity which was fascinating. Her movements were so graceful: she was not just performing ballet or teaching ballet – she lived ballet, she was ballet. The conversation at supper, her hand movements and tea drinking were pure ballet, so much part of herself.

I recall Joan Denise Moriarty with much affection. She brought light and joy into our lives at a time when darkness and trouble stalked the land. Her ballet was for all and was so refreshing.

T. VAL O'CONNOR (CORK)

Both Miss Moriarty and Professor Fleischmann were larger than life. Their love of music, dance and the arts generally was quite unique. Their ability to convey this love and appreciation to their students and the wider public was exceptional. It was an extraordinary coincidence that two such gifted people should arrive on the Cork scene at about the same time. They had a Dream: they set out to dramatically raise the standards of excellence of music, dance and the arts generally in Cork and throughout the country. They worked closely and successfully together, each spurring the other on to ever increasing endeavour and together they scaled the heights. What was quite wonderful to me was the fact that two such strong and powerful personalities could blend so harmoniously and achieve so much at both local and national level. They were completely selfless and their success was at times achieved at great personal sacrifice both physical and financial, involving loss of time with family and friends. But the Dream was everything.

Miss Moriarty created audiences for ballet through her schools and her wonderful stage productions of so many classical ballets. She was surrounded by a small group of devoted acolytes. She was their inspiration and they shared her passion for dance. Their commitment was exceptional and they succeeded in passing on this great love to their many students, who in turn passed it on to their children, in an ever increasing circle. Three of my daughters were members of the ballet school. This gave them exposure to music, the discipline of dance and has developed in them a love of the arts they can treasure and enjoy for the rest of their lives. Miss Moriarty loved her students and they loved her.

Professor Fleischmann's contribution to the arts in Cork was comparable. He loved his work with the students at University College Cork and also that with the Cork Orchestral Society. He conducted the Symphony Orchestra with such precision and style – there was a certain majesty about his performances. His music, his work, his family and his students were his life.

The Cork International Choral Festival was founded by the Professor, Miss Moriarty and a group of friends. This year it celebrated its forty-fifth anniversary. It has been a huge success over the years, bringing choirs from all over the world to sing at the various venues and churches in the city and county. I am a member of the executive committee of the Choral Festival and I am happy to report that it goes from strength to strength. It stands as part of their extraordinary legacy.

They both were given many honours during their lifetime, but the honour they would probably appreciate most is that they will never be forgotten and will continue to live in the minds and hearts of the people of Cork. We shall never again see people of the stature of Professor Fleischmann and Joan Denise Moriarty: they stood apart. They brought colour and excitement into so many lives. I believe they are now in Heaven, heavily involved in celestial music, and planning future exciting productions!

Ar dheis Dé go raibh dá anam dílis.

FATHER PAT AHERN (TRALEE)

My contact with Joan Denise began somewhere in the mid 1960s. I had known of her work since my days studying music at University College Cork, where I graduated in 1962. As a young priest in the parish of St John's in Tralee, I began my early experiments with what was later to be known as 'Siamsa' and from 1974 as 'Siamsa Tíre'.

My aim was to find a way of portraying Irish folk culture, in all its forms, through the medium of the theatre, using the varied skills of traditional music and song, of mime and movement, and of traditional dance. Together with a small group of like-minded enthusiasts – members of St John's parish choir, of which I was then the director – I began to experiment with a visual treatment of Irish music and song. We turned first to some of the work songs, na hamhráin saothair: songs like 'An Spealadóir', 'Casadh an tSugáin', Amhráin na Cuiginne'. Songs such as these provided a ready-made visual element.

We located an old butter churn, still in working order, filled it with water and used it to demonstrate how butter was made – to the rhythm and music of the churn song. It became a kind of dance as we added a jig tune and two dancers moved in and out to take turns at beating the dash of the churn. I found an old flail at my home in Moyvane. My grandfather would have made it. Using it as a model we made some new flails and two of the lads learned how to swing them (knocking each other on the head a few times in the process!) The alternating rhythm and movement looked rather attractive. Using two sheaves of straw we were able to demonstrate how corn was threshed by hand. We added a song and a tune and another dance was born. We went on to twist *sugán* ropes, to milk invisible cows, to feed invisible calves and chickens – all to music, singing, dancing and movement.

What we were doing was very new. It so happened that at this time Liam O Murchú was head of Irish programmes in Radio Teleifís Éireann. He heard about our novel goings on in Tralee and he and a young television director, Seán Ó Mordha, travelled to Tralee to see our work. They were suitably impressed, to the extent that they requested the group to prepare four half-hour programmes for television as part of an Irish music series called 'Aililliú'. That was in 1966.

Among other things, I needed some advice on costume style and design. I thought of Joan Denise and plucked up the courage to contact her. I have never forgotten how readily and willingly she came to my assistance. She very kindly invited me to meet her at her dance studio in Cork across the street from the Opera House, where she had an extensive wardrobe. She brought me through it and gave me invaluable advice on materials, colours, design, etc.

She was keenly interested to hear of the Siamsa experiments in Tralee, especially the manner in which we were using the music and the dance as a kind of working vocabulary through which to demonstrate or relate a folk custom or story. She subsequently saw some of our work during a number of guest appearances we made at the Cork Choral Festival. She would come backstage afterwards to compliment us and talk about our programme.

With hindsight I feel she was engaged in a similar experiment, that we were both ploughing parallel furrows, as it were. What I was attempting with traditional music and dance Joan Denise was doing with ballet music and dance, using Irish folk themes and legends. I saw some of them performed in Cork and was very much impressed, in particular with the use made of Seán Ó Riada's music. She had extraordinary skill and invention and was a woman of indomitable spirit, fired by her passion for her art.

CANON G. H. J. BURROWS (DUBLIN)

The year 1947 marked the beginning of a new chapter in Cork for my wife Rachel and for me: we came into contact with Joan through our two daughters, who went to her for classes. Today I look back with appreciation, almost half a century later, to that teacher of ballet whose training, culture and discipline were formative factors in the lives of our children.

The bond of kinship in the arts and of personal friendship was quickly established between Joan and Rachel. One of the highlights of their association was the occasion when Rachel produced the play by W. B. Yeats, *At the Hawk's Well*, at the Yeats International Summer School in Sligo, in August, 1966. The play was one of three Yeats plays presented by The Ashton Players, a company of which Rachel was a founder member. Joan, on Rachel's invitation, played the part of the hawk. As such she portrayed an awesome mystical figure. At that festival some one took a tape recording of the proceedings: there is no record of Joan's superb dancing. Alas!

Joan had the ability to fill every moment to capacity. During the afternoon prior to her 'Hawk' performance she was able to enjoy, with Rachel and me, a drive to Drumcliffe, where Yeats was buried, and also to Lissadel. But in the course of that drive, she was preparing in her mind a ballet for the ensuing season. Self-discipline in life was a matter of principle for her. It was manifest in her work and in her personal life. While on the one hand she seldom completely relaxed, on the other hand even in moments of stress she seemed never to lose her inner serenity. When we attended her company's great performances in Dublin we would have understood if, as producer-director, she had been unable to take any notice of us. But such was her serenity that she would always find an opportunity to greet us warmly. And, on the other hand, her work was never completely banished from her mind.

A nice reference to the collaboration between Rachel and Joan appeared in the *Irish Times* after the Sligo event under the heading 'An Irishwoman's Diary'. After introducing Joan, the diary recorded:

> ... and between training three groups for the television and one for the German tour Miss Moriarty found time to squeeze in a trip to Sligo with Ashton Productions of Cork. She volunteered her talents to help out the Ashton director, Mrs Rachel Burrows, another woman with her heart and skill in Ireland's cultured future – something of a dismal blank except for the spirit of a few such as these.

One of the tests of friendship is a readiness to share holidays. It was, therefore, a testimony to our mutual regard for one another that Joan would join us for a short time during the summer at our holiday house in Co. Clare, though she took but little time off for holidays. I recall her visit in July, 1970 when she stayed with us for over a week. She brought her caravan which she parked in our grounds. Thereby she could mingle with us, and withdraw, as she wished. She needed – as we all do – privacy as well as companionship. She would work in her caravan during the mornings and then join us for lunch. She would generally spend the rest of the day with us, partaking in our ploys, especially long walks. We always enjoyed her stimulating companionship. That year her arrival coincided with that of the writer Edna O'Brien. By a happy coincidence Joan celebrated her birthday with us three days later.

Joan endeared herself to the local community in Kilbaha where our house was situated. Henry Blake, the blind Irish scholar, himself a good dancer, listened with fascination to the sound of her feet as she danced. Rachel recorded in her diary Henry's comment: 'She's a fine dancer, that Moriarty girl'. Rachel added: 'She (Joan) saw *him* dance in our flagged kitchen, but he could only hear the sound of her feet'.

Joan shared our grief as well as our joy at Kilbaha. At the end of our summer holiday in 1971, a close friend who joined us at Kilbaha every summer for over twenty years, Harry Quinlan, suddenly collapsed and died there. I had already left Kilbaha but Joan was still there with Rachel, to whom Joan's presence was a great stand-by. All through that fearful night, as Harry's life ebbed away, Joan never left him. This was no surprise to me as Joan had a singular gift of compassion for those in distress. I myself experienced her warmth of sympathy when Rachel died.

In 1971, in addition to Harry Quinlan's death, Rachel and I underwent the traumatic experience of pulling up our roots in Cork and settling in Dublin. Inevitably we saw less of Joan from that time. Nevertheless contact was maintained through the visits of the National Irish Ballet Company to Dublin. In the autumn of 1980 – almost a decade after we left Cork – Rachel was invited back to Cork to play the part of Lady Bracknell in Oscar Wilde's *The Importance of Being Earnest* at the Opera House. Lady Bracknell was very much her part, and she played it with panache. She was, however, suffering from emphysema and, as the play continued for two weeks, she was exhausted when the performances came to an end. Furthermore, perfectionist as she was, she felt she had not given her best and was depressed accordingly. It was her last appearance on the stage. Joan invited us to come to her house next morning for coffee, before setting off for Dublin. We felt happy with Joan. Surrounded by the peace and beauty of her home, and by the warmth of her welcome, Rachel felt that the strain of the previous two weeks had been lifted. I, in turn, felt released from my anxiety for Rachel. Dear Joan in her own home had restored for each of us our sense of equanimity, and we were deeply grateful to her.

Joan was a profoundly religious person. While she was diligent in her religious duties, her ecumenical outlook transcended denominational boundaries which, alas, are too often regarded as denominational barriers. She evidenced the truth that when our religious roots strike deep we find that they are embedded in a common spiritual heritage.

The occasion of my final contact with Joan was that magic evening, 24 February, 1988, when a programme, *This is Your Life* was presented by Corks Arts Theatre Club to honour her and to pay tribute to her work. The Committee's aim was to sketch her monumental career. Although I had watched programmes of this kind on TV, I had not realised how deeply moving such an occasion can be. I had one great regret, however: Rachel who so much loved and admired

Joan was no longer with us to share in that special evening.

I remember being much moved when Joan rose to thank the committee for the wonderful evening provided in her honour. The beauty of her diction and the stateliness of her bearing were indicative of her greatness. Her vision and youthful zest were still paramount as she eagerly looked forward to the future of the ballet company, resolutely determined to lead the way. I noted with delight how, after all her years of hard slogging, her dedication and verve had in no wise abated. Looking back today, ten years on, I recall my sense of joy and privilege at being invited to participate in that wonderful evening. It is now a beautiful memory. But it is also a poignant memory, for Joan and I never met again.

DR SÉAMUS HEGARTY, BISHOP OF DERRY

In the mid 1970s, when I was the headmaster of a large post-primary school in north Donegal, I met Ms Joan Denise Moriarty for the one and only time. Prior to that I had seen her on television and I had read about her achievements and her successes as founder and director of the Irish Ballet Company and of her Cork amateur company. Ballet was rather peripheral on my list of interests and for that reason, other than noting the impact which this great artist and visionary was having on ballet in Ireland, I remained uninvolved but in admiration of Ms Moriarty's work. In particular I admired her success in expressing the great sagas of our folk tradition through the medium of dance. Even from a distance, this expression of our cultural heritage attracted my attention. When I was fortunate enough to experience, for example, *The Children of Lír* choreographed, I found the visual impact compelling and my admiration for Ms Moriarty enhanced.

Just as many of the pleasant encounters of life happen unexpectedly, meeting Ms Moriarty was no exception. Her agent, Mr Tom Donnelly, approached me as headmaster to explore the possibility of having Ms Moriarty's group of dancers perform for the school community. My initial reaction was one of muted enthusiasm. Tom Donnelly was a very persuasive promoter. I agreed to consider the matter and to revert to him in due course. Being very proactive, Tom contacted me first. Pobalscoil Chloich Cheannfhaola, where I was headmaster, was very much involved in other areas of cultural expression like drama, Irish dancing, music, debating, etc. The pupils competed very successfully in Slogadh, an tOireachtas, Gael Linn debates and other competitions. Ballet did not feature in our school repertoire of cultural expression. Consequently, on the basis of Tom Donnelly's persuasion and my decision to give my students the opportunity of experiencing live ballet, a date and a venue, Amharclann Ghaoth Dobhair, were agreed upon.

Ms Moriarty herself came at that time. She visited me in the school prior to the performance. Although it is now over twenty years since that meeting, I still recall it with reasonable clarity. Ms Moriarty had a very arresting presence. She was not an overpowering personality but her poise, posture and presence were such as to command respect. She was also gracious in adapting to and accommodating in conversation with one less wise in matters relating to ballet. What I still recall most clearly from that once off conversation was first of all the enthusiasm with which she implemented the clear vision she had about the potential of the old Gaelic myths and sagas to be artistically presented in choreography. The second thing that I recall was how determined she was to make ballet available to an audience, especially to schools, which would not in the normal course of events have either the interest or the opportunity to experience live ballet. I regarded Ms Moriarty at the time as an innovator, a visionary, a consummate professional and a great educator.

In the mid 1980s I had the great privilege of meeting another great choreographer in New York: Martha Graham. Martha Graham was internationally recognised and acknowledged as one of the great choreographers of our time. On the few occasions when I met her in her apartment in Manhatten I was very aware that I was in the presence of an artistic great. I mention Martha Graham here in the context of my meeting with Ms Moriarty. It was a great advantage for me to be able to say that I did have some experience of ballet, limited and miniscule though it was. When I mentioned the name of Joan Denise Moriarty, Martha Graham immediately reacted and she said that although she could not recall having met Ms Moriarty she was aware of the valuable work which she was doing for ballet in Ireland.

When I outlined to Ms Graham the source from which Ms Moriarty drew her themes and her inspiration for her choreography Ms Graham became very interested. She made me promise that I would send her the text of some of our old folk legends and sagas with a view to her working them herself. I did in fact send her the material. I know for a fact that she had these stories read to her, that she was intensely interested in them as potential sources, but I am not sure that she did anything practical about them. It must of course be remembered that by the time I met Martha Graham she was ninety years old, although she was still very active professionally. What is important in the context in which I write is that Joan Denise Moriarty was exploring new sources for choreographic expression which attracted the appreciation and the admiration of an authority of the stature of Martha Graham. I remember these two great ladies with much respect and esteem.

The eventual presentation of the Irish Ballet Company in Amharclann Ghaoth Dobhair went very well. It is still remembered. I, personally, have very good reason to remember it. Briefly it is this. Prior to the performance and indeed for weeks beforehand I had impressed upon the student body how necessary it was to behave properly during the performance and to applaud appropriately, with none of the more exuberant expression of acclamation which could not be entirely excluded from such an enthusiastic, mixed teenage audience. To ensure that proper decorum would be observed I insisted that the performance be exclusively for the school. The teachers were actively involved in ensuring that all the proprieties would be observed. And they were. The student audience behaved impeccably. When the performance concluded I considered it appropriate to say a word of thanks and appreciation to Ms Moriarty and the dancers. I moved to the steps at the corner of the stage and began my short address. Half way into the second sentence I was prompted by someone from behind the curtain to come onto the actual stage. It was very cold and I was wearing a coat. Dress and attire for a ballet performance usually follows proper protocol. I did not observe that protocol because my mind was on other more basic considerations with five to six hundred teenagers present. Anyway, I made my way on to the stage escorted from the wing by the lithe, petite, prima donna who tip-toed on to the centre stage with me in tow – still wearing my overcoat. It was then that the audience erupted into loud and sustained applause. I was had. The audience knew it and they enjoyed it. I knew it too. The pent-up restraint and good-humoured spontaneity found full expression. I even enjoyed it myself. Retrospectively, I can say that I once shared centre stage with Joan Denise Moriarty's Irish Ballet Company – at what ended up being a very, very live show!

GERALD Y. GOLDBERG (CORK)

I first got to know Joan Denise Moriarty early in my career as a solicitor. I was retained to defend her when an action was brought in the Cork Circuit Court by residents of the flat over her studio to restrain an alleged nuisance created by the rehearsal of tap and Spanish dances. After a patient hearing, the Circuit Court judge dismissed the action. I acted for her once more in the early 1940s when in the course of a dance performance in Cobh she fell on an uneven stage and broke a leg. This required hospitalisation. The owners of the hall accepted liability and the matter was disposed of to Miss Moriarty's satisfaction.

When I was elected Lord Mayor of Cork I took the view that it would be proper to confer the Freedom of the City on some of those who had rendered signal services to the city through the arts. I had in mind three outstanding individuals: Aloys Fleischmann, Charles Lynch and Miss Moriarty. Councillor (later twice Lord Mayor) Gus Healy advised me that it was not possible to confer honorary citizenship on anybody born in Cork or County Cork, since they were already citizens. The only person of the three therefore eligible was Aloys Fleischmann. A few years before her death Miss Moriarty, with my wife Sheila, were together awarded the distinction of 'Woman of the Year'.

Tyrone Guthrie, who loved the culture of Ireland and, particularly, the potentiality of the Irish dance form, acclaimed the genius of the Irish dancer, Ninette de Valois. Dame Ninette was one of those who contributed to Joan Denise Moriarty's achievement. There were other influences which had a bearing on her artistic development. There was the great Marie Rambert and her ballet; there was also the friendship between her and Alicia Markova, daughter of Eileen Mary Ruth Marks of Crosshaven, County Cork, who became a patron of the Cork Ballet Company. Both de Valois and Joan initially formed a small company on a shoestring budget; these were both voluntary institutions with dancers coming in at the end of a day's work for classes. They both established schools to lay the foundations for professional dance. Dame Ninette insisted on being addressed as 'Madam'; Joan was always addressed as 'Miss Moriarty' – the name still inscribed on the brass plate of her studio in Emmet Place. Guthrie explains that de Valois' form of address was the 'impress not so much of a great artist as a great general'. This illuminating remark also throws light on the qualities Miss Moriarty needed, and possessed to no small measure, to achieve what she accomplished in times that would have daunted many generals of lesser spirit.

She won extraordinary battles; and she also lost some. Has it not always been from lost battles that most is learnt? Has it not been the defeats, bravely endured, rather than the victories, which have served as an inspiration to others to take up the seemingly lost causes and finally achieve what those who went before so courageously and tenaciously fought for?

Alan Fleischmann (Caledonia, Minnesota)
My Godmother Joan Denise Moriarty

Ms Moriarty was called 'Marty' in our family. She became my god-mother at our mother's invitation and played that role very well. She always made me feel special and while she was somewhat aloof, she always had time for me. Her presents to me were always well thought out and some of them I can remember to this day, 40 years later – a weighted beach ball called a 'Wobbledey-ball' and a swimming ring in the form of a dragon that beeped when its head was squeezed. I remember taking enormous pride in these toys, the like of which neither I nor any of my friends had ever seen before.

Marty played a much bigger role in our lives than just being my godmother. She used to come to us for Christmas and other family celebrations. She would come on picnics with us to the seaside. She would sit with us at my father's concerts and at the Choral Festivals. We would go to her ballets and together we would celebrate these triumphs. I remember well the pride I felt on being introduced as her godson to the famous ballet dancers both backstage and at the receptions.

One of my fondest memories was of one of these occasions when Marina Svetlova, one of the world's great ballerinas, came to dance with the amateur company in Cork. My mother gave a reception at our home for her, for Marty, and their entourage. Being the baby, aged about seven, I was packed off to bed as soon as I had been introduced, while the rest of my siblings, dressed up to the nines (and I have a photograph to prove it!), were allowed to attend the party. Having noticed that I had been exiled, Madame Svetlova requested that I be allowed to return, whereupon I was brought down in my dressing-gown and was allowed to remain for the rest of the evening. I thought Madame Svetlova was the most beautiful creature on God's earth.

On the occasion of my twenty-first birthday, Marty invited me to the studio, where she presented me with a veritable fortune – a pound for every year. I remember her chatting about the important things of life, which fitted well with my own philosophy. For example, where her focus was care and feeding of the arts and being on guard against materialism, mine was care and nurturing of my patients versus materialism. She also spoke of honour, respect, the importance of people over things, the need for hard work and perseverance to achieve one's aims. I remember a slight sense of embarrassment on receiving this pep talk, but it has stayed with me all these years largely because, as the Americans say, 'she walked the talk'.

To me, she was very much like our father though not as warm. She was utterly devoted to her cause of ballet just as he was devoted to his cause of music and I admired her dedication. When I saw her go through the ups and downs of her career, with increasing awareness as I grew older, there was one constant – regardless of the circumstances: what she did was for the betterment of the cause of dance rather than of herself.

I will always remember her with fondness as a woman of great accomplishment, who maintained her idealism despite adversity. She encouraged in me a sense of social justice and to value more highly spiritual than material wealth. She has had a significant effect on those with whom she came in contact. She will not be forgotten.

RUTH FLEISCHMANN (HERFORD, GERMANY)
As long as we children can remember, we saw our father only at mealtimes, which he ate between incoming phonecalls. He spent his mornings composing, his afternoons teaching at university, his evenings at rehearsals or meetings, the weekends preparing his teaching and doing correspondence. There were four seasons of special pressure. Rehearsals began after Christmas for the annual spring concert of the Cork Symphony Orchestra; by March activities became intense for the May International Choral Festival, which he directed; in June the external examiner arrived from England for the university exams; in September rehearsals began for the November ballet week. For thirty years the summer months were given to his Irish folk music research project, on which he worked for at least eight hours a day from his retirement at 70 up to three days before his death at 82. He was the gentlest of fathers: we never once heard him raise his voice in anger; but we five children were brought up by our mother.

Aloys Fleischmann was born in 1910, thus growing up in Ireland during the last decade of British rule, in the heyday of the Irish Revival, the literary movement aiming at preserving the cultural heritage of the past as a source of an independent development for the future. The Gaelic Athletic Association had established a highly popular variety of Irish sport, the Gaelic League promoted the Irish language, the Abbey Theatre provided a forum for new drama. It seemed self-evident to him that within his possibilities he should try to continue in that tradition, applying its principles to music. At the institutional level, he set up new independent national organisations for Irish music teachers and for Irish choirs; he organised the music department of University College Cork to serve the needs of the community by producing competent music teachers for schools rather than specialist musicologists or performers; he founded an amateur symphony orchestra. These were designed to create a basis for active music-making, which he felt was one of the prerequisites for appreciating the art. That was also the thinking behind the International Choral Festival, which provided a forum for local choirs to perform, to compete with their peers, and to learn by hearing some of the best choirs from all over Europe.

We recognise in this many of the principles behind Miss Moriarty's work for dance. They were both primarily teachers who knew that the foundations for appreciation of the arts are laid in childhood and that the young must be given a chance to paint, sing, play an instrument, to dance. Aloys Fleischmann campaigned to attain an appropriate place for the arts in schools; he gave annual schools concerts with his symphony orchestra; Miss Moriarty made sure that all her pupils performed from their first year in her classes. They both wanted to help ensure that the cultural life of the community was fed by local activity, that it could grow and set itself new standards through contact with first-rate artists coming in from outside. Miss Moriarty maintained her amateur company after the founding of the professional one; she felt that professional work which did not have a base in local organisations would have no roots. They were thus pioneers of the community arts concept; and they advocated and practised a cultural policy of regional decentralisation long before such ideas were proclaimed from Brussels.

They were both creators in their respective art forms and, in the tradition of the previous generation, sought to incorporate elements of the Irish tradition, of theme and form, into the classical music and dance developed in Europe. Like the Anglo-Irish writers of the Revival, the special quality of their appreciation of the Irish heritage derived from the fact that they were both partly outsiders to it. Miss Moriarty had been brought up in England, getting to know and value things Irish through the active cultural life of the large immigrant Irish community in Liverpool, where she became a member of the Gaelic League and an outstanding traditional musician and dancer. It was while she was living in England that she acquired the mastery of traditional Irish music and dance, laying the foundations for her later original contribution in Ireland. Aloys Fleischmann's family were of German origin, though his maternal grandparents had been in Cork since the 1870s; he went to school in Cork, spoke fluent Irish and was to become an expert on Irish folk music, but his access through the family to the continental world of music and letters was an exceptional and formative experience, the comparison highlighting to him the value of his Irish heritage.

Only one of Aloys Fleischmann's many causes was based essentially on teamwork: his involvement in the ballet. Without the help of his colleagues in the other fields, he could not have done what he did; but no particular individual was essential to the work, which was his area of expertise and which he had originated. Without Miss Moriarty, however, there would have been no ballet and thus no cooperation between the two arts. On the other hand, without his orchestra, without his original compositions, without his general support, the Cork Ballet Company could not have become what it was, and consequently would probably never have given rise to professional ballet. Theirs was a unique partnership based on equality, on a combining of different talents, on common aims, on a shared understanding of the tradition of the previous generation, which they continued and extended.

But Miss Moriarty had to overcome far greater difficulties than did Aloys Fleischmann. Much more opposition had to be contended with in the struggle to have ballet accepted than in building an audience for classical music, which already had a certain following in Cork when they began. Miss Moriarty was self-employed, depending for her livelihood on her schools; she suffered bad health; she had no immediate family. Aloys Fleischmann had not been trained to teach or to run a university department, and had to work out for himself how to do it, but his academic studies were a great help. There are no courses to prepare artistic directors of professional ballet companies for their work, and even those who have spent a decade or two in them as dancers find it an exacting task. How much more so for Miss Moriarty, who had not had that professional experience. Not very many women in Ireland have directed companies with 26 employees and a turnover (towards the end) of over a quarter of a million pounds. Aloys Fleischmann was aware of the personal difficulties she had to overcome to achieve what she did; he knew that her great will-power was the result of a battle with diffidence, with shyness, with a sense of not being adequately fitted for her task. Like him, she was always afraid that the next show might be a disaster, which could only be prevented by the utmost effort; like him, she was always aware of what had still to be achieved, and she never took for granted that what had already been won could be maintained. Unlike him, in her last years she had to endure bitter personal humiliation and see the destruction of part of her life's work.

It was her perseverance and courage after this disaster, when she also had to struggle with constant pain and illness, that brought her particularly close to our family. We all shared our father's profound admiration for her vision, for her determination in pursuing it against all odds and, perhaps above all, her bravery in enduring defeat. We believe it was the difficulties of the undertaking rather than the successes in which the strength of their friendship lay. They shared modesty, diffidence about the quality of their talents, a strong sense of the urgency of the task to be accomplished, and the ability to concentrate single-mindedly on it despite indifference, setbacks, hostility, or apparently insurmountable obstacles. We children took these features for granted when we were growing up; we gradually realised that they were not part of an inherited character structure, but had been acquired: then we understood that the traits had to be re-established or at least reinforced with every new difficulty to be overcome. We got to know the gentle, shy and kindly woman who had achieved such awe-inspiring self-discipline.

ANNE FLEISCHMANN (KILLARNEY)
My Memories of Joan Denise Moriarty as Family Friend and Teacher
My overriding memory is of a tall, straight-backed lady of quiet dignity who was a regular part of my family and educational life. She paddled among the rocky pools on summer picnics, smiling a little at my father's rather erratic efforts to stuff enough newspaper into the old volcano kettle to get the water boiling for tea. She calmly said it was no problem as escaped pieces of lighted paper floated close to her, or sand blasted in her face from our energetic shaking of wet and sandy towels. 'Marty' was the earliest attempt of one of us to say 'Miss Moriarty' and it became our name for her in the family setting, though she was always 'Miss Moriarty' as our ballet teacher.

We celebrated Christmas in the German manner. Every Christmas Eve her arrival heralded the beginning of the action. We hovered impatiently until the greetings were completed, she had taken up her customary seat and her pile of daintily wrapped gifts was added to those around the Christmas tree. The Gospel was read in German and English, *Stille Nacht* and *Adeste Fideles* were sung, and as the adults discussed mutual friends and the state of the nation, we five plunged into the magic world of presents. She gave each of us a gift, always unusual and clearly carefully chosen with the person in mind, yet she never showed anything other than great appreciation of our far less artistic efforts at small gifts for her. After Christmas we were always invited back for coffee, first to the studio, later to the house in Montenotte which she gradually transformed into a place of austere beauty. There she served us with cakes and goodies and we were allowed dip into the huge books which lay around.

I took ballet classes from the age of four to sixteen, and was fascinated by the whole world of ballet while being far too large to be any good at it. There was an aura of high seriousness about the work, a clear sense that it was important, which left a lasting impression on me. Looking back now from a vantage point of many years teaching I can only marvel at the dedication that Miss Moriarty always epitomised. She created the same sense of importance about our fumbling efforts as she did for the ballet company and later for the professional dancers (I was lucky enough to be allowed attend rehearsals at times for both groups). She set out to motivate us. We were never just doing exercises, she explained the purpose behind them and also challenged us to give of our best. She provided us with short term goals – first it was a chance to be in studio ballets and as we progressed, to take small parts in the Ballet Week. All of this work was set in the context of the Arts.

When eight of us in the one ballet class decided to give up because of the pressure of study in our Inter Cert year, she was clearly taken aback and disappointed. She took us aside and pointed out what we would be giving up. When we still said we were leaving, she accepted it and wished us well. It is only in hindsight that I realise how right she was. In my current work I am trying to find ways of broadening the narrow 'academic' focus, so that students who have other talents and intelligences than the 'bookish' may be able to use them in their learning in school, and get recognition for them. The world of ballet is indeed a rich one, involving music, colour, movement, self-knowledge – in fact most of the intelligences. We were indeed depriving ourselves by curtailing ourselves to book learning. After twelve years of dedicated teaching we were just about ready for the amateur company. We threw it all away and she did not even reproach us.

What I came most to admire about Miss Moriarty was the character she displayed in adversity. I give three very different examples. My father was driving her car one time and had an accident. She told him not to worry: that it was insured. What she did not tell him was that she would lose her no-claims bonus, and having very little money at the time, this would be a serious pressure on her. It was many years later, I suspect when he may have lost his own no-claims bonus, that it dawned on him and he told me about it. It was so typical of her not to say anything, but to face the difficulty with quiet courage.

The second example was when she phoned one night to say that there was a burglar overhead in the studio, the police were coming but could someone come down and keep her company. When the police arrived, I went up with her to her office. It was a nightmare. The contents of every shelf, of every drawer and file had been thrown on the floor, envelopes ripped open, books torn apart, glass frames smashed. The mess lay a foot deep. I looked across at her. She straightened herself, took a deep breath and said it wasn't as bad as the last break-in in Montenotte when they had emptied bottles on to the furniture and thrown food around as well. The police had a difficult time getting the burglar back into the house (he had tried to escape over the roofs) because they said if he as much as scratched himself he would sue for damages. As I watched him and the police scrunch their way over the debris I wanted to shout at him, to make him see the havoc he had caused an innocent person. I was so angry, but Miss Moriarty was already at work, trying to judge just how much damage had been done. It took her many days and nights to sort things out, but it is that deep breath, squaring of the shoulders and quiet return to the hard task that stands out for me. I was to see it on a worse occasion.

She came up to the house one evening shortly after she had read in the paper of the recommendation in the Brinson Report that she should retire as director of the professional ballet company. Her pain and bewilderment were tangible. The focus of all her determined work and efforts of so many years had been whipped away from her. What do most people do when their entire envisaged future is wiped out? When their dreams are snuffed out, and the final insult – when they themselves are seen to be The Problem and named as such? What she did, at this lowest point of her life, was to take that deep breath, square those shoulders and return to her work in her schools and with the amateur ballet company. It was over those months that I came to see what heroism is. For me it is not so much the high moments of dramatic gesture, but rather when hope is gone, when life seems over, to somehow keep living out the values one believes in, to keep working towards one's goal, to continue to show interest in and respect for other people. She managed to do that. For me it confirmed – in blood so to speak – all that I heard her say over the years about dedication and about the value of the arts. It was this being true to what she believed even in her darkest times that made her the most formative influence on my life and on the lives of many others that I know.

ALOYS FLEISCHMANN
Farewell at Miss Moriarty's Graveside, 28 January 1992

Dear friends: we are gathered to pay a last tribute to a lady who devoted her entire life to her art, who nearly half a century ago started to form a company which would bring ballet to the people, not only in Cork but around the country, and who created a whole series of original works, many of them related to traditional dancing and to Irish myths and legends. One might associate her with that famous line of W. B. Yeats – 'A star danced, and under it I was born'.

We have here most of the people who stood by her all through her working life – the members of her dance companies, her board, her teachers, her students, and representatives from her schools in Clonmel, Waterford, Mallow, Tralee, Killarney and Bishopstown. We are particularly glad to see Mr Jack Lynch, with his wife Máirín, who when he was Taoiseach made it possible for her to fulfil her life's dream of establishing a company which would present ballet on a high professional level, and reflect an image of Ireland which had not been presented on the stage before. If Mr Lynch had remained in office for some years longer, the tragedy which befell Irish National Ballet would never have happened. And it is sad that not only did she have this calamity, but that her health began to decline, and over the last six months she endured dreadful pain, mitigated only by the care and kindness of her doctors and of Miss Hunt in Shanakiel Hospital, where she was invalided for so long.

Miss Moriarty loved children. As she so often said, her students were her extended family, and she instilled into them a sense of discipline, of hard work, and of appreciation of the dance, of music, and of all the things which contribute to the finer side of life. It is up to us to see that the legacy which she has left us will be continued. All her schools will remain open, and it is hoped that the Cork Ballet Company will put on *Giselle* in the Opera House next November as a memorial tribute to what she has done for Cork and for us all.

Of the classical ballets, this is surely the most suitable. She herself was a kind of Giselle, a spirit, who has now left us to mourn her artistry, her selfless dedication and integrity – a model for all young people to follow. And it is very fitting that she should rest here alongside the eminent pianist Charles Lynch, who played for Irish Theatre Ballet, alongside Seán and Geraldine Neeson, who wrote critiques of all her companies' performances and whose daughter was a prominent early member of the company, alongside the grave of my wife and parents, whom I shall be joining shortly,[19] and a little further on Sir Arnold Bax, for whom she once gave a performance on her war pipes.

In her early years she was as full of spirit as the month of May, and of the later years as her troubles mounted, one might quote Thomas Moore, and say: 'No chain could that soul subdue'. Ní bheidh a lethéid ann arís – we'll hardly see her likes again. May she rest in peace.

5: The Professional Ballet Companies

(1) Irish Theatre Ballet

Geoffrey Davidson, ballet master (Turkey)
I was dancing as principal dancer in the pantomime *Aladin* in Bristol during the 1961 season when I received a call from Denis Carey from Cork asking me if I was interested in working with Joan Denise Moriarty's Irish Theatre Ballet as ballet master. As I was free I accepted the offer and very soon travelled to Cork to work there. I had just completed ten years with Festival Ballet and, as well as dancing, I had been giving company classes and so was ready to further my career as a teacher and hoped to do choreography.

I found working with Joan easy from the beginning because she demanded the same high standards I was used to demanding from myself and from those I taught. I learnt that I couldn't expect the number of performances that we did in the large professional company, but that gave us more time for preparation and creation. During the years 1961, 1962, 1963 and the beginning of 1964 I learnt a great deal as a result of working with Joan and the Irish Theatre Ballet. I created some ballets as well as dancing and giving classes. I learnt a lot about setting up stages in town halls with no equipment, how to work to taped music whilst on tour and about lighting and staging generally. I also had to deal with dancers' problems, which is not an easy matter. I must say that Joan and I did reasonably well on this score, very seldom having real troubles.

We gave twice-yearly performances in conjunction with the Cork Ballet and so we got to know the wonderful amateurs she had trained; it takes someone really dedicated to get such performances from part-timers. I well remember the extremely complimentary remarks from Michael Mac Liammóir, Séumas Kelly, Norris Davidson and many others after the various classics we performed. During these years I valued the friendship of Aloys Fleischmann, whose dedication to music and the dance I admired, and I loved to watch his infinite patience with the various artists he had to deal with in finally getting the performances on stage.

After the Irish Theatre Ballet sadly ended in the first months of 1964 owing to lack of funds, Joan and myself kept in touch. I worked for Ballet Rambert as ballet master during their last years as a classical company and then taught at the Arts Education School in London. I remember on one of her visits I took her to meet Audrey de Vos, a teacher I admired very much, and was very pleased how well they got on: they had similar artistic aims. During 1970 to 1972 I worked in Portugal with the Gulbenkian Foundation Ballet Company and Joan came to visit. She used to watch the performances and gave very interesting criticisms about them: generally constructive; seldom damning.

After I had moved to Turkey, she invited me to come to Cork to reproduce various works at least twice during the 1970s. In between times I saw her in London when our visits coincided. The last time I saw her was in Joahne O'Hara's home in West Wimbledon: we dined together in the garden on a beautiful summer evening.

MAUREEN WELDON (CHESTER)

When I was ten I suffered from a weak back and flat feet. Our doctor in Cork advised my mother to take me to a dancing teacher called Miss Joan Denise Moriarty, who he thought might cure my disabilities; otherwise I was to be sent to hospital. I well remember mounting the stairs to the studio in Patrick's Street with my mother: we were met by a beautiful tall red-haired lady. I must have looked everything that was wrong: I was small and skinny, as well as having my weak back and bad feet. Miss Moriarty gave me special exercises. It was hard, and for most of the time I was in considerable pain, but the exercises and determination were to pay off, and I vowed I would dance for the rest of my life. That was 1950.

My dancing class for that first year was one hour a week, and when it was finished Miss Moriarty allowed me to stay on to watch the 'big girls' (and boys). In between classes she brought me into the private room where she lived for a drink and a biscuit if she had one. I was a chatter-box, but I knew she was very fond of me, and during this time she taught me that there is no such word as 'can't'. At one stage Miss Moriarty was given a kitten. Whenever she went away on ballet business or on holiday, I was entrusted with the keys of the studio to feed and look after Tinky.

When I was fifteen my father was made redundant, and money became very scarce for our family. My dread was that there would not be enough to send me to ballet classes. I was having two a week; my back had greatly improved and I no longer had flat feet. Miss Moriarty allowed me to attend her classes completely free of fees: all she asked of me was to work hard. My ballet shoes, tights, the green tunic were to become Christmas, birthday and Easter presents from family and friends, as were the costumes for the ballet productions I danced in.

When *Giselle* was staged by the Cork Ballet Company in 1957 with Domini Callaghan (the perfect Giselle), I helped backstage. As a thank-you present, Miss Moriarty gave me a pair of red china ballet shoes, which I have always treasured. The following year I was 'in it': I was given a part in *The Sleeping Princess*; in 1959 I danced in *Les Sylphides*, and when the professional company Irish Theatre Ballet was founded that year, I was chosen as one of the twelve dancers. I will never forget our debut gala performance at the Palace Theatre Cork just before Christmas 1959. Among the audience was Dame Marie Rambert, who stood up at the end of the performance, after the rapturous applause had died down, and in a loud deep voice called out: 'Long live Irish Theatre Ballet.' It was a magic night. Dame Marie and Alicia Markova were patrons of our company.

Our first tour was Clonmel Co. Tipperary, New Year 1960. With Miss Moriarty we were invited to a champagne reception at the Lord Mayor's chambers, where we were given 'the freedom of the town'. This was something unforgettable for us young dancers. Then our work really began: we travelled to perform throughout the thirty-two counties of Ireland. We danced in Waterford, Limerick, Cobh, Skibbereen, Tralee, Wexford, Sligo, Dundalk; in Dublin we danced in the famous Gate Theatre, in Belfast in the Lyric Theatre, and from that base we toured the six northern counties.

We were trained by a series of wonderful people. Our first ballet master came from the Anna Pavlova Company. When Stanley Judson retired, Miss Moriarty engaged Yannis Metsis from Athens, who had been a soloist with the Ballet Rambert. He choreographed a ballet called *Narcissus* based on the Greek myth to music by Debussy, played splendidly on the piano by Charles Lynch. Our third ballet master, Geoffrey Davidson, produced *Carneval*, a ballet of great beauty to Robert Schumann's music. Around 1962 the artistic and cultural range of Irish Theatre Ballet was further broadened when a young Israeli dancer was recruited. Domy Reiter-Soffer was one of our principal male dancers and it was in Cork that he choreographed his first ballet, *Moods*, a jazz ballet. This was something very new to us, and greatly enjoyed by the audience.

Miss Moriarty held the reins in every sense of the word, we knew that nothing escaped her notice. She was the inspiration of 'the Dance.' Often a hard taskmaster, yet our friend and mentor, she brought the beauty of ballet to the highest standard we could reach and took it to people throughout Ireland.

Due to the loving kindness of a very great lady, one small child of ten who could have been deformed for the rest of her life realised her dream and became a professional dancer.

PAT DILLON (CORK)
From Cork Ballet Company to Irish Theatre Ballet and back
The annual Ballet Week of the Cork Ballet Company was the highlight and culmination of a hard year's work, and as the cast list went up, the air of expectancy and sense of excitement was palpable, sometimes followed by elation, if the casting went well. Other times, however, disappointment ensued. A week or so later, the initial feelings forgotten, the whole company put its best foot forward and worked tirelessly to put on the best show ever. This was the way it would be – year in and year out – because this was the way Miss Moriarty would have it. She instilled into us a great sense of discipline, determination and hard work: she both inspired and infuriated us with her passionate drive toward perfection.

Following on from one such highly successful Ballet Week, it finally came to pass after a lot of negotiation that Miss Moriarty achieved her greatest ambition and the first Irish professional ballet company was born, and given a small grant by the Arts Council. It was decided that the company would consist of eight girls and two boys, who were to commence training in autumn 1959. I was ecstatic when I was chosen for this company and thought nothing of handing in my notice and taking a huge drop in salary. I still remember that first sunny September morning when we gathered for class, borré-ing around the studio to the beautiful of music: *Rustle of Spring*. I thought I was in heaven!

But if I thought I was in heaven at the start, I had a hasty descent, if not to the other place, then near enough, as nothing could have prepared me for some of the hard times that lay ahead as the reality of bringing the unknown art of ballet around to every town in Ireland hit me. We had very little money, so we had to rely heavily on bodies such as the Irish Countrywomen's Association, and the farmers' organisation Macra na Feirme, who usually arranged accommodation in people's homes free of charge. In places like Clonmel and Waterford we generally had a wonderful time as Miss Moriarty had schools there and the ladies were very hospitable.

In most of the halls, the dressing-rooms were cold and had no hot water, which was necessary to take off the black body make up which we used for *Voices in the Wilderness*: we had to wash in ice-cold water in the middle of winter. We were often quite hungry too, but we didn't like to return to our hostesses, though we might have been welcome, but it wasn't part of the deal and so we wouldn't do it. If I paint a dismal picture of the downside, I must add that we became accustomed to it in time and we certainly had great fun among ourselves.

We didn't have the benefit of an orchestra on those trips around the country, but we were most fortunate in having Charles Lynch to accompany us on the piano. We took it in turns to buy biscuits for him at the local shop, and then gather the biscuit crumbs and cigarette ash off the piano before he'd play a note, as he smoked even while playing. I remember one night someone had to go to his hotel and get him out of the bath – the fact that the show was behind schedule by an hour didn't upset him one bit. However, we appreciated his considerable talent, and sometimes he used to play requests such as *Liebestraum* and other beautiful pieces for the audience in between ballets while the dancers were changing sets and costumes.

When Irish Theatre Ballet closed, some of the local dancers had to go to Europe, where they succeeded in getting into prestigious companies. Others went back again to Cork Ballet Company, the mother company. This was after all where the greatest pleasure was to be found, and where lasting friendships were forged. I personally feel privileged to have shared my years in the Cork Ballet Company and Irish Theatre Ballet with two such dedicated people as Dr Moriarty and Professor Fleischmann, who served their fellow-citizens all their lives.

JULIA COTTER (CORK)

My memories of Miss Moriarty span over 43 years of both a personal and professional relationship. We had our differences, as would be common between any employer and employee or indeed between friends, but never lost respect for each other and a sense of loyalty on both sides always prevailed. I admired her tenacity, her unflinching devotion to the art of ballet, her enthusiasm and ability to educate – to 'draw out' a hidden talent and to foster confidence. Despite the austere and aloof front she sometimes presented, being a stickler for discipline (her own life-saver), she had a soft core and a heart full of compassion which touched me on many occasions – these are the moments I would like to share with you.

Early in 1964 Irish Theatre Ballet finally disbanded after difficult if not disastrous months of amalgamation with Dublin. Having two directors could not work out (Miss Moriarty in Cork and Patricia Ryan from Dublin National Ballet): two very different characters with different ideas and views. But Miss Moriarty had no choice, for in order to qualify for a grant (which quickly ran out) we had to amalgamate. The final show of ITB in Dublin's Olympia in which Miss Moriarty produced *Prisoners of the Sea* was a disaster for her, as hardly any time was alotted to her for rehearsal of staging, lighting, etc. Apparently everything went wrong and she got no co-operation or support except from her own dancers. I knew nothing of the politics involved at the time but I sensed a boycott and that the Dublin committee was trying to oust Miss Moriarty.

Straight after the performance she came to our dressing-room really upset, trying to choke back the tears. Yet even in her distress she sensed my anxiety (had I failed her?) and reassured me that it was not my fault: 'You danced really well: there was nothing more you could do.' It was, or so it seemed, the 'go-slow' and non co-operation of the stage staff and the 'powers that be' which had caused the disaster. I had not seen her desolate and distraught before; we were her little bit of 'family' in Dublin. I tried hard to console her but was myself inconsolable: I felt my whole world was crumbling around me – was there to be no more ballet in Ireland, no more work for any dancers in Ireland?

In early spring 1964 Irish Theatre Ballet was officially closed down and there were tearful goodbyes as all the dancers (except two of us) left to go abroad in search of work. I didn't know where to turn as I wanted to stay in Ireland. Miss Moriarty had not abandoned me, or any of her dancers for that matter, and had a proposal. She seemed calm: it was typical of the woman – she would never remain downcast for long. She got up and going with plans to develop and expand her school (her first dream child), so 'from the ashes a phoenix rose' and a new dream was born. She told me she had always wanted to spread ballet to outlying districts in Co. Cork – her schools in Waterford and Limerick were already established – and would need an extra teacher. She asked whether I would take the Royal Academy exams.

I was dubious at first, but her confidence in me and her support swept me along – she was giving me another opportunity by creating a job for me in the work I loved, so how could I refuse? Fortunately I took the challenge and worked hard for my major Royal Academy of Dancing exams. Miss Moriarty painstakingly coached me in the RAD children's syllabus and I took my exams in Scotland, Dublin and Birmingham. I was her first Cork dancer to succeed in these exams, to my knowledge, for the purpose of teaching in her school. I was delighted to be able to develop in a new vein with her encouragement and discipline.

So I became the first teacher for the newly established 'outside' schools and we worked closely together as she set up classes in Youghal, Fermoy and Bandon. She would drive me to these small towns in her Volkswagen Beatle called 'Jezebelle' and search for appropriate halls to hire for the weekly classes. Having made sure there was a decent piano on site, she would then have to find a good and patient pianist to play for the classes (nowadays tape recorders are used).

It was on these trips that I got to know Miss Moriarty as a friend, rather than a teacher, and we shared a lot together. Later, once a school was established, I would travel on my own by bus to these places until I came to the end of term and Display Day for parents and children. On one such occasion the display was in Youghal and I was to join Miss Moriarty in her car at 1pm in Emmet Place with all the gear (music, props, costumes, etc.). Not being the best of time-keepers, I was very late on this occasion and had to grab a bike to get me to town as quickly as possible – dropping my gear several times on the road, stopping to pick it up and cursing under my breath. I was on 'high doh' by the time I arrived at Emmet Place, puffing and panting and pouring with perspiration (better than any stage performance!), utterly embarrassed, helpless and frustrated. I flung down the bike dramatically, threw myself into the front seat of the waiting fuming car, knowing I was going to get a lecture and a right good 'telling-off'. I had no excuse, no defence, what could I say, except: 'Please don't say anything: I know I'm late, I couldn't help it and I'm sorry' and promptly burst into tears, sobbing for about ten minutes. Miss Moriarty got such a shock at the state I was in that she never said a word – just looked at me, calmly controlling herself, and let me weep to relieve my stress. Then she quietly said: 'All right, Julia, you are overwrought, shall we go?' I mumbled weakly, ashamed of myself, something like 'Yes, I'm OK now'.

Miss Moriarty clipped the road in silence as I opened up and poured out my tale of woe without interruption. What a listener, what a counsellor, what a friend! I couldn't believe she could be so understanding and supportive, and she gave me all the encouragement I needed to get through that gruelling afternoon. As it happened everything went well, though slightly rushed for time and at the end she said: 'You did very well – the children's dancing has improved immensely'. That was praise indeed from the 'Boss'. But it didn't stop there – her soft heart showed itself once more as she took me for tea to some restaurant and ordered apple tart and ice cream for me! I looked at her in disbelief and amazement – how did she know that was my favourite sweet (the 'forbidden fruit' for any dancer and slimmer)? 'It's all right, dear, you deserve it!' and with a twinkle in her eye and mischievous smile added: 'I used to watch you eating it on tour when you thought I wasn't looking!' I gulped with embarrassment but she laughed and joined me with a cup of tea – you could say our secrets were shared with 'Tea and Sympathy'.

That was the end of term in June 1965 and the end of my year's teaching for Miss Moriarty as I was to be married in July of that year and go to live in England. Miss Moriarty's blessing was to encourage me to continue to teach there. During my early married years I was invited occasionally to return to Cork to dance with the Cork Ballet Company on an amateur basis: in 1965 for the opening of the New Opera House; in 1966 for television work in Dublin. On my final return to Cork from England in 1970 with two children, Miss Moriarty called to see me. She admired the baby; but when the telephone rang, and I thrust it hastily into her arms, asking her to hold the 'bundle of joy' for a moment, she looked surprised and taken aback and said: 'What do I do with it?' as she held it tentatively at arms length. But when I got back into the room there she was holding baby Deirdre close and cooing, laughing and talking to the little one as if she were a mother of six. There was real joy and wonderment in her face – and relief, when she handed back the squirming bundle. Then she produced the most exquisite pair of tiny pink satin ballet shoes for Deirdre.

And then she asked me to dance my old role in a repeat performance of *Prisoners of the Sea*. I said that though it was one of my favourite roles, I was out of practice and didn't think I'd be ready in time. She insisted I could do it and her enthusiasm once again swept me along. She also had John Cunningham home, so she had her two principals back. It was a happy time because in helping her I think we helped ourselves: we both re-established ourselves as professional dancers after a certain gap. She encouraged us to get up and go and never say die! That was her motto and has been mine, ever since – also 'Believe in yourself'. Her influence on my life was decisive.

My association with Joan Denise Moriarty began in 1962: it developed through three decades into friendship and close professional association as her artistic adviser and choreographer. I should think I am one of the few people who really knew her: the teacher, director and choreographer; her struggles, her disappointments and her achievements. To me she was a heroine. That may seem a strange word to use, but I feel that is what she was throughout the struggle. For the building of a professional company was not easy. To me she personified Ireland: with her persistence in adversity, her courage, her humanity, she seemed to me to represent the epitome of what her country stood for.

My first encounter with Joan Denise Moriarty was in London, after I had been working in Copenhagen and was on my way to Israel. I had decided to come and do some classes in London, and there I saw this very striking, tall, red-haired lady auditioning people. Though I really didn't actually want to audition because I was returning to Israel, I was there among the ones that did. Afterwards she came to me and she said that she had a company in Cork, the only professional company in Ireland. I knew of Ireland but I had never heard of Cork before. She told me about Irish Theatre Ballet and said she wanted me to dance Petrouchka. I hesitated. But then I thought: 'Well, if I can dance Petrouchka in Ireland, that's where I'm going to go.'

Two weeks later I took the boat. Little did I know that the journey on a boat in December would be absolutely awful. So my first encounter with Ireland was through the Irish Sea. It was gales from here to Christmas and by the time I arrived in Cork, I was so ill that I could hardly stand. There she was waiting for me at the docks. I looked at her and when I saw her glittering eyes, I thought 'My goodness, it was worth doing all this journey, to come and meet this woman'.

I was whisked off to the studio first. I was really taken aback because the studio in Emmet Place was so very tiny. Then she took me to breakfast. I remember being very touched by her account of what she wanted to do through Irish Theatre Ballet: to bring dance to every small place, every town, every city in Ireland. It sounded really far-fetched to me at the beginning, but her enthusiasm was contagious. She offered to take me to the hotel so that I could sleep the journey off, but how could I have done that when she was so energetic, so open and so friendly? She had a class at 10 o'clock – this was about 8.00 – and I said I would come to the studio. The hotel was nearby; I had only to cross St Patrick's Bridge to get there. It was what the Irish call a very soft day, with a little rain, a drizzle, a constant drizzle indeed; but the weather seemed to me beautiful and people were smiling at me, I think because I was dark, differently dressed and looked foreign.

When I got to Emmet Place I heard the piano going, and saw Joan Denise standing with about ten dancers. I was introduced to everyone in the company as well as the teacher, who was Geoffrey Davidson. She sat very quietly during class, and then left and came back dressed in rehearsal gear and said we were going to rehearse our first ballet. I of course was delighted I was going to dance Petrouchka. Then I got a surprise. She said 'No. *Petrouchka* is next month. We are doing the repertory ballets, which we are going to perform in different places in Ireland.' *Petrouchka* was for the season in Cork and probably Dublin.

The rehearsal started. The music was very strange indeed and I became apprehensive. I loved the rhythms of this music but I knew nothing about it and what she was going to do. She said this ballet was going to be called *West Cork Ballad* and that the music was by Seán Ó Riada. Well, I was intrigued but also devastated because I knew nothing about Irish dancing. When she started to demonstrate I saw it was absolutely and utterly foreign with all the batterings and the intricate steps. I thought I will never, never be able to do it. I couldn't very well say to her 'I'm sorry, I do not want to do it'. All my training was in classical and modern ballet and nothing like this. She took my hand and did the first battering and said 'Think of it as a tap dance, but it is not tap dance; it is Irish'. And I said to myself: what do you mean: it is a tap dance, but it is not a tap dance; it's Irish. But somehow, I managed to do a few steps and she kept on praising me: 'Yes, that's it, that's it'. But I knew damn well what I was doing was bloody awful. Then she began to tell us all about *West Cork Ballad*. At the break we sat round her and she told us about the folklore of Ireland and what the steps mean, about the fiddler that goes from town to town to play at funerals, at weddings, for birthdays and all sorts of occasions – and I could see it, for what she had told us was so vivid. She was a real storyteller: it was fascinating. She got us into the very essence of what the *West Cork Ballad* was about and we understood the intricate rhythms of Seán Ó Riada's music.

She had a wonderful capacity of understanding and knew how to deal with people, and through the months we grew to love her because she was just what you have to be as director. Although one of us, she was nonetheless a little bit aloof, in a nice way. That is what I thought a director should be – very caring, wanting to know our problems, but on the other hand, aloof. She was very lonely: indeed an extremely lonely person.

Anyway, the first performance I did in Ireland, would you believe it, was in Skibbereen, in the town hall. My idea of theatre was the Danish Royal Theatre or Tel Aviv's Habima Theatre and London's Covent Garden. When they said Skibbereen, I had no idea where Skibbereen was or what kind of people would be attending. When we got there, I found it a rather beautiful and quaint little town. It was a bright sunny day but very cold because it was January, as I distinctly remember. And then they took us to the theatre. When we went in, I kept on looking for the stage: I looked and looked and thought: 'Well, there is no stage'. Eventually I was ushered to a small, minute, tiny, but tiny stage, which looked more like a double room than a stage. And they said: 'This is it'. I was quite horrified and I thought: 'My God, how are we ever going to perform on this?' We went for a short lunch while the workers were fixing up the stage and checking the lighting and we had a short rehearsal after lunch. I was very upset, and said to myself: 'I didn't come to Ireland to dance in a tiny little hall. This is absolutely ridiculous.' The hall would probably have seated a maximum of 200 people, if that, and I felt I really hadn't studied all those years to come and work in Ireland for this kind of performance. This was for the birds, not for me. I remembered being embarrassed and I did not say anything about Skibbereen or how much I hated the hall as Seán Cunningham, one of the dancers, was from Skibbereen and all his family entourage were coming to see him. So I shut my big mouth.

There was another ballet in the repertoire called *Slavonic Dances*, which Joan Denise had also choreographed and that was classical. I thought it was a very beautiful ballet, with very good dancing. I found it most choreographic and so different from any other choreography that I had seen. I remember that it struck me as being so musical and thinking 'Here there is a choreographer who really understands music.' Anyway, the performance started and I could hear a lot of hustle and bustle and noise and I looked through the little peephole of the curtain and the house was packed. There weren't 200 people: there were 500 at least. They were all standing, fathers with children, and children with dogs, and the entire town of Skibbereen seemed to have arrived on the scene. It was rather wonderful. We did the first ballet *Slavonic Dances* and then *West Cork Ballad*.

I was also dancing Don Quixote, which went so well. I was very pleased and I remember well what that performance did for me – I recall saying to myself that when in the future I would be with a bigger company and would be doing Don Quixote again, I would know that if I can dance it under such circumstances, then I can dance it anywhere. However, it was the *West Cork Ballad* which was acclaimed, and I could not believe it. I was the Fiddler and the public were clapping, were singing, were shouting at the end of the show. They had enjoyed it, indeed loved it, and the whole was a great success. People came up to me afterwards and they shook my hands and said they thought that I was the most wonderful Irish dancer they had ever seen. That was very amusing to me, because I had known nothing at all about Irish dancing until I was taught by Joan Denise. We were all invited out after the performance. I will always remember how Joan Denise Moriarty came up to me afterwards and said 'Domy, you may have hated every minute of rehearsal, you may not have liked doing this ballet, but I'll have you know that from tonight, for me anyway, you have become an honorary Irishman!' That was enough for me, because coming from her that was a big honour, loving every crevice of her country as she did.

I toured with Irish Theatre Ballet to so many towns and cities. I will never forget those tours: they went west and east, north and south. Her enthusiasm somehow translated to every one of us dancers and I suddenly started seeing Ireland through her eyes. The long journeys to wherever we went to perform were quite extraordinary. We travelled at night and we travelled in the daytime; we travelled in winter and in summer and suddenly I felt as I thought she felt about Ireland, beautiful and exciting place that it was and is. I got to know the people, I got to love the people the way she loved her people. That rather amazed me because I was finding things hard at that period until I got to dance Petrouchka. But I was completely taken by her vision, by her enthusiasm, by her love of dance.

When we dancers talked about her, though we were very young, we still could see the sacrifices this woman had made. At times we realised what she was going through. She was a workaholic. She used to get up at about five o'clock in the morning and do a class herself. Then she went to open the studio and she had to deal with all the paperwork that had to be done for the company. Then she sometimes taught class and sometimes she worked on music that she was going to choreograph. Then she started rehearsing. And after rehearsals that went on to 5.00 or 6.30, she used to teach classes in the school until about 9.00 o'clock and then from 9.00 till 11.00 o'clock there was the amateur company, the Cork Ballet Company, that used to come and do classes and rehearse for the season. And that was daily – every single day. We could see that this woman really worked herself to the bone and we decided that she was possessed: possessed by her determination to introduce dance theatre to Ireland.

When we were travelling, we used to help with everything: building the stage, carrying props and costumes. It was certainly very tiring, because we also had to do class and then we had a performance, but I think we forgave everything, because during the performance and after the performance there was such enthusiasm and people always came up to us and thanked us for dancing for them. We went to such small places, including convents and schools, and remote communities – we really saw Ireland. And we loved it, we loved the people. Here was I, a Mediterranean, completely involved in a country that was so utterly different to my own. Yet the family values were very similar and I got to really love being there. The other thing which I found quite extraordinary were the productions we managed. We did *Cinderella*, full length, *Les Sylphides* and we did *Petrouchka*, we did *Giselle*, we did *Swan Lake*, we did many other productions which were quite a handful to do. But she somehow succeeded. She brought a tremendous amount of dance culture to the city of Cork and to the surrounding area, and to Dublin and beyond.

She did not get a salary from being a director of Irish Theatre Ballet, but she earned her living from her schools and many of those children were not paying full fees because their parents could not afford it. She wanted to give them dance, music, and in particular discipline. She always felt that discipline is the epitome of life and without it there can be no growth, no progress. Since the beginning of her work in Ireland, generations of her students had become mothers and fathers, and realised the importance of the arts; these were the people who had followed her throughout the years and had helped her to continue. She opened dance schools all over the south of Ireland.

It was only later that I realised her predicament, her lack of financial support. She was putting money from the schools into the company, as well as trying to raise money in all sorts of different ways, like organising flag days in which most of the dancers took part. Needless to say, I was one of them. She also had jumble sales at least twice or three times a year to which people brought all sorts of costumes and clothes and bric-à-brac, and the money went into the company. She had a form of bingo, for which once a week city salesmen and women actually went out and sold tickets, and every week there were winners. That went on for years. I left Ireland after the fall of Irish Theatre Ballet. She just couldn't keep it up: there was no government subsidy at that period.

I was invited from time to time to dance with her Cork Ballet Company in the season, which was usually in November, which I enjoyed. In the meantime I had a career in England, Israel and the United States in which I was also a choreographer. It was she who had encouraged me to choreograph. I had choreographed in Israel before for workshops, and the works were received favourably, but she wanted to see for herself, and of course there were no videos in those days. She asked me if I would like to choreograph for a workshop in Cork. I started with a duet and quartet and I called it *Moods*. She liked it and invited me to choreograph for the company. At the time I was dancing a lot but with her encouragement I did the ballet which got a wonderful reception, both from the audience as well as from the critics. From then on, though I was away working all over the world, she would invite me every so often to choreograph for the Cork Ballet Company.

One day early in 1970 she phoned me and she said they were going to do a production of *Coppélia* in Cork and in Dublin in the Abbey Theatre and that this would be a very decisive time because people from the government and Arts Council would be attending. She invited me to dance for the production, which I did. The Abbey Theatre was absolutely packed as well as the performances in Cork; then we went to Waterford and then to Clonmel with the Cork Ballet Company. Then everything was dissolved; we all went home, and that was the end.

In June 1973 she phoned out of the blue and said she was coming to London. So we met and had dinner. She was full of mystery and excitement, and I couldn't work out what the matter was. Finally she said: 'I think I am going to have a subsidy from the government to build up a professional ballet company again.' And I said: 'What do you mean you think?' – either you have it or you don't.' She said: 'I actually have it.' But she was sceptical whether the government was going to go ahead or not. I think it was because she had had so many knocks in life that she really could not believe it, and she would not believe it until she saw the official letters in her hand, but I am sure that when she spoke to me she had already had letters galore from the government. Anyway, she asked if I would join the company. I was in full swing directing plays and musicals, I was also choreographing for very big companies like the Dance Theatre of Harlem and the Bat Dor company, American Ballet Theatre and so on, and I really was not available: But when I looked at that wonderful face of hers and her eyes and she said: 'You know, Domy, it has taken me almost a lifetime to get to this; the government is actually handing out money to create a company, a ballet company!' – what could I do?

So she persuaded me to come to Ireland and to become artistic adviser to the Irish Ballet Company. Of course, there was no repertoire whatsoever. We had to start from scratch. We had auditions in Ireland and Britain. I knew some dancers who I had worked with in the past; but her main concern was to get as many Irish dancers as possible, and Irish technicians and managers. Then the repertory had to be chosen. We felt that we needed a popular repertoire as well as an international one, so that if the company was ever invited abroad, it could represent Ireland. So, many choreographers apart from me were invited to produce works for the company: people of high international standing.

The first performance was in Cork. As well as Irish critics, a number had also come from Britain and France, so, needless to say, she was nervous and apprehensive, not knowing how they were going to take to the newly born company. Her intuition was very strong, especially about the repertoire. She chose an Irish ballet which she choreographed herself and it was very good. There were also modern ballets as well as classical, so we had a mixture of different repertoires. I must say the critics were terrific because not only did they hail the company: some of them said that as a first season it was astounding, because the standards were so high. Once she got this recognition I think she relaxed somewhat. She surrounded herself with highly professional people: her stage hands were good; her administrator, Muriel Large, was well-known, having been with Sadler's Wells and Western Theatre Ballet and Scottish Ballet. Pat Murray, too, was very important in Irish National Ballet: he made all the scenery and designed all the costumes.

I remember the first two years in the life of the company. Joan Denise wanted to know how the ordinary public felt about the company, so questionnaires were handed out wherever the company performed and believe me, that was all over Ireland from the north to the south. And the questionnaire asked: 'How did you hear about the company? What ballets did you like best/least?' and 'What did you think of the company?' The outcome was revealing: the majority liked the modern ballets, because they could relate to and understand them better, because they were very emotional. The first-timers, who had never seen classical ballet before, often felt it was high-brow, especially the girls *en pointe*. I'll never forget one of the questionnaires read out from Clairemorris, which is a very small agricultural town, and it said 'My favourite ballet was *Women*' – a very modern ballet – but the comment on the same questionnaire about a classical piece was: 'Why are these people dancing on stilts?' meaning the *pointe* shoes. These questionnaires went on for two years and she built the repertoire, not only based on what the general public liked, but also on what she felt was artistically suited. And I think she was generally right in her choice.

The company ran on a shoestring. I cannot think of any company having such a large and varied repertoire, having such good dancers, surviving on such limited resources. But she kept her sense of humour. I don't know how she did it all. Her musicality, her energies, the choice of dancers were really quite extraordinary. I think what she accomplished was wonderful. She took many girls and boys from the Cork Ballet Company and also from Dublin. She gave scholarships to students who would rehearse and learn repertoire from the company, who later on became members. It was a very work-intensive time.

My relationship with the company grew. I created about two works a year. She gave me carte-blanche, except that I had to tell her what I was creating and write a scenario for her and let her hear the music. She was careful from that point of view, because she did not want me to go way out, although I did, and she understood the importance of daring to create things that Ireland hadn't seen. She was a great encouragement to me and throughout all those years we had a wonderful relationship. Reflecting back on that time, it strikes me that most of the ballets that I created for Irish National Ballet were later reproduced for other major companies, all over the United States and Europe, with great success. *Yerma*, for example, was one of the first ballets that I created for Irish National Ballet; I have done it since in five different places: in New York for the New York Contemporary Company; I did it for La Scala Milan, for the Ballet Metropolitan, and for Pittsburg and Chicago Ballet. It was the same with *Chariots of Fire* – I did it in Chicago, I did it all over the place. *Women* I did for six or seven different companies: La Valse, House of Bernarda Alba. Most of the ballets I did for Irish National went into the repertoire of other companies. So you see the seed was sown in Ireland. I am very proud that I created them with Irish National Ballet, and it was Joan Denise who encouraged me to go on and do them in other places.

The first time she went to New York, she was invited to a big symposium of directors from different countries. I also attended. Of course nobody really knew who she was. When she was introduced as the Irish artistic director of Irish National Ballet, they asked a lot of questions and she answered every one with dignity and panache. She really was a lady in every sense. People loved her because she was so straightforward and no-nonsense. Naturally, when they heard what subsidy the company was getting from the government, they nearly fainted. They couldn't believe that this repertoire was all done on such a tiny budget. It was wonderful to see how those 'important people' took to her, and how interested they became in the Irish scene. Some of them later came to Ireland and they visited the company, which was a great compliment.

The company within a relatively short period of time achieved critical acclaim, especially from critics outside Ireland. Most of the British critics who came every season to look at the company were astounded at the standard. Of course, I wasn't there all the time: I spent about four months or five months a year in Ireland, but we were on the phone constantly discussing the repertoire and the needs of the company. There was a great trust between us. I don't think we ever had a bad confrontation, but that does not mean that we agreed on everything. I was there to advise and it was for her either to accept my advice or not. But most of the time, she did accept it.

Her hope was to be able to bring back the Irish dancers who were dancing all over the world, to have an out-and-out Irish company, with Irish dancers and Irish staff. She encouraged me to do a work based on James Joyce's poetry. She encouraged me to bring in Irish themes, Irish music. Many Irish artists owe much to Joan Denise Moriarty. Her artistry encompassed much more than just dance. She was an ardent pipe-player; she read and loved music; she encouraged musicians. She urged all her dancers to read works by Irish writers. I remember her giving us dancers Irish poetry for Christmas. She had a goal in life and that goal was to bring dance all over Ireland. To accomplish that, Joan toiled incessantly. She had no family; but though she had friends, yet she was very much alone. Her greatest happiness was to see the company working hard, performing in Ireland, bringing joy to people in small places, which anybody else would have considered impossible to dance in. She herself, her encouragement, her belief, swept me off with her. Coming myself from a pioneering country and realising the importance of being a pioneer, knowing you have to dare in order to create, I realised that this woman had a dream and that I was caught in the web of it, as were so many people. That dream was nothing selfish:

it went far beyond any individual. Joan Denise Moriarty will live on in the hearts of very many people: artists, dancers as well as those she brought joy to, whether in Clonmel or Clairemorris or Dublin or Dunmanway. They took pride in her pride. I for one owe her a great deal; and I for one will never forget her.

JOAHNE O'HARA, ROYAL ACADEMY OF DANCING (LONDON)
Marie Rambert was a person with a vision of a company of dancers as an artistic entity: she had a vision of something she wanted to create, and which she saw lacking in England at that time. And she, like de Valois, and in Ireland, Joan Denise Moriarty, gave all her energy to this. Such people, so utterly focused on the vision that they have, inevitably 'teach' something to all who come into contact with them, I believe. It is not a question of whether or not Joan Denise was qualified as a teacher of technique: she was a teacher in a far wider meaning of the word. In those days, no one was qualified. The greatest teachers, including Karsavina, Preobazhenskaya, *et al*, had no formal qualifications. But like Marie Rambert and de Valois, she inevitably 'taught' all who came into contact with the great work she was doing *in* her own country and *for* her own country – something precious about the beauty and the purity of the ballet and of the theatre.

In my own experience during my time dancing with her company, Moriarty took ballet, then an unknown art form, to tiny towns all over Ireland, to places where, I remember, the local farmers would ask at the box office 'What is ballet, Miss – do they talk?' Those same farmers and their families were there to see us dance again the next time we arrived, and the numbers doubled and trebled as time went on. If there was not a stage, we built one. There was no end to the courage and invention of Joan Denise. She was, in her way, a teacher of what she loved in giving the art so valued by her to people all over Ireland.

Her absolute focus and drive did from time to time give rise to certain problems. She was no angel, for example, on the score of saying 'thank you' once in a while. I think she simply forgot about such things, being so involved in what was coming next; what had to be done next. I remember once saying to her that we never know whether she thought we'd done a good performance or not and that it would be great for us all (the dancers) to be told once in a while that we'd done well. She seemed surprised, and after that did occasionally make a point of saying something about our work. Probably if we'd all stopped to think, no one had ever complimented her on her own!

The words 'Courage' and 'Determination' are the ones which come to me when I think of Joan Denise, and the feelings which overwhelm me when I think of her are of the utmost gratefulness, of thanks, to a woman who gave me a chance to be a part of something which was important, not just for myself, but more significantly for the people of the country which she loved above all.

(2) Irish National Ballet: Administrators and Dancers

DONN MCMULLIN (CARRIGALINE, CO. CORK), MANAGER OF THE IRISH BALLET COMPANY 1973–76
Speech at This is Your Life *in 1988*
I was twenty-six years in hotel management before becoming manager of the Irish Ballet Company – I don't know how I got in there.

Before going on our first tour, we wrote to 110 venues; fifty replied and forty were selected as viable – we thought. We went to Charleville for the Cheese Festival, and had to sweep the hall first before we started. We were in Coolea because of the Miss Moriarty – Ó Riada connection. The girls' dressing-room there was a caravan – there was no room inside the hall – so there was a plank between the caravan and the entrance to the hall. When we went to Clonmel we were announced as coming with Burt Lancaster: we performed in the cinema, and our notices were pasted under the heading of the old one – Burt Lancaster with – and then underneath came the Irish Ballet Company.

We went on a 28-day tour, giving 23 performances at about 18 different venues. In the early morning we would pack up, take the bus to the next venue, take a break, then there would be class, a break, a warm-up, the performance, and the next morning it was on again. Everybody did everything: it was a wonderful experience, there was no faulting it, as behind you was somebody who had done it all before!

Donn McMullin ten years later
On first acquaintance Miss Moriarty was seemingly remote and aloof, but in time I realised that this was a kind of shyness. She was an immensely private person and respected your privacy too. Her passion in life was ballet – it is as simple and as complex as that. She had enormous drive, vitality and determination – and above all a vision that she followed through thick and thin all her life. She ac-

cepted the honours which came her way – she did not seek them. She drove herself hard, and in consequence felt free to drive all others equally hard, as I remember only too well. An example. On our early tours she came to nearly all venues, if it did not conflict with her school commitments. Once we had arrived in the town, she would tour the streets to see how many posters were displayed in shop windows, if the billboard was prominently placed outside the venue for that night, if the local paper had written up the company and used the photographs sent to them. I would then be informed of each and every shortcoming! This was not done nastily or in a schoolmarmish fashion, but firmly and factually. It was often tough to take, knowing how much effort had been put into the organisation; I sometimes would have relished an odd word of encouragement, or a better understanding of the realities. You had to rely on local good-will and interest to ensure that posters would stay in place between your pre-performance postering visit and the actual performance date. Even the most interested local editor might have to push ballet off the pages if ploughing competitions, horse trials or a visit by an important political, clerical, or pop personality appeared more news-worthy. At times like this her tunnel vision was hard to cope with.

Yet I knew that, though she was tough, she had to be; and above all that what she demanded of others, she first demanded and delivered of herself. I was always conscious of how rigidly she judged herself and drove herself. Congratulate her on the opening night of one of the annual Cork or Dublin shows and you would receive a gentle and rueful smile and the warning: 'It's the next performance that counts. People forget easily.' It was always tomorrow to conquer, never resting on today's laurels. And this meant another challenge, another pushing out of frontiers. There was no time for sitting back or being pleased with your efforts. She was valiant, resilient, resourceful, with a will of steel and total commitment. But this remarkable, complex, brave, selfless, unique personality could be difficult to live with: she could be infuriating, demanding and single-minded to the point of obsession. There were times when you would have loved to have said 'Excuse me, Miss Moriarty', left the room, closed the door and seeking some place out of earshot, given vent to a long, full-lunged scream! But you didn't. That was a tribute to her unending fortitude even in the face of adversity – and there was adversity.

There were many occasions when the Dublin ballet world and associated arts ventures showed only too clearly that they considered that any artistic organisation using the word 'Irish' in its descriptive title should be based in Dublin. The vibes were very strong when one met with such Dublin colleagues. But who in Dublin or elsewhere had dedicated his or her whole life and all their energies to guaranteeing a place in our culture for an indigenous Irish ballet company? The one woman who fought massive battles to achieve this, at personal sacrifice, is dead. So is Irish National Ballet, and indeed professional ballet in Ireland.

Perhaps I should end by saying she was a lady, a perfect lady in the old-fashioned and sadly neglected sense of that word: she was a woman of sensitivities and inherent graciousness, a unique and enriching personality. I shall always be deeply grateful that I met her, knew her a little, worked for her and with her, admired and liked her a lot – flaws and all. One thing is very certain: without her there would never have been a professional Irish ballet company. Long may her memory live!

DAVID GORDON (CORK), BALLET MASTER OF IRISH NATIONAL BALLET
in conversation with Anne Fleischmann
A.F.: You were ballet master in Cork with Irish National Ballet from the very beginning in 1973. How did you come to Cork?

D.G.: I had seen an ad in the paper *Equity,* which is the Actors Union, advertising for a ballet master for the Irish Ballet Company. I was with the Royal Ballet, at an age when I was coming to the end of my dancing career, so here was an opportunity for me to step straight into the role of ballet master. Of course, the difference between the two was enormous, as you can imagine. It really was very glamorous where I was: I had been there for 17 years. It was wonderful touring all over the world – I was dancing with Margot Fonteyn and Nureyev. It was all like a dream. But the dream was coming to an end. It was Dame Ninette de Valois who discovered me. She was very interested in the fact that I was Irish and she was a kind of mentor to me. So I was really extremely lucky.

A.F.: Had you heard anything about the Irish Ballet Company at that stage?

D.G.: Practically nothing. I was born and brought up in Belfast and moved from there to the Royal Ballet, and it may have been the prospect of coming back to Ireland that made me decide to go and see this lady. When I arrived in Cork, it was the night of an election around the Watergate time and the Nixon affair; my room in the Imperial Hotel was opposite a television shop and for some reason or other they had left all the televisions on, including the sound, so I didn't get any sleep. Next morning I went for a walk. I remember the smell of the river: I couldn't get over this and wondered what I was doing there. Then I went into the cafeteria of the Imperial, and Miss Moriarty was sitting in a corner at a table alone. It was like a blind date.

My first impression was of the stern face. I asked her about her aspirations for the company, and she certainly impressed me. I have to tell you that in those days I was very grand. It was I who was interviewing her more than she interviewing me, which I regretted a bit later. I thought I would have trouble with this lady. It wasn't so much that she was obviously very strict and austere, but she clearly had her own personal ideas about how the company should be run. However, all these things, apart from frightening me slightly, were positive. She certainly had a very clear vision about what she was going to do, even though I wasn't sure that our methods would be the same. But she had a vision.

We had lived under a very strict and disciplined regime in the Royal Ballet, but then change began to creep in. There is a basic discipline which you must accept, but nowadays there is much more give and take, and much more scope given to the dancers' own personalities. She wasn't *au fait* with the changes that were happening in the ballet world and I knew that that was going to be a problem. But I made up my mind to accept. My family were delighted at the idea that I would be moving back, because they all still lived in Belfast and do so to this day.

Miss Moriarty was always very aloof; it was as if she had an electric fence around her. But despite all this, her heart was in the right place. I felt that she was going to allow nothing to stand in the way of her vision, and that I tremendously admired. She reminded me of de Valois, except de Valois had a tremendous sense of humour: she was always sending herself up and laughing. She had a funny walk like a duck, and everybody used to make fun of her. She knew this, and she used to make fun of herself. But Miss Moriarty was never like that. She was always her own person and I don't think that in the fifteen years I worked with her I ever got close to her, which was a great pity. I saw her laugh occasionally, but otherwise she was very withdrawn. I don't think I ever heard her give a belly-laugh. I don't really think she was a very happy woman. Her career was, I suppose, horrendously difficult. And the way it all ended was so ghastly.

A.F.: But to go back to your first arrival in Cork: it must have been a huge cultural shock for you – from the Royal Ballet to the conditions of the Irish Company.

D.G.: It was, and at that point we didn't even have a rehearsal room. I just had to go out and find one – it was a billiard room in the Father Mathew Hall. Then we got a rehearsal room in the Presbyterian School, where we stayed for many years. But that was all pretty awful.

A.F.: And how about the dancers? Did you find that you were taken aback by the standard of the Irish Company when you got there?

D.G.: Not so much by the standard, but by the mishmash. Not only were they different sizes and had different figures and different looks, but they all came from different cultures, from different schools. I was used to the Royal Ballet, where everybody had all gone through the same training – I suppose we all looked like automatons compared to them.

Our inaugural performance actually was in Dublin. That was the first time that Domy Reiter did a ballet for us. Ninette de Valois came to the inaugural performance in Dublin. I remember she wrote me a note which I got at the stage door. It was just signed 'Madam' and said that she had just been given the Erasmus Prize, which is a kind of Nobel Prize for the arts worth a lot of money. It's the custom, it seems, that whoever gets it only keeps a small percentage of the prize, and the bulk of the money is donated. So she was considering giving it to the Irish Ballet Company, but she wanted to see them first.

A.F.: That was great for your work with the company – your link with her.

D.G.: Yes, it was really. Those ladies were all very strange – she was exactly the same as Miss Moriarty, or Miss Moriarty was exactly the same as she. She wrote on her note to me: 'David, I am coming to see the performance tonight, but I don't want anyone else to know'. She also said she wanted to sit away from Miss Moriarty and the others. She was well known at Covent Garden, where the people used to hate having her sit near them, because she used to talk all the way through the performances. In those days you had paid, I suppose, about £35 a seat and if you had a woman next to you talking all the way through, you would be very upset.

A.F.: Would she be criticising?

D.G.: Oh yes, and you would be black and blue from her elbow. Anyway she was coming. That opening performance was frightening. We were all very nervous: Miss Moriarty was too, though she didn't know that de Valois was there and would see the performance. There was a ballet by Joan Denise herself: *The Devil to Pay*, with Seán Ó Riada's music. I thought this was the shakiest bit of the programme; to me it was old-fashioned, old hat. But de Valois loved it! She thought it was extremely well constructed, absolutely superb.

We all met afterwards in the manager's office. As I walked in, Miss Moriarty said 'Who is the friend you are bringing?' That was the kind of regime that annoyed many people: I had had to beg for those seats, not being able to tell who it was I was bringing. You can imagine the faces of all assembled when I walked in with de Valois. Afterwards de Valois had a long talk with Miss Moriarty and she said how much she had enjoyed it. She donated her Erasmus money to the company. She quite often came back to see us, even though she was very old by then. (She is still alive; she is older than the Queen Mother). I think Miss Moriarty was pleased about that, but we didn't know. I feel Miss Moriarty tended to distrust people because she had obviously had to fight all her life to get where she was. So none of us really knew what she was thinking. But though I always felt that she did not completely trust me either, in her capacity as artistic director I always had her full backing.

About five years later we had a row – a huge row, in fact, and I resigned. She tried to talk me out of it, but I being so grand would not hear of it. It was about halfway through the year, so I did say that I would stay and see my contract out. I had also fallen in love with Cork by then. I began to review the situation: during my five years in Cork things had declined tremendously in ballet – there was much more unemployment, there were fewer ballet companies, money was getting very tight everywhere in the world. So I would probably have had to go to America. As an old friend of mine used to say: 'Ballet companies are like ash-trays; as the company grows up, you get a lot of butts and there comes a time when you have to pick up the ashtray and get rid of the butts.' It is a horrible fact of life, but this is what you have to do in a ballet company. Miss Moriarty had some tremendously difficult decisions to make. Some were terrifying. But artistic directors all over the world have to do this. Anyhow, I went back and said I had reconsidered. Typically, Miss Moriarty said 'Well, I'm sorry, you can't: you've made your decision' – and she wouldn't budge! So there I was. I had to ask for my job back; and then she gave in. I always admired her for that, because it was a big issue for her to reverse her decision. In a way she slightly lost face, and we never thought she would do that. Otherwise she never did.

We made great strides with the company. We visited nearly every town in the country: we took ballet to the people. Some places there might be only two men and a dog. I'll never forget one show we did in Kilkee. That was disastrous. We would have ten, twelve people a performance. We did that for about two seasons in the summer. But they were beautiful summers, and it was a beautiful place, I used to think: 'Heavens, if I were on holidays, the last thing I would want to be doing would be going to a ballet performance'. But anyway we did it. And in other places we used to do tremendously well.

A.F.: It was Miss Moriarty's policy to bring ballet everywhere – had she spoken of this to you right at the beginning, when she met you?

D.G.: Oh, yes. Everything she said to me on that very first day in the cafeteria in the Imperial Hotel she carried through. She stuck to her guns the whole way.

A.F.: How had you felt when she told you she wanted to bring ballet to every corner of Ireland?

D.G.: I thought it was a great idea – and it was. But I didn't realise what it would entail. In some of the places we went to, we would have to clean the toilets before we could even go in. I remember in Cavan, I had to stand in the wings putting in ten-pence pieces into a metre at the side of the stage to keep the lights on! We used to go to these places by bus; we'd get to the hotel and straight to the hall; there wasn't any time to spare. Some of us helped with the get-in, and then we would have class, and then we would do the performance. She wasn't often with us, because she had her schools, and also on account of what we used to call her 'penny-pinching philosophy'. In fact, there was not a lot for Miss Moriarty to do on these tours, and she felt that her time was better employed back in Cork. That was another thing I didn't agree with: her presence there would have made a difference.

We were like a family when we were on tour. Travelling for dancers is strenuous, but it wasn't for me because I didn't have to get up and give a performance when we got to the next town. It was so nice. We knew the people who were always there and we built up an audience we could trust, and who were obviously our fans, and they would get others to come. It wasn't on such a grand scale, but it was tremendous fun. I had my dog on tour with me. Basil was the best looked-after dog in Ireland, because all the people who knew us in the various hotels would mind him and the hotel staff would take him for walks.

The people everywhere were very kind to us. For example, the Essames of Clonmel. She used to cook the most delicious meals for us. We used to go there every time. But they were very anti-drink. They used to serve lemon and orange, so those of us who liked a drink would have our flat bottles in our bags and we would top the orange up. Of course, they knew! Actually very few of the dancers drank at all: it is the technical staff I'm talking about. We thought we were getting away with it, but, of course, Miss Moriarty knew. She wasn't that sticky: she just kept her composure. She knew perfectly well what we were up to.

A.F.: And were you involved in the Birr Castle visits?

D.G.: Of course. They were marvellous. What an extraordinary woman she was, Anne Countess of Rosse. We always performed during the Birr Vintage Week in the Marion Hall, an average town hall with a tiny, tiny stage. She would arrive with huge floral arrangements to decorate the entire stage all the way round. At times I used to have to say to her 'Countess, would you mind?' – you could hardly see the artists behind the flowers! But it was so well meant. There was a little door in the walls of the castle, which were about seven feet thick: it was right opposite the front door of the Marion Hall where we were performing. But she wouldn't use this door: there had to be a ceremonial entrance. They would leave from the front of the castle, in order of lineage, get into cars – about four – and drive all the way through the estate, which was over a mile, to go through the gates and come all the way back for the state arrival! We would all be there to greet them and then she would arrive last with two of her staff, with cushions for herself and her husband, because there were wooden seats. She would be the last to come in and everyone would stand and she would walk down the aisle. Then she would sit and everyone would sit. Then I would walk down the aisle and say to her 'Madam, may we begin the performance?' It was a performance within a performance. And at the end she always made a speech.

A.F.: And did you then go back for drinks after the show?

D.G.: We did. On one occasion RTE made quite a long film on us and our visits to Birr. It was a super programme. We all had lunch by the lake, and after the show we went for a full buffet-meal. It was an absolutely beautiful world of its own.

And then we used to have visits to Lota House for the handicapped children. Miss Moriarty always kept us going, she was always thinking of things for us to do. The idea of us having a day off – that was out of the question. We would always know her mood. She used to often wear a tam o'shanter or a beret, and from the angle of the beret, we would know what we were in for. We used to call it the TAM ratings.

Her schools policy was great: I used to enjoy that. The dancers did too, although it didn't go down well at all at the beginning. Because, within the theatrical circle, dancers really have a very glorified idea of their own position within that sphere. Of all the theatre careers a dance career is the hardest and most exacting of all. So dancers are always pushing themselves to create something; and to be able to keep up this dedication and sense of purpose, they have to boost their egos. So they may sometimes seem to be imperious, but it is just part and parcel of being a dancer.

One of the problems was that we had a considerable fluctuation of dancers. Miss Moriarty wasn't always tremendously popular, but as time went on we got a core of people who began to understand her vision and to understand what she was at. And we all began to respect that even though we might find her trying. We all respected her. And I often think now she was a bit like the queen, whereas we wanted her to be 'Diana', but she couldn't be like that: it wasn't in her.

A.F.: There has been a lot of criticism about Miss Moriarty's choreography. Obviously it was not her number one area. How did you find her choreography – apart from *The Devil to Pay*, which you mentioned? What would you have seen as her best efforts in choreography?

D.G.: The best thing was the *Playboy*. It was a huge success There was a wonderful feeling in the company, a wonderful feeling. Again, it was her little world. It was something that no one else would have dreamed of doing for fear of being thought old-fashioned, being thought behind the times, being thought non-technical. And yet, it worked. It was utterly beautiful: it had tremendous quality. Its innovation was this marvellous, naive, theatrical, childlike experimentation. I found it very moving. It was said 'They are doing a bastardisation of Irish steps and ballet mixed up'. But if she had had a little more technical knowledge of the classical Irish technique, we would have been *Riverdance*!

A.F.: Well, you were in a way!

D.G.: But, let's face it, *Riverdance* has a more artistic outlook, a more magical outlook. I love *Riverdance* and Michael Flatley is incredible. But you see, the whole idea of theatre has changed. You don't have the de Valois or the Moriartys any longer, because things are ruled by the stars that come up. Nureyev had exactly the same problem when he came. He had to leave the Royal Ballet, because he did not fit in with the class system, as against the star system. He wasn't allowed to change choreography to suit himself. The establishment strangled him. And the same would have happened with

Miss Moriarty. She couldn't understand. We had people with us who thought they were or who were, within our context, stars, and who had more talent than the average person with us. They wanted to do things more their way, but that wasn't allowed. But, when I look back on it, in fact they did. She turned a blind eye. In other words she wouldn't admit it, but in actual fact, she did. It was exactly the same with de Valois when Nureyev came. Everyone else hated him, because when you went on stage with the Royal Ballet a hair wasn't allowed to be out of place (we used to use no end of tins of hair lacquer a week!). But he allowed his hair to fly all over the place. I remember de Valois one day slapping his face and saying: 'Naughty boy'. She had this great idea: he was a naughty boy. The same kind of relationship existed with Miss Moriarty and Richard Collins. I couldn't get away with a thing, but he was allowed to because he was a 'naughty boy'! She in fact did what de Valois did.

A.F.: How did the Ballet Company, these professional dancers with classical backgrounds, how did they react to her Irish ballets?

D.G.: They weren't the most popular, because the dancers did not have her vision. How could they have had? But if *Playboy* were to be done today, it would be tremendous. She thought of it way ahead of Flatley. But his dance form is not classically based, it is just theatrically based. It has Spanish touches, it has ballet touches, it has all kinds of touches, whereas ours definitely had a ballet feel or ballet look. Whatever it was, it was absolutely wonderful.

A.F.: Looking back overall, what stood out for you as a supreme moment in all your years with the company?

D.G.: The visit to America with *Playboy* was tremendous, though the Americans didn't take to it on the scale that the Irish had. It was being viewed from a different angle and we only got middling houses. Though I suppose that is very good in America. At that time, back in 1979, dance was the big thing: they were selling more tickets for ballet than they were for football matches. But the big thing was with the big stars, and with the classics: we didn't fit into those categories, which was slightly disappointing. Then there were the Domy Reiter works, which were absolutely fabulous. We had a production every year and she had the vision to keep bringing him.

A.F.: May I ask you about the Brinson interview with the company?

D.G.: I knew Brinson well. At that time he was the wine critic for the London *Times* and a ballet fan. I remember going to a lecture given by de Valois about the critics. He was there and he sort of wormed his way into de Valois' heart. He loved ballet. At that time the Royal was being knocked a lot by the critics and he was one of the people who wasn't knocking it and he became friendly with de Valois. And he started an offshoot of the Royal Ballet called 'Ballet for All'. They used to do pocket versions of the big companies' repertoire, with young students. So when you left the school to enter the company, you would do a period of six months or a year with this little group. They did it extremely well and it was most popular in schools. It made money, too. (Miss Moriarty developed work in schools as well with Irish National Ballet. It was a great innovation.) The 'Ballet for All' was closed down later: it lasted for about ten years. Then he got a job with the Gulbenkian Foundation, which made him quite powerful.

The whole thing was very sad, and it was Brinson's doing really. I was so confident, knowing him so well. I felt there was something Machiavellian about the whole situation. I think someone had made their mind up even before Peter Brinson arrived: that there was something of a *fait accompli* about the whole thing. No one knows, but that was my personal opinion. And the way the whole thing was done was just so awful.

A.F.: And the actual report itself, did you feel that it gave a valid account of the company and the situation at the time?

D.G.: I did, because in most cases he was very positive about the company, and in no way was he suggesting that the company should be axed. But it was anti-Moriarty, which we all disagreed with.

A.F.: It said a new policy was needed, but did you people on the ground get from Brinson a sense of what the new policy was to be? Because I remember my father asking 'What exactly is it you want done?' and he never got an answer to that.

D.G.: I would say that they did not know themselves. Everybody was groping in the dark. I really think the whole thing was a financial affair. And in situations like that, heads have to roll. And they did here, with that awful headline 'Head of the Irish Ballet axed'. It was just dreadful. We all felt so terrible about it, because by that time, love her or hate her, we all respected her. That goes for everyone. It was unanimous.

The problem was that everything had changed. The unions had become stronger. We were all complacent. She was the only one, I feel, all the way through, that wasn't complacent. We all thought this money would go on forever. And we didn't realise that this woman was battling away by herself all the time, the main object being to keep the company going. That meant doing the things that she was doing. To have experimented, to have gone outside her field of knowledge would have been much more expensive for a start, and that was one of her big worries: that we were going to become so expensive that there would be a huge lobby against us. After all, they had axed the Irish Theatre Company. The unions were raising their sights: we were being paid something like £35 a day subsistence allowance in addition to our salary, which in those days was a lot of money and there were 15 dancers, plus stage crew working day and night on double time. It was a very expensive business. And she had all that as well to worry about, whereas we never thought about it at all. But we were all very, very sad about the way she was treated.

A.F.: Could it have been done any other way, do you think?

D.G.: Yes, I think it could. They could have brought her up to Dublin, sat her down and said 'Look, this is what we think'. I know she would have said: 'Fine, give me the money to do it'.

A.F.: Were they afraid she wouldn't take no for an answer so they had to do it publicly?

D.G.: Possibly. My opinion is that the decision had been made for quite some time, but I suppose we'll never know.

A.F.: Do you mean that Brinson was more or less told to close it down?

D.G.: No. I think his report was very positive. He liked Cork. He thought we were doing marvellous things: I had many a conversation with him.

A.F.: So was his report just used, then?

D.G.: I think it was. I think that was the whole reason they wanted a report. In fact, I would say that his report concerning our company was a little bit of a disappointment to them because it was so positive.

A.F.: And when they brought in the Finnish lady to produce presumably this new policy ...

D.G.: But Anneli didn't really have any particularly different policy from Miss Moriarty. She had certain ideas which she wanted to give, but they weren't any different from anything that Miss Moriarty ever did. And the vision wasn't as clear as Miss Moriarty's had been. If they had really been looking for a change in policy, they would have got someone from a different genre, a contemporary person, a contemporary policy.

A.F.: And did you sense that the writing was on the wall at that stage?

D.G.: Well, we had just believed it would go on for ever. But what was done to Miss Moriarty was such a kick in the teeth, I never

186

really believed in anything after that. I would have if they had cleared the decks and if there had been something obviously new, a new goal, a new vision. But there wasn't. It was just a different person in Miss Moriarty's place, who was giving us nothing more. She was simply performing the function that Miss Moriarty herself had performed before her. It was about then that I began to realise that the writing was on the wall – even though we thought it could never happen. But it had happened with the Irish Theatre Company as well, and they were a most successful company. Towards the end, they stopped doing the tiny places that we used to do: they then only did the bigger centres, Limerick, Galway, which some people say was more sensible. But Miss Moriarty stuck to her guns and we went to every single town hall.

A.F.: If she had been able to relate more warmly with the company and the people, would things have been very different? Would that have been her biggest drawback, as you'd see it?

D.G.: I think so. If she had been a little more 'Diana', I think people would have rallied. And yet people did rally to her cause. We thought: 'She is Miss Moriarty: no one would ever dare to do anything to her'. It wasn't until they had done it to her that, too late, we all began to realise. I had still been hoping. I really thought we were safe after the huge success of the *Playboy* in Dublin. I thought then that her confidence would have grown so much from that experience that she would be able to feel open, to involve people, at least myself, to understand her more. But she still kept her distance.

A.F.: It was a lifetime habit.

D.G.: Yes, it was indeed. She didn't know how to open up.

A.F.: It's a bit like with Shakespeare's characters – it was probably the thing that preserved her and helped her to survive for so many years and then it became her downfall.

D.G.: Yet she never lost face right through all that awful time during the ending of her work with the ballet company. It must have been terrible for her.

I think the Arts Council of the time wanted then to put into place the policy they have at the moment. But they have put us back so far. Instead of investing in what we had and changing what we had, they stopped us. It has now taken ten years to get to a stage where good things are coming out of the new policy. And though some of the new things are excellent, they could have come out of the existing framework, and it would have happened so much quicker and would have cost a lot less. I feel it was a very sad thing to do. There is no one with her kind of dedication and discipline around now: that sort of person just doesn't exist any longer. Instead of recognising it and trying to lead it into a new direction, they stifled it and cut it off. I am distressed they didn't give her a chance: they just chopped. If they had decided to make changes with her, I am certain she would have adapted, because we must remember that her fundamental concern was to keep the company. The fact that she took that appallingly painful step of resigning in order that it would survive shows that if she had been given any other choice, she would have taken it.

MURIEL LARGE (EYE, SUFFOLK)
Administrator of Irish National Ballet
The first impression of Miss Moriarty was of someone not of this world. We met in the foyer of a London hotel – an unlikely setting for this distinctive woman with the severe hairstyle, centre-parted; classical bone structure of face and brow, and pale clothes with long fluttering scarves.

I worked closely with Miss Moriarty, almost on a daily basis during her 12 years as artistic director, and although in many ways she could be infuriating, I developed a strong respect for her. I may not always have agreed with her opinions and attitudes towards the work of the company, its dancers and repertoire, but I admired the way she lived her life by self-imposed precepts and the personal discipline which this entailed – and I had a fondness for her which overrode all.

I know that for many years Miss Moriarty had longed for the establishment of a ballet company of national status, recognised and grant-aided by the government, which would crown her lifetime's work in Cork, but I do not think she ever foresaw the consequences this would have on her life. The great sadness to me is that this dream, once realised, created for Miss Moriarty (despite the success some of her ballets achieved and the many awards she received) so much trouble and so little pleasure.

TOM DONNELLY (CROSSHAVEN, CO. CORK)
Manager of Irish National Ballet
Speech at This is Your Life *in 1988*
Miss Moriarty's *Playboy* was put on for the Dublin Theatre Festival in 1978 and was the success of the festival. It was then put on in the Opera House in Cork; in April 1979 in New York, later in Sadler's Wells during the Sense of Ireland Festival, and in Rennes in 1985 to celebrate the twinning of the city with Cork. As well as being a box-

office success, the *Playboy* made theatre history. For the first time in living memory, the audience left their seats at the end of the performance, and danced jigs in the aisles to the music of The Chieftains, something which was never known to have happened in the history of the theatre. And that happened again in New York, which was even more extraordinary with a multi-national audience. Miss Moriarty created magic in that performance. Of course she was magnificently served by Seán Cunningham as the Playboy. He was brilliant, dazzling, marvellous. And also Anna Donovan as Pegeen Mike, and the splendid comic performance of Patricia Crosbie and every member of the whole company. Some magic happened that night at the Olympia and we all shared in Miss Moriarty's dream.

The *Playboy* got a great reception in London too. But despite packed houses in the Opera House and in the Olympia, Miss Moriarty was convinced that in London it would be a disaster. 'The house will be empty, nobody will know the Irish Ballet and nobody will come', she said. I had the great pleasure of meeting her off the plane and bringing her by taxi to Sadler's Wells Opera House. Over the Opera House there was the Tricolour – it was very nice of them to fly it – and a huge lighted sign which said: Irish National Ballet in Joan Denise Moriarty's *Playboy* with The Chieftains. But underneath in equally large lights, two words: SOLD OUT – before we began. So I stood her in front of the theatre and had a professional photograph taken so that for all time if she ever dared to say again we were going to have a disaster, I could show her this.

But I understand her pessimism. I think why everything she did was so marvellous was that she never trusted on past triumphs: everything was a new experience and it always had her one thousand per cent attention to the minutest detail. That's how she succeeded.

LORETTA KEATING KLEANTHOUS (CYPRUS)
Director of Irish National Ballet
I was invited to join the board of Irish National Ballet in about 1981. For some years I was the only director residing outside Cork. Once a month I drove from Co. Kildare to Dublin, some 25 miles, and took the train to Cork. From the station I enjoyed the walk to the Imperial Hotel, where our board meetings took place, commencing at 6pm and lasting until about 11.00pm. I was always received with enormous warmth from my Cork co-directors. I never resented the travelling I had to do over those years; rather I felt privileged to be a member of the board. It was close to feeling a member of a family. I en-

joyed listening to 'the Professor' and Joan Denise batting ideas back and forth; there was always the worry in my mind that I was not contributing enough. By being part of what was happening I felt I had gained so much.

Before joining the board I voiced my worry, since I had enjoyed the friendship of a number of the dancers and I hoped this would not be endangered. I was assured, however, that this closeness could be an advantage. Thus, when asked, I would meet a few of the dancers before the board met, so that I could bring their worries or grievances to the meeting. In due course, it was agreed that a representative of the dancers could attend whenever they felt the need.

Joan Denise Moriarty was a lady of vision, and I believe she achieved an enormous amount, considering the attitude to ballet in Ireland in the early years. Classical music and the Radio Éireann Symphony Orchestra emerged during the Second World War years, but even thirty years on, ballet was not a high priority for audiences. Opera took precedence. It was, however, the persistence of Miss Moriarty, with the continuous encouragement of Professor Fleischmann, which finally made the Irish National Ballet possible.

Perhaps because of Joan Denise's Cork Ballet School and Cork Ballet Company (the amateur company which was the performing group of the school) her attitude towards the members of the professional company was more than a little dismissive, and she often treated the dancers as irresponsible children. She liked many of them, though, and likewise many grew fond of her; but, generally, from what I recall, there was not the great rapport between Joan Denise and the members of the Irish National Ballet as there was with the Cork Ballet Company. Her work with the school, however, was extraordinary. It was wonderful to watch young people, and sometimes not so young people, from varying walks of life, factory workers, typists, professional people, on stage, utterly transformed by the dream world, giving all of themselves to create something extraordinary. (Norris Davidson made a truly poetic film about the school.)

Irish National Ballet, not unlike other ballet and opera companies in other countries, was dogged by financial problems. Contributing to this was the fact that 'Equity', the union representing the Arts, insisted the company be paid top touring rates. Other dance companies such as Dublin City Ballet did not have to do this. However, miracles were achieved on a small budget. Pat Murray gave so much of himself: his stage designs were ingenious. When he had little money to play with, he could still create something special. When he had more in hand financially, he could produce something fantastic.

Only when I was invited by the Arts Council to meet Brinson did it emerge that there were doubts that Miss Moriarty was the right person to be artistic director of Irish National Ballet. Brinson did ask me about Miss Moriarty's rather strained relationship with some of the dancers, and I answered him honestly, and also told him I felt privileged to serve on the board. What emerged from this meeting was that it was felt for practical reasons the ballet should be centred in Dublin and, of course, Miss Moriarty was adamant it should remain in Cork. How ironic it is that so many years later the policy for the arts (especially in music) is to decentralise! Thinking back, perhaps the fact that Miss Moriarty had not been a professional dancer may have been held against her. But I never heard this voiced. The Arts Council, which funded the company, then started insisting on certain measures, one being that some members of the board step down and new members be recruited. I was asked to remain; Joan Denise was asked to resign as artistic director. This was perhaps the beginning of the end for Irish National Ballet because it was like a ship without a sail.

The company could only afford to be modest in size, but it was unique in that so many new exciting ballets were staged. Domy Reiter-Soffer created a number of these. Joan Denise herself provided one particularly successful ballet: her *Playboy of the Western World* which did so well in New York with Ireland's beloved group of musicians 'The Chieftains' to provide the music. I only missed a performance in Dublin and some in Cork if I was out of the country. Many of the ballets performed were created for the company and so were new, fresh and exciting, and this excitement and freshness was reflected in the performances.

In the 1970s I accompanied Justin Keating, to whom I was married at the time and who was Minister of Industry and Commerce, on an extensive tour – he was trying to entice people in industry to open factories in Ireland and I, at the invitation of Coras Trachtála, to publicise the arts in Ireland. We travelled 23,000 miles in 19 days. There was a reception given in the Irish Embassy in Washington to which, amongst others, Henry Kissinger was invited. Someone in our group, knowing my love for ballet, obtained tickets for the resident ballet company in Washington. I shook hands politely with Kissinger and made a quick departure. Alas, the performance that night was incredibly mediocre and dull. I remember at the time feeling that with all their money and choice of dancers, how lacking in fire and magic it was compared with our own small company, which always had to battle against such odds, led by two extraordinary people, who gave of themselves so unsparingly and contributing so much to the arts in Ireland.

DENISE ROBERTS (ESSEX)

I trained at Bush Davies School in East Grinstead, Sussex, and then joined 'Ballet for All' in 1978. This company was part of the Royal Academy of Dancing. When it was closed down I moved to Dublin to join the Dublin City Ballet in 1979, dancing lead roles. Miss Moriarty would sometimes come to Dublin and watch the Dublin City Ballet; I knew several Irish dancers in the company would be quite nervous that she was watching. I stayed with the company for a year, then returned to England where I joined British Ballet Theatre. I missed Ireland very much. There was an audition for the Irish Ballet Company in 1982: I joined the company in that year; little did I know that I would stay till the closure in 1989.

Miss Moriarty was always very kind to me and I found her a caring lady. I liked her classical ballets *Reputations, Invitation to the Dance. Playboy* was a great success and I enjoyed the time when Miss Moriarty set the ballet in the studios and will always remember her Irish screws.

I did find, however, during those years in the company that there was an 'us and them' situation between Cork Ballet and Irish Ballet. I think we all felt let down sometimes; we wanted Miss Moriarty to be more involved with us professionals, to recognise our commitment to our company and not just that of the Cork Ballet. But though we sometimes complained, we all recognised that what she managed to do was amazing. She really did bring dance all over Ireland, into the small towns, into the big places – she even took us out of Ireland! I always got on well with her, always admired her greatly, and was so sad to hear of her death. I was so proud to have been asked to go back to Cork to dance the peasant *pas de deux* in *Giselle* with Preston Clare for the gala performance of 1992 in memory of Miss Moriarty and Aloys Fleischmann: it was a very special honour.

I now have my own school with 40 little dancers; I teach adult ballet classes at our local council schools. My husband is from Cork and I visit three times a year. I do feel sad sometimes walking around Cork and remembering the good times we had with the company. I wish the Irish National Ballet were still going strong. It would be wonderful to put on some performances in the Opera House in

Cork to recognise Miss Moriarty's works and her life. I would be willing to help in any way I could.

KATHLEEN SMITH-EPSTEIN (OREGON, USA)
I feel that all credit is due to Miss Moriarty and all those who helped her to succeed at making such a good company in a country where there was no classical dance tradition. As a choreographer she had an excellent idea to combine the Irish culture with simple ballet steps, and *Playboy of the Western World* was her crowning glory – a great show in the best sense of the word. In my opinion, her strength lay in the way she chose to present the dramatic side of each ballet she made. She herself was always modest about her choreographic abilities; for example, she would explain what she wanted from us and then add that she hoped it would work as she had tried it out in a small space in her kitchen! But this isn't so strange when one knows the conditions under which the national ballet company worked most of the time.

Conditions could sometimes be rather primitive. One story comes to mind. It was June or July of 1976, and we had just finished our most successful Dublin season ever at the Abbey Theatre. It was the first day of the summer season, and we found ourselves at St John's Hall in Tralee about to do our first performance (we would travel each week for six weeks to Tralee and Killarney for three performances on quite small stages, often performing to half an audience or less). Miss Moriarty seemed less than pleased at the rehearsal and lectured us afterward. She told us to forget the Dublin season (the icing on the cake as she called it); our true mission as a ballet company was to bring ballet to every last town and person in the country. To tell the truth, it was very difficult to perform in *most* of the towns on tour in Ireland, and the conditions at St John's represented some of the more difficult ones. It could be quite depressing and took a lot of discipline to make a performance of which one could be proud. At the time, what Miss Moriarty said had the effect of depressing me even more; however, I knew she was completely sincere and certainly respected her for that.

Miss Moriarty gave me my first chance to choreograph and was very complimentary of the first piece I made. Through the years I made several small pieces which were shown at 'Dance-ins' and twice at the Everyman Theatre in Cork. On the strength of this work I also received a bursary from the Arts Council in 1985 which, unfortunately, I was never able to use as we left Ireland that year.

In my career I had the good fortune to dance in 14 different companies. As a mature dancer I spent the last ten years of my career in Ireland, in part because of the interesting work that I was doing with Domy Reiter-Soffer. This was my 'icing on the cake' as I had already danced almost every classical ballet, much Balanchine, other neo-classics and ballets of many contemporary choreographers throughout Europe and also in the States. I say this only to put a perspective on my opinion. Miss Moriarty as a choreographer of pure ballet did not achieve an international standard, but her Irish works are certainly worth preserving should there ever be another national company. As a director, she was quite shy with everyone; she was not in the studio every day; thus, David Gordon played a major role in the running of the company from a dance point of view. In Muriel Large she had one of the best administrators I ever worked for, and I am sure that Miss Large played a key role in the success of the company.

So what is a good artistic director? In my opinion, choosing key people to help run the company is a great part of it. Having a choreographic speciality is a bonus. But the main asset that Miss Moriarty brought to the company was that she *was* a leader as indeed an artistic director must be. She was Irish, she was respected, she was ambitious in the best sense of the word. As far as my personal relationship with her is concerned, she was always unpretentious and seemed to appreciate my work for the company. I was sad to learn that she had died.

Ireland had something very special in its own national ballet company which was due to the efforts of many people; Miss Moriarty, Miss Large, David Gordon, Domy Reiter-Soffer, Tom Donnelly, Desmond Graham, Lucette Murray, the entire board of directors, the technical crew, wardrobe mistress/master (Moira MacNamara, Tony Kelly, Vera O'Driscoll), Mrs Barry who made most of our costumes and, last but not least the many dancers throughout the years who did their best to create some magic for the audience. (Please note, this is a partial list of people; I'm sure I will remember many more having mailed this!) It is a pity that it could not have continued. I was quite interested in working to become the director myself when Miss Moriarty would decide to retire; but, in the manner that events unfolded, I would not have been strong enough to save the company.

CATHERINE MCMAHON (HOLLYWOOD, USA)
I am writing the following from memory as I am now living in Los Angeles, and all my diaries and papers are in London or Ireland.

However, I do not need them to revive my recollections of the woman who inspired me to have the courage to follow my dreams; I remember Joan Denise Moriarty, as do so many others, for her incredible courage and determination and for all she achieved for dance in Ireland.

I grew up in Limerick. One of my earliest memories is of dancing for my grandparents as a very small child to a record my father had bought of *Swan Lake*! I took my first dance lessons in Limerick. When I was around seven years old, it was discovered I had fallen arches (flat feet) and I was told to give up dancing. In fact, dancing, especially ballet, would have strengthened my feet. However, in the meantime, I took up speech and drama classes, but on the rare occasion I saw some ballet on TV, I got a tremendous urge to do it. I was fascinated by the plasticity and physical control of the dancers. I eventually hounded my parents and at the late age of 15 I went to have my first ballet class at Joan Denise Moriarty's 'Friday School' in Limerick. We had seen a series of dances Miss Moriarty's girls had performed on television and my parents were impressed. These were like Irish folk dances in style and beautifully costumed, well rehearsed and executed. My father also remembered having seen Miss Moriarty's first professional company, the Irish Theatre Ballet, which he said was the most professional of all the dance groups he had seen in Ireland to date.

When I left school, I couldn't afford to train as an actress in England; I hadn't had enough training to become a dancer, so my third choice was to go to the Cork School of Art, which was located right opposite Miss Moriarty's School of Dance in Cork. Well, if I was 'behind' in Limerick, I realised I was even more behind in Cork. I was fine at the barre as there was someone in front and behind, so I just copied everything. However, when we went into the centre of the floor and the teacher would set an *enchainement*, the other students all knew the French terms for the steps and automatically set off across the room looking wonderful. I charged after them and hit the position, but they were already reversing and going into something else. It took several months of two to three classes a week before I began to do better.

I am writing this to illustrate how difficult it was for anyone growing up in Ireland (outside Dublin or Cork) to have any chance of breaking into the world of dance. This was in the 1970s, so one can only imagine what it must have been like in the 1930s and 1940s. When Miss Moriarty came to Ireland and later set up her school, it was a poor rural country, recovering from a civil war, trying to establish an 'identity' and culture and Second World War had begun devastating Europe. Even Dame Ninette de Valois had a struggle to keep Sadler's Wells Ballet going in London.

Once I started at the school in Cork I had regular contact with Miss Moriarty, as she taught the weekly Monday night 'company class' (for the amateur Cork Ballet Company) and she was regularly at the school overseeing things. She was already well on in years but she was very fit and agile and well able to teach the Cork Ballet 'company class' These were the dancers she had trained over the years plus the senior students from the school. She always brought in teachers who were either registered with the Royal Academy of Dancing or with the Imperial Society of Teachers of Dance, who were trained teachers up to date with the current syllabus and methods. The worst we could ever say was that Miss Moriarty was a little bit 'dated'.

The company classes that she taught were invariably enjoyable and entertaining. Of course, some of the young dancers would argue over certain ways of doing things (i.e., from the syllabus being taught in the school) but this is quite normal as there are several different 'schools' of training in classical ballet (e.g., Cechetti, Russian, ISTD, RAD, etc). Miss Moriarty had a commanding presence, but she also had a warm, humorous side and always chatted with the company before starting class. We felt like 'family' and she once said we were all the children she never had. She had tremendous energy which drove these classes along. Nobody slacked off when she was teaching and many of these dancers had come after their day job or a long day at school or college. Several of her students went on to become professional dancers, for example Carol Bryans, Patricia Crosbie, Jill d'Alton; others, like Kilian O'Callaghan and myself, went to London to continue our training. She also trained a teacher, Mary Madden, who taught at the Cork Studio for many years. Whenever examiners were brought over from England, Miss Moriarty would arrange for them to coach Mary and update her on any new additions to the syllabus.

So, while attending Art College in Cork, I did classes at Miss Moriarty's School of Dance three times a week and managed to gain the Elementary and Intermediate Certificates (ISTD) in classical ballet. Once I gained competence, I got asked to perform with Cork Ballet Company in their annual November productions at Cork Opera House. Miss Moriarty would bring over guest choreographers to 'set' these productions. It was an incredible experience for us to have the chance to perform on a large stage in a fully equipped theatre,

196

beautifully costumed and set, and to dance to a live symphony orchestra. Guest dancers were usually brought in for the leading roles. We would start rehearsals in August in the school studio and learn the choreography to taped music. It was always a big event when we had the first orchestral rehearsal. Of course it sounded different and the tempo may have been a bit faster or slower. As dancers absorbed with perfecting our sections it was frustrating to have all this stopping and starting. I remember Lavinia Anderson, one of the principal dancers with the Cork Ballet Company, being held high in a difficult 'lift' by her male partner and quipping when the music stopped: 'Professor, can you play a bit more music so I can get down!!!' However, all this made us appreciate what it takes in teamwork and cooperation, patience and, of course, the ever present 'blood, sweat and tears' to mount a large-scale ballet or musical, with good production values.

At the Royal Ballet School in London a few very lucky children get to perform at the Royal Opera House each year (the children's roles in *Nutcracker*, etc.) and of course the graduating class has its performance there each summer. This was our chance in Cork to have that experience of being in a large production. Much of what I learnt about stagecraft then I was very grateful for years later as a professional dancer and actress. I remember the usual chaos on stage during one of the scenes with all the *corps de ballet* doing their thing for the first time, with scenery and drapes in their way, and lights in their eyes, and Miss Moriarty's voice commanding over a microphone from the dark auditorium and somehow keeping control and shaping it all into a coherent production. I think an organisation like the Cork Ballet Company is a very valuable asset to any city. Only a few talented people can actually make a living as professional dancers and even then their performing career is so short. The amateur company was a wonderful way for all those who had a certain amount of training to practise that which they loved doing, even into their later years. There were some marvellous 'character' performers always needed to play the courtiers or the wicked witch, etc. It also provided a great social structure for meeting people, and a guaranteed audience of all the parents and relations of those involved. However, it took someone like Miss Moriarty to keep it going with her vision, dedication and drive.

She was passionately interested in Irish history and folklore and spent a lot of time researching traditional folk dances and steps. She was involved in the annual Cork Choral Festival, held at the City Hall, in which choirs and folk dance groups from Europe and the

Eastern Block countries took part. I remember performing in *The Strawboys* one year in the most amazing tweed costumes, huge straw headpieces and wooden sticks. The rope holding my trousers up got loose and I spent a very anxious 15 minutes on stage desperately trying to keep them from falling down around my ankles, while wielding my stick in the other hand and trying to keep up with the fast and furious pace of the dance, all the while sweating profusely under the 'tweed'!!! However, it was great to be representing your country with its own unique folk dances in front of all those other nationalities.

When the professional Irish Ballet Company (it later became known as the Irish National Ballet) was set up in 1973 with a grant first from the government and later from the Arts Council, most of the dancers had to be brought in from abroad. There was no professional training school in Ireland to produce dancers to international standards. The best of Miss Moriarty's students joined and some from Dublin. David Gordon of the Royal Ballet was the ballet master and taught the daily class for the dancers and oversaw rehearsals. Guest teachers of the calibre to coach professional dancers were regularly brought over to Cork, usually for two-week stints. I was lucky enough to spend a year as a student taking classes with the company before going to London Contemporary Dance School, and during that year I had teachers such as Brenda Last (Royal Ballet), Richard Collins and Elena Mordinova (Bolshoi), Rachel Cameron (Royal Acadmy), Tony Hubbard and others. Miss Moriarty's ambition was to maintain it at an international standard and to make it something that Ireland could be proud of. She was the driving force behind that company and at the time was the only person who could, and did, get it up and running.

During the year I spent as a student dancer with INB there was a certain unrest and dissatisfaction among some of the dancers. As in any company, some may not see eye to eye with the artistic director. Many of the dancers had worked in Europe and the USA and perhaps felt a bit cut-off from the rest of the dance world in Ireland. There was the question of why the national ballet company was not based in Dublin. Many of the dancers would have preferred this and perhaps politically it would have strengthened the company's position. Of course, dancers used to the more established 'conditions' (and greater funding) in Europe and the United States must have found it difficult to tour in Ireland often dancing on tiny stages in freezing school halls without proper dressing-rooms and showers and sometimes to small audiences. However, they enjoyed the warm reception and hospitality of the Irish people.

The first time I saw the Irish Ballet Company perform was the summer of 1973 at a hall in Kilkee, Co. Clare. We sat on benches and watched a beautifully executed classical *pas de quatre* followed by a modern piece and then by a lively piece with an Irish flavour. The company travelled all around Ireland and brought their expertise and quality to many people who were seeing dance live for the first time. It was an uplifting experience. I remember being saddened years later when the Brinson Report was published which advised cutting off funding for the professional company in favour of lesser funding to small 'community' dance groups. A noble intention, no doubt, but I am still not convinced that watching a group of untrained or 'not as well trained' community outreach dancers in a workshop style performance could ever move, touch or inspire 'ordinary folk' as the professional company had. There is something about dance and movement that when skilfully performed and when what is performed (the content) is of a certain quality, regardless of how classical or how avant-garde it is, how sophisticated or how uncultured the audience, a special human impact is made through the virtuoso physical form of expression.

Joan Denise Moriarty believed there was a need for a professional training school for dancers in Ireland. Having the professional company around during that fifteen years gave many of us something to aspire to and at least the possibility of employment once we were 'trained' and up to standard. Young dancers coming up through the schools in Dublin and Cork still had to go abroad to complete their training and often never came back. The company could only take one or two student dancers at a time, and it wasn't a school anyhow. They would get a daily professional ballet class, but they would not get the intensive all-round training, including ballet, contemporary, jazz, folk and historical dance, plus the increasingly important body conditioning and anatomy studies. This marriage of sports science with dance is vital for the increasing physical demands placed on today's dancers. The tragedy is that her dream came so close to all being pulled together. There has been in recent years a National College of Dance in Dublin but unfortunately there is no professional company attached. A national company needs a school to supply it with dancers and, likewise, a school needs a company for its dancers to aspire to when they graduate. It is universally appreciated that in order for dancers to be fully expressive, they must be highly trained instruments and not hampered by a lack of technical ability. This implies a solid classical ballet training along with contemporary and jazz styles, etc.

Miss Moriarty realised that Ireland could not afford a large-scale professional company that could mount the classics (*Swan Lake*, *Nutcracker*, etc.). In itself, this was a Catch-22, because they consistently play to packed audiences and can 'fund' a company's season. However, she developed the idea of touring a programme of three one-act ballets each season, with contrasting styles (classical, modern and something with an Irish feel). I remember as an art student being bowled over the first time I saw Royston Maldoom's *Adagietto No. 5* for its sculptural quality and Domy Reiter-Soffer's *Yerma* for its passion and drama. The first full scale 'Irish' ballet by Moriarty, *Playboy of the Western World* to music by The Chieftains went to New York and Sadler's Wells in London and helped put the Irish National Ballet on the international dance scene.

No one else in Ireland achieved what she did and to such a professional level. I remember that I feared the worst on hearing that Miss Moriarty had been advised to resign her position as artistic director of the company in 1985: I felt that without her (or someone like her) at the helm, the company would not survive. It had taken a long steady fight to set it up and the tragedy is that no one was groomed to assist and eventually replace her. In Europe, Britain and the USA, it is quite feasible for artistic directors to move from one state or country without too much difficulty. However, in a small country like Ireland, without an infrastructure of dance already established, without large funding, this required someone with a particular understanding and knowledge of the condition of dance in Ireland and also with the vision of what it could be!

I feel it is important that her legacy be preserved and documented. To all the dedicated followers of dance in Ireland, it seemed we were badly let down by our Arts Council, who felt they were acting in the tax-payers' interests. The success of *Riverdance*, which combines Irish music and dance with a modern day sex-appeal and show-business pazazz is surely proof that Ireland's rich cultural heritage can be a success commercially and artistically in the 1990's, both at home and abroad. Music and dance transcend many boundaries. I can imagine the tall figure of Joan Denise Moriarty, hair swept back in a headscarf, her stern features breaking into a smile, giving her blessing from wherever she is now. May she rest in peace.

PAT MURRAY (CORK), DESIGNER

Member of the Arts Council up to 1998, in conversation with Anne Fleisch-mann

P.M.: At the age of 18 I started in the Crawford School of Art in Cork in Emmet Place, which is across the road from the ballet studio. I was there two days when I was summoned by Miss Moriarty, and in the presence of Michel de Lutry and Domini Callaghan, who were doing *The Sleeping Beauty*, asked if I would make some props: they gave me a little list. The biggest mistake I made at this stage was to make them too well. 'Oh,' they said when I presented them, and gave me another list; and before I knew it I was making all the props. From that ballet of 1958 on I designed every ballet for Miss Moriarty for over 30 years. It was a life sentence! You'd have got time off for good behaviour anywhere else.

Miss Moriarty was very nice to me. I always thought she and Professor Fleischmann were great fun, though some people were terrified of them. I remember poor Professor sweeping the orchestra area when they had all gone home after rehearsal, and collecting the chairs. He'd have to go up to some houses to fetch an instrument and then return them. He was always tortured with musicians as she was always tortured with the dancers.

She was faced with a very difficult task in the Ireland of the 1940s. To get a man on stage was nearly impossible, and often girls had to take the man's part. She stuck it out until people got very fond of her and then she gathered a group of loyal men and women around her who helped – people like James W. O'Donovan and Leslie Horne, Alec Day and myself at a later date. Once you were involved, you were involved. She and Professor were very loyal people and they demanded loyalty too. As people got to know her they realised she was very simple under that veneer.

A.F.: You often went on holiday with her – what did she enjoy?

P.M.: She loved the circus. We were on holidays once in the Canary Islands and all she wanted to do was go to the circus because she thought it was the most honest art form. The circus performers did everything. Of course, she had the same idea for the ballet, that the dancers should be selling programmes in their dressing-gowns, ushering people to their seats and doing everything, just like in the circus. So we always went to the circus everywhere we went. In Cork when the circus came, there were always flowers for Miss Moriarty because she always came to see them. She did the ballet *The Big Top* for children. She loved children, but she was very shy, though strong as steel under it. She would ferret away until she got the thing done, like water on granite. She always said you can lead the Irish but you can't push them. She was right, and she'd lead everyone, even the army; she got everyone in at some stage.

Any time we were on holiday on a beach we'd watch all going by and we'd try to guess their occupations. She loved a game of sevens and scrabble. 'That's how I spell it,' she'd say when her spelling was wrong and it wasn't the best, I must admit. She loved a good movie. When you go to a movie, she said, you're not worrying whether it is going to work or not: it's in the can and you can relax. She loved concerts, anything well done, in fact.

When the *Playboy* went to France, to Rennes I brought her over, as I had a bit of money at the time. We were going down the Champs Elysée and she said 'I must tell you something. See that shop? When I was studying here that's where I worked: in fashions in the ski department'. Of course, she was tall – you could see her modelling the ski-wear. There was a lovely silky dress in the window which she admired. I suggested she try it on. 'I couldn't afford it'. I said we were in Paris, just to try it on. So I had great pleasure saying 'Wrap it up'. It fitted her like Isadore Duncan, all oranges and blues and pinks. I asked if she had ever been at the Follies Bergères and she hadn't. So all dressed up we went there and sat in the second row. She adored the show. In the penultimate scene, the star – a tall black woman with a jewel of a figure – came down the steps, took me by the hand and brought me up on stage with two other men. I was caught: JDM was under the seat laughing. We went on to Maximes afterwards and she made an entry there. She had a glass of pink champagne, only one glass. I bought her a bottle of pink champagne which was still in her place when she died: she was keeping it for a special occasion.

A.F.: What was she like as a teacher?

P.M.: She only taught the younger kids, but what she did for them was great. She made them go to exhibitions and concerts. I know, as they all called over to the School of Art, and anything musical they went to as well. They got great deportment. A lot of them were never dancers afterwards, but she helped them become self-confident women, able to enter a room with poise and elegance. They all speak very highly of her. Some of them did become professional dancers. She was a great teacher. She was always going back and forth to London to courses to make sure everything was being done right. She was very conscientious. She'd have been knighted in England, and of course she got the doctorate here.

She would do anything connected with dance. She trained the

men in things like *Guys and Dolls* and did the dance for operas in Wexford and Dublin. She loved story ballets. She once said to me: 'I'm not a very good choreographer, you know.' I said 'You are.' She had great humanity. She didn't care about small things, but in big things she was there to help you. When other choreographers used come over, they'd pick the best dancers or dancers of the same height. She, however, would take the other dancers that the guest choreographers were not using and she'd create something around them. She created wonderful works for Anna Donovan who was very tall, works like the *Táin*. She was great like that.

She was above all a catalyst. If she wasn't in Cork there would have been no dancing: nothing at all. Being a catalyst she knew who to select and whom to mix and match – that was her great gift. I remember when she brought *Playboy* to London to Sadler's Wells, both Peter Darrell and Dame Ninette de Valois were there and they both said if only they could do for their national dance what she had done for Irish dance. But they couldn't do it. She was far ahead of *Riverdance*. They valued her for what she was doing in Cork. Dame Ninette came over for the very first night of the Irish Ballet Company in 1973 and did a cartwheel on the stage. That was her speciality. It was a great night.

Then there were the choreographers who all adored Miss Moriarty, and who kept coming back. Richard Collins adored her altogether. She loved him, he was like a Peer Gynt and she'd forgive him anything. They all respected her integrity, her honesty and her art. They'd invite her in to ask her opinion. You see, she'd look at it from an Irish point of view. She was very good like that. Domy Reiter-Soffer was going to do his *Othello* and was going to bring in a black dancer. She wondered if that man would be happy in the Cork of the 1960s. What would he do after the rehearsals? She felt it wasn't right that for a twenty minute ballet he should be brought to Cork for a year. She could always pin down the issue. If the choreographer wanted to do an obtuse ballet, she'd say it wouldn't work and she'd be right: it didn't. She couldn't take too much of the abstract. 'What are they doing? They're bluffing, it's too long,' she'd say. As she'd say herself she wasn't the world's best choreographer, but she was an entertaining choreographer. She said the public come in and see a thing once. It is no use going through the subtleties. They are not going to sit down ten times and watch the same work. If you can't get it across in 25 minutes you are not able to do it at all. She was a great believer in the visual too. 'The eye must be entertained, the ear must be entertained.'

She hated awkward movement or ugly movement or positions of the body. She was all for line and purity because she was a very pure person. She couldn't even curse. When she was exasperated at something she'd say: 'Pat, curse for me.' I would and she'd say: 'Thanks. I was brought up so strictly that I can't say that.' She always said Irish dancers were like the Russians: they danced with their whole bodies, heads and all, whereas many British dancers moved from the head down, with no expression. She also said that technique was fine, but you must also have love as well. She used call the professional dancers factory dancers sometimes, because they were watching their watches at ten to five, whereas she'd work day and night. But she'd forget that these kids were exhausted and it wasn't the end of their day when they left at five or so: they'd be going out again. She used terrify some of them, but if they were in any trouble, in real trouble they used always go to her. JDM would listen. Even the men would go to her because she was a strong woman. Nothing shocked her or Professor, though they might pretend to be shocked.

A.F.: What was your understanding of what she wanted to achieve?

P.M.: She wanted her people, as she put it, to express themselves as Irish people. 'Don't treat London as the capital of Irish theatre: we are Irish,' she'd say. 'Our people are as good as anybody else or better and I want to make sure that they have dignity and a sporting chance in all the arts because as they get older they'll need them. The disco will be gone when they are twenty; the dance and classical music won't.' All she wanted to do was to make the arts available to people, for their choice. That was her vision, and to make the quality of life the same for people in Cork and around the country as it was in Dublin. She said that was an uphill struggle as everything was in Dublin, and she stayed in Cork and she fought cleanly.

No one else could do what she did. And there has been nobody since. I know because when the Arts Council decided they wanted to revive dance, I was given the job. The ballet was gone in Cork. There was the schools, but the days are gone when you can get a professional orchestra or ballet. What we did was to revive the contemporary ballet in Dublin. The first thing was to get money. The money was down to £135,000 a year, but we got that up to £900,000 a year and there are three companies. Now we are trying to start a small professional ballet company – where it is based doesn't matter.

A.F.: Was that one of the problems regarding the last professional company, that it was Cork based?

P.M.: It probably was. The Brinson report didn't help it, although it did say, in fairness, that there was nothing else in Ireland like Irish National Ballet. What happened was: the amount of money given to the Ballet Company was very high in those days – £400,000. The theatre needed more and got it. Miss Moriarty not appointing a successor was a problem too. We begged her to have an assistant but she never did. A prophet in his own land is hardly ever accepted as a prophet, but she was held in great respect by people in Cork: they could see what she was trying to do. The dancers will tell you as well, even though they might have laughed at her behind her back because she was old fashioned, but they loved her and had great respect for her.

A.F.: What about the Firkin Crane?

P.M.: The Firkin Crane was her idea. She wanted a building in the city centre where the people are. That was wonderful. But then the ballet collapsed and we had the Firkin Crane but no ballet company. I have great hopes for it now. It is a dance centre and I'm hoping that we'll get a small classical ballet company in there. The facility is there, the tradition is there. JDM was ahead of her time. If she was only here now. But she will never be forgotten because she has done it. I think they made a big mistake when they closed the professional company down because they did not put anything in its place. They recognise now how difficult it is to start from nothing.

About her gravestone: Ken Thompson did it. When he showed us his first design, I said: 'That's not JDM. She was a warrior.' I wanted an ogham stone six foot six tall, her name, and just dancer: no more. I wanted it taller than Fleischmann and Lynch, or she'd have been lost among them all as they have big slabs. So that's what she has now.

PRESTON H. CLARE, SCOTTISH BALLET (GLASGOW)

Irish National Ballet was my big break: I joined straight from dance school in May 1982. I was nineteen when I met Miss Moriarty for the first time and got a contract for five weeks to be a gollywog in her children's matinée, a new venture she was starting so as to bring in a younger audience. She was the first choreographer I had ever worked with and she had a wonderful way of getting things as she wanted. She had her own names for her own steps – 'walking on eggs', 'Irish screw' were all new to me, but you learnt to know what it was she was after.

She was certainly a woman who knew what she wanted. She

would walk into rehearsals and sit down, watching with a stern face, taking in every detail, and making sure everything was as she expected. This earned her the nickname among the dancers of 'The Face', because we would long for her to smile a little, letting us know she was happy with our work. But with Miss Moriarty you had to earn her respect.

I must have done something that impressed her because after the five initial weeks I was offered a full-time contract. The following March the Black Swan *pas de deux* was in the repertoire with Kathleen Smith and Roger Wade. David Gordon, the ballet master, wanted Denise Roberts and myself to be the second cast and do a few performances. He had many arguments with Miss Moriarty, who thought at nineteen I was too young – and in a way she was right – but in the end David won and after weeks of rehearsals we did our first performance for a schools' matinée. It went very well indeed and after the show Miss Moriarty met me back stage and gave me a book of Frank O'Connor's short stories, which was inscribed inside: 'Preston, congratulations on your first "Black Swan", Wednesday March 23rd 1983 – Joan Denise Moriarty'. As she handed it to me she said: 'When your name is up in lights, remember us in Irish ballet.' I guess it was her way of saying she was wrong and that I had earned her respect, and in doing so she was respected and admired by me.

Another book came to me on my twenty-first birthday. One of the dancers organised a surprise birthday party for me and everyone was there. Miss Moriarty gave me the Irish comic classic – *The Irish R.M.* by Somerville and Ross. As usual she wrote something inside: 'Happy twenty-first Preston, Wishing you every happiness and fulfilment down the road of life – have an enjoyable day. Joan Denise Moriarty March 30th 1984'.

It was Miss Moriarty who recognised my talent as a character dancer. It was she who cast me as Seán Keogh in her *Playboy of the Western World* in 1984, and in the same year I was asked by her to dance in Cork Ballet's production of *The Nutcracker* as Dr Drosselmyer, a role I am well known for today in Scottish ballet. I also danced as the Fiery Tinker in her production of *Puck Fair* that year.

We dancers of Irish National Ballet always had the feeling that Miss Moriarty was happier with the amateur Cork Ballet than with us – probably because she had started Cork Ballet twenty-five years before INB and some of her closest friends were in Cork Ballet. I think she felt that Cork Ballet worked for the love of art, whereas we in INB, the professionals, did it for money, as our living. I don't think you could say we didn't love what we were doing. The wages were not good, and the facilities were poor, but every dancer was passionate about what we were doing in Ireland. Anyway, Miss Moriarty asked me to perform with Cork Ballet, which made me feel I was trusted by her and taken into her circle of friends. To add to that I can tell you how honoured I felt when Denise Roberts and myself were asked by Cork Ballet in 1992 to dance the peasant *pas de deux* at the memorial production of *Giselle* in honour of Joan Denise Moriarty and Aloys Fleischmann.

I left Irish National Ballet on 31 August 1985 to continue my career in Scottish ballet. Miss Moriarty left the same day under different circumstances – she had been asked to leave. She was very upset and didn't come to the last performance. This meant I couldn't say goodbye to her, so I wrote to thank her for all her help and wish her good luck. This is what she wrote back: – 'Dear Preston, Thank you for your card of good wishes. I felt sorry not to see you before you left but I know you will understand how painful the past three months have been and I felt to be at the last performance would be just too much. Thank you for being such a nice person to work with – I shall miss you. All good wishes – keep in touch – success. Joan Denise Moriarty 3/9/85'.

Well, Miss Moriarty, my name isn't up in lights yet, but I will never forget my time with you or Irish Ballet.

CAOIMHE NÍ HEINIGH (HOLYWOOD, CO. DOWN)
I first met Joan Denise Moriarty at the Abbey Theatre when I was ten years old: she made my day by signing my programme. Later, I attended classes run by the Irish Ballet Company for young dancers during their Dublin season, where she made a point of talking to us all after class. When I began professional training at the Hammond School in Chester I wrote to her, telling of my ambition to join the IBC one day. She replied encouragingly, asking me to keep her informed of my progress. At the end of my first year in England, I was invited to do company class in Cork. She watched class and afterwards told me to go on working hard – she also hoped I would grow a little taller! I pestered her with letters throughout the following year and, in the summer of 1983, I auditioned and was accepted into what was then Irish National Ballet as a student member.

To be honest, I can't say I got to know Miss Moriarty during my first year – she seemed very distant. However, at the end of my year's 'studentship', I was summoned to the office where Muriel Large informed me that Miss Moriarty was pleased with my work and that I was therefore to be offered a full dancer's contract. Walking back to the studio, I wondered why she hadn't told me herself, but thought no more about it. That afternoon, Miss Moriarty beckoned me out of the studio. I followed, assuming she was going to mention my new contract. She didn't say a word however, pointing instead at the company notice board, where she had just pinned up the cast list for the revival of her ballet *Reputations*. I gasped when I saw my name – my first-ever 'first cast' role. Still JDM didn't speak: she just stood and giggled at my delighted reaction.

My saddest memories of Miss Moriarty come from the time leading up to her retirement in the aftermath of the Brinson Report. She was obviously terribly hurt: one dreadful afternoon she came to the studio and asked the dancers what exactly they had said to Peter Brinson. In what became a very emotional and angry meeting, she accused the dancers of stabbing her in the back, running her down at every opportunity. Despite our protests, she refused to discuss anything, just repeating over and over again that we had betrayed her. This was the reason that on what was officially her last day with the company, she didn't attend our performance at the Everyman Theatre. After the curtain fell, the entire company waited onstage to pay tribute to her, wondering how she had felt watching the company she had founded for the last time as artistic director. When she didn't arrive, it was left to Donal Walsh, the chairman, to break the news that she hadn't been at the show. We were all devastated. It was the saddest possible ending.

Looking back, I don't feel Joan Denise Moriarty ever thought she was a success. But she was: without her there would have been no Irish Ballet Company or Irish National Ballet, no jobs for Irish ballet dancers, and audiences from Gweedore and Ballycastle to Tralee and New Ross would never have had the opportunity to see ballet. I loved my time in Cork and feel privileged to have been one of the few Irish dancers to have danced in our National Ballet Company. I am glad I took the opportunity of expressing this to Miss Moriarty, in a letter I wrote to her when she left the company. She sent me a lovely reply which I have to this day.

(3) Irish National Ballet

Guest Artists, Choreographers, Guest Teachers

MARINA SVETLOVA (VERMONT, USA)
I greatly admired Joan Denise Moriarty, ever since I came to perform
in Cork, and after seeing what she was doing in Ireland for the art
of dance I offered my services free of charge to tour in Ireland's provinces, which I did between my other engagements. I enjoyed the
artistic atmosphere: there were inevitably many problems, which
she always channelled due to her knowledge and devotion to the
company.

I always did admire her and feel very sad that she is not any
longer among us, but the beautiful memory will always be with all
of us.

DOMINI CALLAGHAN AND MICHEL PASCHOUD DE LUTRY (MUNICH,
GERMANY)
Message to JDM at This is Your Life *in 1988*
Would there ever have been a Cork ballet or an Irish ballet company
without her courage against insurmountable odds, her teaching,
artistic integrity, iron discipline and initiative disguised within velvet gloves?

Her name conjures up for us a kaleidoscope of exhilarating
memories. She first impressed us with her beautiful Titian hair and
soft, gentle voice as she met us at the quay in Cork when we disem-
barked from the lamented *Inishfallan*. We were involved in the productions of *Swan Lake, Giselle,* and *The Sleeping Princess* for the Cork
Ballet Company between 1956 and 1958 and will never forget how
she conjured up the impossible: décor and costume-designers, dressmakers, not to mention dedicated students and dancers prepared to
devote exhausting hours of rehearsal at the studio in Emmet Place
after daytime school and work.

In those days she was obliged to beg permission for extra food
during the Lenten fasting period so that the dancers did not fade
away during the rehearsals, which sometimes lasted till nearly mid-
night. Also she had to fight prejudice so that the boys could appear
on stage in tights, because there were nuns at the dress rehearsals.

But due to her untiring engagement all Cork seemed to do their
bit towards making these productions a success. We remember with
fondness coffee sessions at the Green Door over the sometimes hys-

terical discussions about seemingly unsolvable problems and then Miss Moriarty would listen quietly and immediately go and solve them. The whole atmosphere of working with the Cork dancers was unique: a feeling of idealism, joy of dance and performance – which the Irish certainly possess – came to fruition with Miss Moriarty as the tireless generator.

Ireland must thank Professor Aloys Fleischmann, Pat Murray, Hilda Buckley (a marvellous Carrabosse), and many unnamed, dear people, but first and foremost Miss Joan Denise Moriarty for the wonder of the Irish ballet. Her use of Irish culture in her choreography is without example in the dance world and one wishes that those ballets could be seen in even wider perspective.

Congratulations dear Joan, good luck, three cheers for you, keep healthy, happy memories and affection!

Domini Callaghan and Michel Paschoud de Lutry ten years later
Our feelings towards Joan and Aloys are those of great respect and admiration. We enjoyed so much working with them during the pioneer days of the Cork Ballet Company and will never forget the unique atmosphere of idealism which they inspired during rehearsals and performances. It 'fired' the city of Cork to champion 'their' company and the public expressed their enthusiasm by donating their applause, thanks and full houses.

Joan's work as a teacher proved without a doubt that it was possible to cast and produce the full length classical ballets with her pupils and students together with supplementary professional guest dancers.

When Michel was deciding on the cast for the first production of *Giselle* in 1957 it was obvious that Joan was the ideal choice to dance the role of Myrtha, the Queen of the Wilis. After watching her teaching and dancing in class, no one could deny that she possessed the requirements for the part. At first she turned the suggestion down because she would have liked the full cast to have been chosen from among the students. However, after preliminary rehearsals Michel persuaded her to take over the part. She possessed the smooth *bourées* on *pointe*, regal carriage, lyrical *adage*, excellent flowing arms and the cool dominant aura required. She definitely projected with authority her interpretation of this far from easy role.

We will always remember her and Aloys for their devotion to music and the dance and their friendliness as colleagues. The orphaned Cork Ballet Company must miss them; is there no one with the same courage to revive the Irish National Ballet? Surely all the heartbreak and effort which went into those years of development and practice must be able to earn fruition permanently.

RACHEL CAMERON, ROYAL ACADEMY OF DANCING (LONDON)
Joan Denise Moriarty gave me the impression of being a true Irish visionary. Her knowledge of Irish folklore and her empathy with the people of Ireland appeared indicative of a deep love of her country.

This love, combined with the desire to extend dance education throughout Ireland, means that all Moriarty's energy was directed towards the development of an Irish National Ballet, which, in spite of continual difficulties she eventually achieved. Unfortunately this achievement came too late for her to appreciate and enjoy. For so long she had acclimatised herself to failure that she was almost unable to accept success.

At her best in adversity, Moriarty was able to disregard reality and maintain faith in her dream. Not only did she keep her own faith, but she motivated others to assist in the work towards her ideals. It was easy to recognise her failings as director of a professional ballet company. Such failings appeared to be caused by an inability to communicate directly with company members of all departments. I found during our discussions that I had an understanding of and sympathy with her future plans. She always insisted that our discussions of the plans should be confidential. I respected her wishes, but often wished she would talk to the company as she did with me. But the protective barrier she built for herself prevented the sharing of ideas and plans, resulting in misunderstandings, which in turn obscured her view of actuality. However, had she accepted reality, it seems unlikely that she would have been able to overcome the apparently insurmountable obstacles and disappointments.

Whatever her faults or limitations, it must be acknowledged that without her commitment there would have been no Irish National Ballet. There is no Irish National Ballet today. It is to be hoped that Ireland will produce another visionary to re-create and extend Joan Denise Moriarty's dream.

KIRA STRAKHOVA (DEVON)
When I first was in Ireland, I only watched Irish National Ballet classes and performances; while there I was asked to come back to teach, which I did – I was teaching at that time in Dartington Hall, so I could only stay for a few weeks. I enjoyed my time teaching in Cork enormously. Miss Moriarty was a kind, gentle person, whom I

admired for having formed Irish National Ballet entirely through her own efforts. Unlike the major companies, who have their pick of dancers, choreographers and décor artists, this company had to work within limits, lacking in funds, etc. But her dancers made up for it: they were young, enthusiastic, and very hard-working.

TONI BECK (DALLAS, TEXAS)

It gives me great pleasure to write about my experience with the Irish Ballet Company under the direction and guidance of Ms Moriarty. My association with the company was for a period of four years in the mid 1970s, when I was choreographing for a number of ballet and modern ballet companies in both the United States and Europe.

My personal experience with the company and with Ms Moriarty was most rewarding and uplifting. I found that I was always given the support that was necessary to produce the new ballets – I did four with the company. Although the company was small and on a tight budget and we had to work in a very compressed period of time, we all felt productive and inspired. I was there when Anton Dolin was working with the company, which was a most enriching experience; I was there twice when Domy Reiter-Soffer was in Cork, and I also knew him when I taught and choreographed in Israel.

During the time I was working in Cork, one of my dancers, Mr Babil Gandara, was dancing with the company. This made for a great deal of continuity and cohesiveness. I have only positive memories of my involvement with the Irish Ballet Company and with Ms Moriarty. I found her to be a most gracious woman who supported her company and its standards in a most professional fashion.

HAZEL DURANT (WESTON-SUPER-MARE)

I was in Cork twice around 1964 for a couple of weeks at a time conducting ballet examinations for the Royal Academy of Dancing in Miss Moriarty's school. She certainly made a great impression on me. She was an excellent teacher, with vision and ambition. I had a great admiration for Miss Moriarty and her pioneer work in Ireland. She was, I felt, a person of great integrity and courage, and the self-dedication and determination to devote herself to the cause of establishing a National Ballet in Ireland.

ALAIN DUBREUIL, BALLET MASTER OF THE ROYAL BALLET (BIRMINGHAM)

It was in the early 1970s that I went to Cork and danced with the Cork Ballet Company: in *Giselle* in 1971 and in *Swan Lake* in 1972. I found Miss Moriarty and Professor Fleischmann both charming and utterly committed to their respective form of art. Miss Moriarty was indeed a formidable woman, her drive and her love of dance communicated with all who worked for her. She had a great knowledge of dance – of ballet, folk, Irish.

I recall being present at a dinner with Jack Lynch where Miss Moriarty put forward her ideas of forming the Irish Ballet Company. She was obviously very persuasive, as Mr Lynch's government gave her a grant to start the company. My personal memory is of a very beautiful woman, wonderful red hair, always immaculate, and a real charmer.

SANDRA CONLEY, ROYAL BALLET (LONDON)

In 1972, I was invited to dance in *Swan Lake* with the Cork Ballet Company. Miss Moriarty impressed me as being a woman of some considerable vision and energy, with the ability to gather around her talented people and encourage them to use their gifts in a common purpose. This was what the great Diaghilev did – and few people achieved more artistically than he.

Soon after our visit, I recall Miss Moriarty was given a professional company: a remarkable achievement surely. Although, sadly, I was not able to see them perform, I read some very good reviews in the ballet press. I have memories of an extremely happy and stimulating time spent with Miss Moriarty's energetic and enthusiastic company, I recall Professor Fleischmann's professionalism, and what was achieved by a very talented designer on a limited budget.

HELEN STARR JONES (LOUISVILLE, KENTUCKY)

I remember I was delighted to accept Miss Moriarty's invitation to perform *Giselle* with the Cork Ballet Company. Alain Dubreuil my partner and I thoroughly enjoyed ourselves: we were well looked after and given adequate rehearsal time both with the dancers and then with the orchestra, which was in the capable hands of Aloys Fleischmann. I loved him for his incredible energy, his love for ballet and his enthusiasm which would be hard to match anywhere.

Giselle went very well and I found a group of very dedicated people of all ages, the like of which I had never come across before. Now, after 20 years in the USA I have a yardstick, as this type of company – basically a school with a visionary at the head of it – is the mainstay of ballet in America today. Because the big companies no longer tour widely, the exposure of many of the American people to ballet or dance in any form is dependent on what are known here as 'civic companies'.

When Miss Moriarty approached me about producing and dancing in the full length *Swan Lake* the following year, I was able to accept the challenge willingly, on the strength of what I had seen with *Giselle*. Obviously some changes would have to be made to *Swan Lake* as I knew it, since it required a large cast, but with careful planning we were able to put together a very presentable version, utilising all the people in *Giselle* plus a few more from the school who had matured during the year.

It must have been late January 1972 when I returned to Cork to begin teaching *Swan Lake*. I was glad that we did not work until later in the day as, just before leaving for Ireland, I received confirmation that I was pregnant with my first child. This news meant that I would not be able to perform in the autumn but at least there was plenty of time to find another ballerina. I thoroughly enjoyed staging the ballet, and I believe this was accomplished in three weeks. When I left for home, the principals in the *pas de trois* in Act 1 and other leading roles already had the promise of what they would become, but the *corps de ballet* was, understandably, a mess. They barely knew their steps, but then Miss Moriarty had nine months to work on them and judging from *Giselle*, all would be well.

Hannah was born in September and was I think six weeks old when my husband and I took her to Cork to put *Swan Lake* on the stage. I always stayed in the same hotel, so they were very accommodating now that I had a baby in tow. I had a pram, the top part of which became a carry-cot and Hannah went everywhere with me. Rehearsals stopped at feeding time (I was the source of the food so couldn't get anyone else to take over) but nobody seemed to mind and really all that was left for me to do was to add some production details and get the visiting principals fitted in. The *corps de ballet* were dancing well together, in straight lines and the orchestra sounded good. Alun dealt with the scenery and lighting and we were both very pleased with the end result.

So much so that we began negotiating to join the professional company which was about to be formed. My husband Alun Jones was employed as assistant artistic director of the Irish Ballet Company and I joined as a dancer. He really did very little for the whole year. Miss Moriarty, having waited for nine years to see her dream of another professional company in Ireland come true, was not ready to hand over any of the reins, except the financial management to Muriel Large. In Miss Moriarty's defence, she really did not need an assistant director that first year as she employed Domy Reiter-Soffer as resident choreographer and David Gordon as ballet master. So that is why we returned to England after a year.

CHARLES CZARNY (THE HAGUE, HOLLAND)
The Irish Ballet Company, later named The Irish National Ballet, was one of my most loved places to work. For a small company running on a shoe-string budget in physical circumstances that I had seen nowhere else in all my travels around the world, it provided a *superior* professional environment. The artists were first rate and were ideal for the repertory that was the company's aim: a contemporary one.

If there is one thing I miss now, in my retirement, it is the thought that the invitation to come back in the future is not part of my future. I loved the letter that would come asking me to return to set another ballet. And when I arrived I was greeted by the dancers with enthusiasm, professionalism, discipline and love of work in the studio. David Gordon was there constantly watching and asking questions and keeping the dancers aware of the corrections and demands I had made in previous rehearsals. No time *ever* was I frustrated by a lack of complete assistance by him. He was the communication officer, also, with the management, technical division and Joan when necessary.

I always went away *fully satisfied* by the team that the artistic director provided for me to get the most out of full days that were allowed for me to work. And the result was some of the most beautiful reviews I had ever seen. And, with all humbleness, (don't you believe it, ha!) I was used to good reviews in other parts of the world.

If I ever was invited out by one of the dancers I would accept with the announcement that I would not talk about the company or its politics or their frustrations. About dance and their experiences and their lives in the dance, etc. yes, but never specifically about the ballet master, the management, gossip, etc. I had learned to avoid that very early in my choreographic career. And since I had twenty years of professional performing experience with companies, I knew that dancers are chronic complainers and since they are mostly all the time tired from the physical exhaustion, having to diet, and often with no 'personal life' due to the dedication the company demands (unannounced tours, long times away from home, etc.), most dancers are 'unhappy'. (No I am not a pessimist. I presume *all* artists are dissatisfied, or 'unhappy'.) However, for me the atmosphere in the studio was so conducive to excellent results from the ballet master and the dancers I could deliver my most positive, inspired energy.

When I was asked to write for this book about my experiences with the company I was asked to also describe troubles, tensions and tribulations. I can't. There were none. You have to believe me! I always had the feeling that I was welcomed with open arms. And my rehearsals were not complicated because I would always bring a ballet that had already been tried and true. They were bouncy, happy and sometimes humorous ballets, so we had a 'ball'. And in the three which were more 'poetic' or 'serious' the dancers took to them like ducks to water. The Schubert for four women and four chairs got one of the most glorious write-ups, a la critique, that I had *ever* had on it.

I mentioned in the beginning of this account the difficult physical circumstances of the ballet. Can you imagine my horror on my first visit in January coming into an abandoned church with a stove in the corner of the room and dancers bundled up like explorers to the north pole? Nowhere in the world had I seen such 'poverty'. I was used to *studios*. But then after a few hours with David and the dancers I did not feel the cold or see the environment. Joan would come to watch and take off her coat and sit there smiling as if it was the middle of summer and in the studios of the Royal Danish Ballet.

Isn't it ironic that when Joan was removed by the Englishman and those who believed him, and someone was found who had all the qualifications to really do the job, the whole thing fell apart?

I am guilty, like so many who 'failed' her. I should not have come on that last visit when she was no longer artistic director, and no one was there to replace her yet. I should have visited her and told her I cared about and valued her, but didn't. In the first instance my loyalty was to the special dancers with whom I had a bond and who I wanted to support in a struggle to, at least, have the company go on. In the second instance I did not want to explain to Joan why I was there, or excuse myself for putting the company and my own work above her. When the company fell apart it broke my heart. I still correspond with five of the ex-members who all seem to be getting on with their lives, as dancers do because they are now at an age when they have to, but with the feeling of having been 'cut off' at the prime time of their artistry.

Now to what I feel and what I have experienced with artistic directors, and what I think. Definitely *not* needed are diplomas and 'qualificatory papers'. Joan was a *pioneer*. She set up an amateur company that was so impressive, and it so satisfied the needs of her community that she was encouraged to accept the leadership of a professional group. She gave herself completely to the dance and built something no one else would have wanted or *dared* to do in the extremely poor physical circumstances and financial limitations. But then when she began to get financial recognition, and the company became 'National', and it looked like this was going to be a 'comfortable' and enviable position to hold as artistic director, or member of the board, etc., people began to ask for credentials.

I came to work for the first time with an honorarium of 200 Irish pounds. That was about one-eighth of what I usually got. The *per diem* allowance was what I had to use to pay my hotel and daily food expenses, etc. – in every other country the hotel was paid for by the company and the *per diem* was for food. They did their best to offer me as much as they could. The last visit was rewarded with an honorarium that was about one-fourth of what I got elsewhere. But the *per diem* was worth less because the hotels had gotten more expensive.

To teach a ballet that was already created some place else, thus not an original one for the company, I worked five hours a day for twelve rehearsal days. The money was not important because the artists were so great, the ballet master terrific and the city a joy to be in. Here was a company most choreographers who worked in the modern idiom would certainly want to work with. The dancers earned a pauper's wage, they performed on stages the size of postage stamps with dressing-rooms that were depressingly inadequate and the tours were hard labour. I heard their stories. They too were pioneers. All this was held together and led by a woman who had the *charisma* to win their support and the support of the community for one of 'their own kind'. And *if* she had no 'credentials' she knew how to get the people around her who could do the work needed to produce an artistic organisation. She was a choreographer. And no credentials are needed for that. No company of the highest standard will ask anyone for credentials or diplomas if the person's ballets are exciting or moving or valuable for a public. She certainly did not use the company to 'push' or promote her own work. Otherwise she would not have invited outside choreographers. I *never* felt on any one of my visits that an artistic director was lacking or someone else was needed to take over.

HARRY HAYTHORNE, ARTISTIC DIRECTOR
of the Royal New Zealand Ballet
I have only the most pleasant memories of the times spent in Cork at the invitation of Miss Moriarty. Admittedly as an artistic director she did not have the background in professional theatre that one

might have expected, but that would also be true of a great number of founding figures in ballet, particularly those operating in situations remote from the international mainstream. Most ballet companies in Australia, New Zealand and the United States (and I daresay elsewhere) emerged wholly or partly from an amateur background. What is more important is the enthusiasm of their founders and that their aims and operations be as professional as circumstances will permit. Miss Moriarty had these qualities in abundance.

Through an introduction by Muriel Large, I was twice invited to Cork by Miss Moriarty. On one occasion I came to stage *Coppélia* for the Cork Ballet Company, during which visit I was also a guest teacher of the Irish National Ballet. On the other occasion it was purely as a guest teacher of the Irish National Ballet. Apart from the times I was in Ireland I have been in other places associated with dancers whose initial training was under Miss Moriarty. There have been several but most recently Kilian O'Callaghan, who was a soloist with Scottish Ballet, West Australian Ballet and finally a principal of The Royal New Zealand Ballet.

The Cork Ballet Company was conceived as an amateur company and as far as I am aware deliberately maintained that status. Nonetheless its aspirations were very high and near professional standards were achieved. The Irish National Ballet was fully professional and on the occasions on which I saw it perform attained standards of dancing and production of which any regional company would be proud and on many occasions reached heights which were comparable with those of national companies from other of the smaller nations.

Criticism can be levelled at some aspect of any ballet company but perhaps only those who have had to work with very limited funding trying to build an audience from a limited population base can fully appreciate the considerable achievements of Joan Denise Moriarty and the artists and staff she gathered around her.

She was proud of her Irish heritage and unselfish in her determination to give Ireland a ballet company of which it could be proud. The great pity was that there were not those with the will or perhaps the wherewithal to carry on the work she staunchly began.

RICHARD COLLINS (COLUMBUS, OHIO)
who died in 1991, formerly of Balletmet

28 January 1988

Dear Miss Moriarty,

I've been meaning to write you since I left Ireland after *Swan Lake* in November, but with my usual lack of organisation I never got round to it. However, after two months my feelings are unchanged, even strengthened, so I just want to say two things, one of which leads directly to the other.

The first is that I have never seen the Cork Ballet perform better. I was delighted, impressed and thoroughly proud to have contributed towards what seems to me a really professional, moving and dedicated performance of *Swan Lake*. I love your company, and it seemed to me they gave back to you, to that production, all the care and hard work (not to mention relentless discipline!) that you have lavished on them through the years. I provided only the framework, it was you who brought it to life. I feel privileged to have been a part of it.

The second feeling is an extension of the first. When I look back over my years in Ireland, with the Irish Ballet Company (as it then was), I realise what an immensely rewarding period it was in my life, how much I learned, and how much I benefited artistically from working 'on the road' with such a lively and growing concern. Those were indeed the days, and they were more real and down-to-earth than anything before or since. Thank you for all your love, patience and experience.

We may argue about some things (I know I can be almost as obstinate as you sometimes!), but it is always I who am the learner, and I want you to know how grateful I am to have met you. Thank God for the truth!

With much love
Richard

(4) Critics

MARY CLARKE, EDITOR OF THE DANCING TIMES *(LONDON)*
I was introduced to Joan Denise Moriarty by the late Betty Hassall, then principal of the famous Hammond School in Chester and a greatly respected examiner of The Royal Academy of Dancing. I liked Miss Moriarty immensely and after she had left, Mrs Hassall strongly commended her work to me and said I should visit Cork to see for myself.

I obeyed her!

I visited Cork several times and travelled to Dublin for the historic occasion when Professor Fleischmann proclaimed the company should be the Irish National Ballet. I also saw and enjoyed the London season at Sadler's Wells with The Chieftains. Over the years my admiration of Miss Moriarty's work, especially when she was dealing with Irish themes, increased and I observed with respect the loyalty and devotion she won from her colleagues from the worlds of music and design.

I am delighted that her great contribution to ballet in Ireland should be recognised in this book.

CAROLYN SWIFT, DANCE CRITIC OF THE IRISH TIMES *(DUBLIN)*
Joan Denise Moriarty as Choreographer,
Long before *Riverdance*, Joan Denise Moriarty was trying to develop Irish dancing into a performance art which would tell a story, rather than merely demonstrate a skill. Even before Fr Pat Ahern founded his Irish folk theatre Siamsa Tíre in Kerry in 1974, Joan Denise Moriarty was combining her love of ballet with her experience of Irish dancing and musical knowledge gained through her skill on the Irish war pipes to choreograph short pieces for her company in Cork, using Irish traditional steps and dance rhythms.

Seán Ó Riada from Coolea in West Cork was at that time pioneering the development of Irish traditional melodies, rhythms and instrumentation in both classical and popular music, and Ms Moriarty eagerly seized on his scores as settings for short ballets. The first of these was *West Cork Ballad.*

This was choreographed for Irish Theatre Ballet in 1961 and later revived for the amateur Cork Ballet Company, which she founded in 1947, to perform for Cork Ballet Week in October 1970. Its slight plot was taken from a well-known tale about a strolling fiddle player who, after flirting with the daughter of a shopkeeper, beats a hasty retreat when she shows signs of taking him too seriously. The traditional nature of the story is emphasised by the other characters bearing names like Paddy the Stone and Biddy the Still.

The choreography of this piece was simple, but it was an early attempt to marry traditional Irish dance steps with ballet, just as Ó Riada himself had married Irish traditional music with classical techniques. The piece proved extremely popular and was revived for her second professional company, the Irish Ballet Company, later to become Irish National Ballet, during the first year of its existence, when it was performed both in the Cork Opera House and the Abbey Theatre for the latter's 1974 Third International Theatre Season, prior to a countrywide tour. The part of the Strolling Fiddler was danced by Domy Reiter-Soffer, the Israeli choreographer, who had originally created this role. As late as 1984, this piece was still in the repertory of Irish National Ballet, when it was danced at the Saturday matinée at the Abbey Theatre by the late Carol Bryans, Howard Epstein and Anna Donovan.

Ms Moriarty choreographed another short piece to an Ó Riada score for the January 1974 opening of the Irish Ballet Company in the Cork Opera House before a tour which included the Gaiety Theatre, Dublin. This was *Billy the Music*, in which the music of a melodeon-player has a strange effect on a young girl, who is revived by a mysterious stranger. The latter is at first acclaimed by the crowd but, when Billy the Music plays again, the mood changes and the crowd turns against him. The role of Billy was created by Terry John Bates, now best-known in Ireland as the Toni Award-nominated choreographer of Brian Friel's play *Dancing at Lughnasa*.

A similar blend of Irish traditional and contemporary-style dance was used in *Devil to Pay* (1962), again to the music of Seán Ó Riada, performed by his group Ceoltóirí Cualann. This piece was, however, more elaborate in structure, having four scenes and an epilogue. From kitchen to shebeen to the open road and back again we follow the fortunes of a man who goes off with the gypsies, but has to return to face his angry wife when his money runs out.

These three Ó Riada pieces were presented together to great acclaim at a festival in memory of the composer, held at Coolea in September 1974. *Devil to Pay* was also kept in the repertory and was danced by the Irish Ballet Company at both Saturday matinées in the Abbey Theatre in 1981, with Seán Cunningham as Eoinín, Anna Donovan as his wife and Carol Bryans as the Beggar Girl. It was also danced throughout the National Ballet Company's 1984 autumn tour.

In 1977 came the last of her Seán Ó Riada ballets: *Lugh of the*

Golden Arm. Originally devised as a solo piece for the Mexican dancer Babil Gandara (later ballet master of Dublin City Ballet and subsequently artistic director of his own, new Irish Theatre Ballet) as Lugh, the piece was later expanded for a cast of six, the music being performed not only by Ceoltóirí Cualann but also by Eamonn de Buitléar, now better-known as a wild-life film director, with his group Ceoltóirí Laighean.

For this piece, Ms Moriarty left the world of Irish folktales, which had inspired her work ever since her first substantial piece *Seal Woman*. That was set to Hamilton Harty's Irish Symphony and choreographed for the Cork Ballet Company in 1956. Later she created a sequel under the title of *Prisoners of the Sea* for performance in Cork in 1961 and at the Olympia Theatre in Dublin in 1963 when Irish Theatre Ballet, the professional company she was at that time directing, amalgamated with Patricia Ryan's Dublin-based National Ballet Company at the request of the Arts Council, who held out the hope of proper funding for one company, which they were unable to provide for two. The partnership, however, lasted for less than a year.

The plot of this early work was a development of the well-known Irish folktale of the seal which assumes a woman's form and gains the love of a young fisherman before returning to the sea. In this version, however, the seal woman is no innocent who makes a perfect wife until her husband fails to keep her sealskin cloak hidden from her, but a siren who lures the fisherman to leave his betrothed and follow her (the seal woman) into the sea. Moreover, unlike the traditional story, the piece had a happy ending for the betrothed throws herself into the sea in pursuit, finds her fisherman again in the undersea realm of Mananaan MacLír and successfully pleads for his release.

The world of the seanchaí was also evoked in Moriarty's 1974 piece, created for her amateur Cork Ballet Company as a curtain-raiser for *Swan Lake*. This was *Full Moon for the Bride*, set to the music of A. J. Potter, in which faery folk mingled with strawboys at a west of Ireland country wedding in an attempt to lure away the bride.

With *Lugh of the Golden Arm*, however, Ms Moriarty went further back in time for her sources to the mythological hero, thought of as the Mercury of the Celtic Gods. A ritualistic mourning procession, followed by the grieving widow, in which a dead warrior's sword, shield and cloak are borne aloft, is interrupted by his murderer, who attempts to slay the widow also. Lugh appears and defeats the attacker in single combat, fulfilling his role as protector of the weak and easing the widow's grief by avenging her husband's murder. The ritual of the opening procession is echoed at the close by a ritualistic folding by the widow of her husband's cloak and, as with the ballets based on folktales, traditional dance featured amongst the more contemporary movement.

I saw this piece danced several times, including a performance at the Abbey in June 1980, and will always associate the role of the widow, Fidelma of the Long Hair, with its proud but passionate performance by the tall, dark-haired Anna Donovan, later ballet mistress and chief repetiteur of the Dallas Ballet Company.

In 1978, Ms Moriarty choreographed her first full-length ballet: *The Playboy of the Western World*. For this work, based on John Millington Synge's well-known Abbey play, she took the imaginative step of collaborating with the hugely popular music group The Chieftains. Seán Ó Riada, on whose music she had relied so heavily in his lifetime, had been a founder member of The Chieftains and now that he was dead it was only natural that she should turn to music with the same ethnic exuberance. But what gave the performance added excitement was that the group performed live each night in the orchestra pit of the Olympia Theatre, something made financially possible by the additional funding available from the Dublin Theatre Festival, for which it was staged.

The production was a commercial triumph, for the folk-ballet had vivacity and charm to match the music, but artistically it was only partially successful. As I wrote in the *Irish Times* of its revival at the same venue six years later:

> It has the advantage of Synge's humorous yet moving storyline, combined with the excitement of The Chieftains in the pit, although both present subtle traps which the choreographer did not altogether manage to avoid. The very success of the play tempted her to stick too faithfully to the original script, much of which can only be told in mime, and the exuberance and popularity of The Chieftains tempted her to extend some of the dances for longer than they could hold. But there is much inventive wit and delightful business, particularly surrounding Katherine Lewis' marvellous Widow Quin (a part originally and equally well danced by Patricia Crosbie) and I particularly enjoyed her final scene *pas de trois* with Jonathan Burnett and Preston Clare as a pair of saddle-drunk roisterers ... Moreover, any reservations I had about (the choreographer's) failure to integrate the jigs and reels successfully into the narrative were swept away in the triumph of the scene on the strand, where she felt free to portray the races without sidelong glances at the script, since in the play they take place offstage.

In 1979 *The Playboy* was recorded for television by RTE and presented by Noel Pearson at the City Center Theatre, New York, where it was received with greater enthusiasm from ethnic audiences than from ballet fans. It was, however, an undisputed commercial success in March the following year when it was performed in London as part of the Sense of Ireland Festival. It played to full houses at Sadler's Wells, original home of the embryo Royal Ballet but, for the most part, English ballet critics were unenthusiastic about this very ethnic folk-ballet.

Invited by the Taoiseach to create a short ballet for the Pádraic Pearse centenary in 1979, Ms Moriarty chose his poem 'Renunciation' on which to base *Diúltú* (the poem's title in Irish). This was an augmented *pas de trois* with Carol Bryans as the poet's earthly love and Anna Donovan as the Mysterious One who represents Ireland, for whom his love ultimately proved stronger, the *corps de ballet* representing the Shadows of the Past. The theme, with its symbolic casting of cloaks at the poet's feet to represent centuries of oppression, seemed too heavy for the choreographic vocabulary and the work received only one further performance in 1983.

In 1981, Ms Moriarty created her second full-length work for the Dublin Theatre Festival. This was *The Táin*, based on the epic tale from the Ulster Cycle of Celtic Mythology *Táin Bó Cuailnge* (The Cattle Raid of Cooley) with an original score by Aloys Fleischmann, performed by the RTE Concert Orchestra conducted by Proinsias Ó Duinn. It also had the advantage of Patrick Murray's splendid front gauze, showing two gigantic bulls, their horns locked in battle, and the contrast between his costuming of the Ulstermen and women in glittering blues and silvers, with the Connachtmen and women wearing warm reds and browns.

The choreography, as I noted in my review, though 'Irish in every detail, this time avoided the jigs, reels and hornpipes.' It got maximum comedy from the famous 'pillow talk' scene between Maeve and Ailill and nicely contrasted the relationship between the dashing, athletic Cuchulainn (danced by Roger Wade) and his compliant Emer, with the warrior couple from Connacht, whom I noted were made delightfully human in Anna Donovan and Seán Cunningham's portrayal, 'while Jonathan Burnett as the Fool continues to develop the talent for comedy he showed to such good effect in *Reputations'*.

This was the 30-minute piece specially commissioned by RTE and televised that autumn. Inspired by a print called 'Another Reputation Gone', which hung on the wall of Le Chateau, a well-known Cork theatrical pub, it was directed for television by the Ballymena-born Norman Maen, who has been RTE's first and only resident choreographer, and who must take some of the credit for its success on TV. Evoking an Edwardian café, with gossiping society ladies, dashing hussars and starry-eyed honeymooners, it was set to Charle Lecocq's 'Mam'zelle Angot' Suite and, when staged in the Abbey that June (between the spring tele-recording and autumn transmission) came across as a partially-successful attempt at a light-hearted curtain-raiser in the manner of Leonid Massine, chiefly memorable for providing the aforementioned Burnett with an opportunity for a fine Massine-style performance as the waiter.

In 1982, Ms Moriarty created what was virtually her last work for the company, *Invitation to the Dance*, though she continued to choreograph short pieces for children's matinées, like her *Golliwogs' Cakewalk*, until she resigned as artistic director of Irish National Ballet in 1985. Set to Weber's music *Invitation to the Dance* was a slight period piece for five couples exactly illustrating the title.

In 1986, however, Irish National Ballet, under its new artistic director Anneli Vuorenjuuri-Robinson, performed a revival of her dances for Act 2 of *Orfeo et Euridice*, which she had choreographed for the Dublin Grand Opera Society in 1980 as she had previously done with *Tannhäuser* and *La Giaconda*. When all her other pieces are added, such as her 1948 *Golden Bell of Ko*, based on a Chinese legend and set to a score by Aloys Fleischmann, her 1974 *Overture* to Tchaikovsky, her only attempt at modern contemporary dance *Blobs*, a piece commissioned for performance in the Crawford Art Gallery, Cork, for the opening of the Rosc Exhibition in 1980, to say nothing of very early pieces such as *Sugraí Sráide* (Street Games) to music by T. C. Kelly and E. J. Moeran, and *Puck Fair*, with a score by Elizabeth Maconchy, this all adds up to a considerable choreographic repertoire, the majority of it using Irish composers.

It is therefore clear that Ms Moriarty played a valuable role in sustaining her various companies with regular injections of original work based on Irish themes and with Irish music. Viewed retrospectively, these showed an ability to visualise Irish mythology and folklore using strong characterisation, but sadly showed the lack of experience she would have received from working regularly as a dancer in a professional company. This might have given her the choreographic vocabulary to realise her undoubted vision to a much greater extent.

Nevertheless, in envisaging a blending of Irish, classical and contemporary dance movement as a means of expressing Irish mythological and dramatic themes more than fifty years before Michael Flatley began thinking on the same lines, she must be regarded as a pioneer. When to this is added her single-minded determination in the face of all obstacles to establish and acquire funding for her several companies at a time when there was even less understanding of and sympathy for dance in most establishment circles than there is today, she undoubtedly deserves her place in Irish dance history.

NORRIS DAVIDSON (DONARD, CO. WICKLOW)

Most people called her Miss Moriarty; those of us who Joaned her were few, dedicated to ballet and to her. One had to be dedicated to her and to accept her views as being the right ones and the only ones because she never questioned them herself, or if she did it was in private and between her and her artistic self – which was more or less her whole self. She was approachable for discussion provided that a certain distance was kept and she would listen, giving all her attention, but her decision would almost certainly remain the decision of the ballet mistress/administrator/artistic director. It was a self-appointment, from student to teacher and then to the very top of the organisation, such as it was, because if there was to be ballet in Cork she was the only one who could create it and, because she was the only one, her words alone represented the only possible course.

I think government by committee began the disintegration of the ballet company after years of moving in various directions; the young imported dancers missed a strong and single authoritative voice. JDM had it but in the end she often gave way to her friends through a sort of loyalty. And yet she was a woman of steel. I used those words to describe her when I had been summoned to Government Buildings where discussions about a national ballet (which meant a Cork-Dublin ballet) were beginning. I was sitting in the office of a sympathetic civil-servant whose name I no longer recall who said he was more of a rugby man than an arts man and he asked for enlightenment. I told him what I could of companies, choreographers and managements I knew and he rather glumly said: 'I suppose she'd want to take this company on a world tour'; but when I told him it was her view that it would be two years before she showed anything anywhere (her words to me) things brightened and he was not a bit perturbed by the idea of two years with nothing for the public to see. He was in the end to become a strongly interested supporter of the company. It was when I was leaving his office that he said: 'What sort of a woman is she, really?'

and with her unquestioning determination in my mind I told him about her steely quality. She drove herself with the same determination that she pressed the cause of ballet, travelling very long distances from class to class to get the money to keep alive and to forward her real work. When her company began to travel in a minibus, she would take them from dancing in Co. Clare back to Cork on the same night. She saw nothing odd in it; it saved money. But it was part of an attitude that eventually discouraged the young imported dancers of some years ahead. Something very representative of Joan's attitude to life was in her driving; she never shared the experience with me. She used to make trips to Dublin, usually same-day return trips and the journey times she gave me were terrifying. I am sure she didn't see any obstacles on the road, if she saw the road at all, so intent was she on getting her business done and returning to Cork's shelter.

I knew her to make a major change of mind once only and it was a giving way to circumstances. In the early days she told me of her dream of a professional company, not the shows put on by her classes or the yearly full-length ballets of the Cork Ballet Company but a regularly performing Irish company built up into professionals. When I asked her about soloists she said she would create her own, build them up. That was not to be and never could have been. It was something she would never have thought of if she had spent longer with Rambert before striking out on her own; and she admitted this to me in the end.

The first time I met Miss Moriarty was in 1944: *A Midsummer Night's Dream* was being put on in the Sunbeam-Wolsey grounds in Millfield, Cork. I didn't see it there because it rained and was swiftly matinéed into the old Opera House. I remember it because it seemed to me to be a rare example of co-operation in Cork: the Cecilian Singers, the Symphony Orchestra giving us the Mendelssohn, and the drama people, among them Charlie MacCarthy as Puck. There was another meeting backstage in the Wexford Theatre Royal where I was with other radio people at a dress rehearsal of the very first Wexford opera *The Rose of Castile*. It was during an interval that this female figure pushed its way through us to a vast old inefficient iron radiator filled with hot water. She touched it with her toe, raised toe to the top of the bars and then up and up the wall, such an extension as I had never seen, and the warmish air flowed under the flowered skirt of a Spanish costume; Joan Denise Moriarty was preparing for her solo 45 years ago. She was engaged from Cork because even in those early days she was beginning to be known and Cork was associated with dance because no where else was.

Without Aloys Fleischmann, her musical partner, this whole ballet venture would never have been; he brought strings, brass, woodwind and enthusiasm to her aid. Some of her work might have been given to cobbled-up two-piano arrangements but she was ambitious from the beginning though tape had to be used in the end. Time was against her. The modest approach with small music would never have done for her and would have prevented the City Hall, Gaiety Theatre and Cork Opera House appearances whose fame brought about the smaller but technically more interesting performances by her own professional company, the Irish National Ballet. But it didn't really do for an uninstructed public: it wasn't *big*; it certainly wasn't big enough for a Cork used to the occasional Cork Ballet Company presentations with music visibly made and much spectacle. When the organist Mr Horne was gushed at about Cork's wonderful appreciation of music he said, mildly, 'Ah, Cork likes a tune.'

The early Cork Ballet Company performances were always under the auspices of the Cork Orchestral Society and Professor Fleischmann and Miss Moriarty were determined to give Cork more than a tune to hear and a dancing-class show to see. I first met Aloys Fleischmann when, I imagine, he was at the end of his student days; still far from the professordom. He was with his parents and it was several years before the war in a little hotel near Steague Fort. I was making a film nearby, a documentary for the tourist board. Aloys, with mischief, spoke of the ladies who owned the hotel and compared them with the whispering and rattling of the palm trees outside. He grew more serious as I was to find in my meetings with him. But they were not frequent. I was aware of him and his music; I had been at some of his concerts but it was not for ten or a dozen years after his comments on his hostesses that I began to meet him regularly, starting with rehearsals of the Cork Ballet Company's *Sleeping Princess* with the Cork Symphony Orchestra and it was to be *big*: everything Cork does still seems a little bit too big so as to be worthy of Cork.

The Cork Ballet Company had done quite a lot, among the productions had been *Pulcinella*, but now this was one of the big Tchaikovskys with an amateur *corps de ballet*, a more or less amateur orchestra and no more than four imported professionals – all things considered, why were they risking it? 'Because it's there to be done' is the Professor's recorded answer. 'Recorded' because it's there on tape; I was making a radio-documentary 'Mounting a Ballet in Cork'.

Doing was the thing, keeping the company before the public in a big way so that its support might continue, standards were as high as could be managed. I once murmured to the Professor some politeness or other about something the orchestra had just got through: 'They ought to be shot', he said, 'every one of them', but he said it smiling, with warmth and affection.

DECLAN HASSETT, EDITOR OF THE CORK EXAMINER
Obituary in The Cork Examiner, *1 February 1992*

Tribute to the First Lady of Dance

Around four p.m. on Tuesday last, a funeral cortege moved gently through St Patrick Street Cork, as shoppers stood in the grey cold in silent tribute. It was the final journey through a beloved city for Joan Denise Moriarty, who has bequeathed so much to its citizens. Earlier the large St Patrick's church had been thronged at the Requiem Mass. There was no generation gap in this grief; the extended artistic family of Joan Denise, young and old, shed quiet tears. There was tangible emotion expressed with silent dignity; Joan Denise would have approved of this right sense of control. Father George Murphy, in a moving verbal portrait of a life, gave us the broad canvas, but did not miss the essence of Joan Denise: her influence for good on those who came in contact with her.

Hers was a quiet influence too in the way people who have much to give do so with unstinting generosity and the receiver may not be immediately aware of the gift. Joan Denise may not walk our streets but her spirit will continue to inspire others to move on to other artistic heights. In that church on Tuesday there was not so much that cold sense of loss at her going, but more of a warm inner glow for those who had come in contact with her during that very full life.

In my work as a journalist I met Joan Denise on many occasions and was always somewhat in awe, had that sense of being in the presence of someone special. In recent years my admiration for her work grew with each meeting. Joan Denise in the material world never had it easy; hers was a continuing crusade for the spread of the love of the dance form. Battles were lost but not the war. Ballet is alive and will live, because she did not know the meaning of surrender.

In recent years her Cork Ballet Company produced some of the brightest and best evenings in the Opera House. Each late November, for a week those colourful shows would herald the approach of Christmas. This year was no exception with a wonderful *Cinderella* reaching the stage against seemingly insurmountable odds.

And it does not end there. The first steps have been taken to present *Giselle* on the same stage next year. This perhaps best of all confirms that Joan Denise may have gone to her eternal reward, but for those whom she leaves behind, the dance will go on, as she would have wished it to do.

Robert O'Donoghue (Cork)
Speech at This is Your Life *in 1988*
When Robert O'Donoghue came up to speak, the moderator, Michael Twomey, introduced him and proceeded to tell him to apologise at once for action his ancestors had taken against Miss Moriarty's ancestors in 1195. Robert O'Donoghue refused point blank. He gave the following reason:
The Moriartys at that time were allies of the O'Donoghues, who were the principal clan chieftains. We raided Farranfore and had an arrangement with the Moriartys that they would stay put until we had taken the best of the cattle and the women back to the Macgillycuddy Reeks. But the Moriartys, being Moriartys of course, got in before us, and when we landed there all we got were two calves, one bondswoman and one old man with a stick.

I began in 1964 and commented on eighty-five per cent of Miss Moriarty's work. The job of a ballet critic is very difficult, as is that of a painting critic. It is impossible to convey in words: one has to see the performance to get the kind of empathy the art form requires. I was very aware of my inadequacy in this respect. I was also a historian of Miss Moriarty's career evolution. I always realised once the job was done what I should have said but hadn't – I would wake up in the middle of the night realising it, and would feel like running down to the producer or director and apologising profusely.

The word 'magic' has been used, a word I suspect. It does not exist in art. What I witnessed was the work. Ballet was a new substance: a combination of colour, music and dance; we were seeing embodied on the stage a new form of the music we only knew through records. Colour is an essential part of the persona of dance. In the beginning I was aware of the struggle, how the elements were seeking to come into some kind of unity – this was the early days. When I saw the *Prince Igor Dances*, with Joan herself dancing, I was so filled with emotion that I rushed home and wrote a poem, which I have lost. I'm glad I did, because it was probably terrible. But it occurred to me that what I was looking at was a strange combination of imagination, sensibility and intelligence, and that the source of these three elements were emanating from the spirit of one particular person.

Nobody, but nobody at that time had any idea of what ballet meant: it was a new conception. This was her great contribution. This woman had come in from the shadows, come into Cork city, and with nothing, absolutely nothing, made what we've got today, a national ballet company. Now I know, as Joan knows I know, what a terrible struggle she had, the agonies of spirit that she had from the outset. From the very beginning, and in the mid years, and even up to the very end: right through it was struggle. I don't think that at any stage she could sit back and say to herself: I have done it; I am fulfilled. And the great thing about her dance was that you felt all the time there was some place else we could go: we can walk still further. And I began to think and write about the integration of the indigenous dance and the classical form and – lo and behold! it was happening, happening in three or four marvellous cases. She had filled a void in which there was no dance and now she was taking national Irish talent and combining it with the most difficult of all forms: the classical ballet form. That was one of the great things.

The word 'struggle' is foremost in my mind. Everything came out of the struggle, the struggle of one person, first with herself, then with her friends – God knows about her enemies, but certainly with her friends she had to struggle as well, and they with her; dancers with her, she with dancers; music with her, she with music – out of all this comes the furore of personal dedication, of courage, and tremendous knowledge. I keep on thinking about that: the knowledge of one person there in the centre, doing exactly what she knew could be done, having faith in it, and doing it. And we have it today.

While I stand here now, trying to find the words I want for a tribute to a great, great lady, I keep thinking of Lady Gregory, Miss Horniman and many great Irishwomen who under curious circumstances came into Irish art and influenced it in so many ways. I would consider that Miss Moriarty has gone ahead of any woman in Irish art, mainly because she came in on her own.

While I was watching and listening tonight and wondering what I would have left to say – after all those grand things and the true things, and the delightful things said, what could I say? I was watching Miss Moriarty in profile on the television (yes, you're on TV!) and I know she was a bit bewildered by all she heard and I hope she was thrilled too, seeing that it's all so sincerely meant. But I couldn't help feeling the loneliness that is at the heart of all. All of you close friends can get so close to the artist, yet the artist is that much remote even from the closest of friends – has to be. And it is that loneliness that is of her spirit, and it is of that loneliness that courage is made, because to be lonely in a crowd of friends, in a crowd of partisans, in a crowd of fellow-artists, is the loneliest of all.

But the rewards are also personal, and I hope and trust that she is now at this moment beginning to get some little feedback from the love shown here tonight and I do indeed congratulate her.

Robert O'Donoghue ten years later
When I delivered that unscripted speech I was above all else concerned with expressing what I *felt* about the achievement of a remarkable woman. The achievement itself is self-evident. That it was denied its ultimate fruition was the result of the inability of others to understand its significance and consequently to ensure its development. She had harrowed virgin ground. She had planted the seed. She had reaped some harvests against the odds of a climate inimical to her purpose. She persisted. In 1973 an Irish ballet company came into existence, subsidised by the state. It was the best part of forty years agrowing. It took the stroke of a pen to destroy it.

From beginning to disastrous end, Dr Joan Denise Moriarty had to wrestle not only with the insatiable demands of an art form depending on so many varied elements and a synergy of talents, but, also, with the petty politics – not to say, downright nastiness – such a collective inevitably involves. On top of which she had to deal with the ballet's voracious appetite for finance. Even when she managed a state subsidy, in the 1950s and 1960s, for her Irish Theatre Ballet, she had to scrounge out other resources to survive – as, indeed, she had to do also for her later national company. When the Arts Council ignominiously dumped her, I believe it had more to do with the cost of the matter than to any other rumoured cause: i.e., that Dublin was sore at the idea of a decentralised dance – though grapes were the colour of their arrogant dismissal!

Without the Cork Symphony Orchestra, under its founder and conductor Professor Aloys Fleischmann, there is no way she could have done what she did. The Cork Ballet Company could never have been and without that beginning there would have been no Irish Theatre Ballet and no National Ballet. Nothing but a dream that remained a dream.

* * *

(5) Transcript of Miss Moriarty's unprepared speech of thanks at the This Is Your Life Tribute of 24 February 1988

I don't know where to begin – dance is a silent art and we hate talking. But it is true what the last speaker said: one has very, very dear friends; yet it is a very lonely life because you have to keep to yourself all your problems. Nobody is interested in hearing about problems: all they want is for you to put something before them, and success. I suppose people think it is hard to get to know me – well, that's because one lives in a kind of cocoon and must get on with the work, with the job.

So it has been a lonely life, but a very interesting one, and I see so many here who have done so much to help me fulfil the burning desire I have had all my life to share with as many people as possible of all age-groups in the wonderful art of movement and dance. So many dear friends have helped. I have got all the tributes tonight, but one person cannot do it. It is not just me; I don't like taking the credit – though I've been the bully behind it! – but so many have helped: the dancers, the people backstage, the people frontstage, my board of directors. The directors keep me on the right track and don't let me get too fanciful. All the people who are here tonight have helped, and many hundreds of others.

We've got so far, but there is so much to be done yet. The ballet companies are always on a shaky footing financially. Both the Cork Ballet Company and Irish National Ballet mean a great deal to me as people, as friends, as performers. All I want in life is to continue producing works that people are going to enjoy, and also will have to think about a little bit. My motto has always been to give audiences a lot of what they want and a little of what they don't want.

I am so unprepared to speak here – I got a telephone call from Miss Beatrice Hunt out of the blue one night and she said that a big presentation was being made to Professor Fleischmann, and that they would like me to be there. She said that it was a big secret, that he knew nothing about it, and thought he was going to a meeting. But when I opened the door here tonight! Now I know how it feels. I often saw this show and had wondered: 'Do these people really not know?' I thought they'd surely been tipped off. I can guarantee you that I was not tipped off! But it is lovely to see so many people, so many people who mean a great deal to me. As you know, I have no family – and yet I've the largest family in Ireland! You are all my family – whether you're dancers, whether you're producers, whether you're friends: it's all family.

Before I finish – as usual I never just say 'Thank you'! – I have a request. None of us know how long we've got on this planet, on this earth, but I've got two desires, one you could still help me with. I do want before I leave this planet, this troubled planet of ours, that the Firkin Crane will be opened before I disappear. I would like everybody to help towards that. We've got into the second phase of the building, and it isn't only a building for ballet and the dance: it's for everybody to be able to use, and it's very dear to my heart that that should happen before I leave. I can still remember the first time I saw that building – it was always in my mind that it would make a beautiful studio. One day, due to a traffic jam in the city I had to make a detour and go up that way, and I saw a notice that it was for sale. That's how it came about. I know you wouldn't be here tonight unless you approved and were behind me in my work: please give the Firkin Crane as much help as you can.

The second thing I don't think I will see. I've always wanted a first-class, top national ballet-dance school in Ireland – we have a lot of talent, but it all emigrates. I don't mean just another school: it would be a school where the cream of our dance world would be trained, not just to be dancers, but to be artists as well. There are two kinds of dancers, two kinds of musicians, two kinds of actors I suppose: there are the people who dance and play nicely or act well, and then there are the artists – that is a different thing. That is what I want to create: artist-dancers that we can be proud of, who can go anywhere in the world and represent Ireland – that is my idea of Irish National Ballet: for Irish dancers to be able to bring this art to the whole people of Ireland. The goddess of dance is like that red light up there: she's always there and she's always prompting me to do more, to go on, to get more done. I hope I will be allowed to do more.

There are so many people here, but I must say a special word of thanks to you, Mr Jack Lynch: I well remember that meal after the ballet in Dublin in 1972 that's been discussed. And there's somebody else here I must mention. There are not many people I've been nervous or frightened of in my life, but I well remember on the company's first performance in the old Opera House, I got my very first radio interview with Norris Davidson – I was terrified of him, that man with the microphone shoved up to your mouth and the question: 'What do you think?' and I didn't know what to say. I always remember what you said: 'I'll meet you on the summit' – do you remember?

Thank you all – it was a tremendous surprise. It will give me more courage to go on and fight. All the arts are in difficulties financially; it gets more expensive to put anything on, and ballet is the most expensive of all arts. It's a silent art: it's got to look beautiful, it's got to look elegant, it's got to have style, it's got to have lighting, it's got to have costumes – you can't stint if you want to have something beautiful to look at, and these days more than ever, as I think you will agree, we need beauty.

Thank you very very much: I'm deeply moved and it will give me strength and new vigour to go out and fight more battles.

APPENDIX A:
WORKS CREATED BY JOAN DENISE MORIARTY

Entries give the name of the work, the name of the librettist if not Joan Denise Moriarty (JDM), the name(s) of the composer(s) of the music, the performing company (abbreviations: CBC = Cork Ballet Company 1947-1993; ITB = Irish Theatre Ballet 1959-1964; IBC/INB = Irish Ballet Company 1973-1983, Irish National Ballet 1983-1989), and the year(s) of the performances (rptd = repeatedly performed by the professional companies).

(1) *Alphabetical List*

BALLETS:

A la Degas; Delibes; CBC; 1954, 1967
At the Hawk's Well (Yeats); Charles Lynch; JDM solo; 1966
Big Top; Rossini; CBC; 1956, 1982
Billy the Music; Ó Riada; IBC; 1974, rptd
Blobs; Rivier; IBC; 1980
Bolero; Ravel; CBC; 1948
Calinda; Delius; CBC; 1947
Cameo; Tchaikovsky ; CBC; 1955
Capriccio Espagnol; Rimsky-Korsakov; CBC; 1950, 1957
Carnival des Glisseurs; Meyerbeer; CBC; 1956
Casadh an tSugáin (Hyde); Ó Gallchobhair; CBC; 1954, 1958
Castillan; Massenet; CBC; 1987
Catalysis; Roussel; CBC; 1967
Children of Lír (O'Reilly); Friel; CBC; 1950
Classical Variations; Glazounov; CBC; 1988
Cóitín Dearg (Mac Liammóir); Fleischmann; CBC; 1951
Comedy Opus for Twenty; Prokofiev; CBC; 1971
Comus (Milton, Horne); Lawes, Purcell; CBC; 1947
Contrasts; Traditional Irish Music and Jazz; CBC; 1987
Coppélia Act II (reproduced); Delibes; CBC; 1951
Coppélia (reproduced); Delibes; CBC; 1955, 1970, 1971
Cry Havoc; Roussel; ITB; 1961
Devil to Pay; Ó Riada; ITB; 1962, rptd
Dissy Opus; Jazz; CBC; 1989
Diúltú (Pearse); Buckley; INB; 1979, 1983
Fairy Queen (Horne); Purcell; CBC; 1948, 1964, 1985

Festival Impromptu; Sullivan; CBC; 1985, rptd
Fickle Princess (Hans Anderson); Handel; CBC; 1950
Francis of Assisi; Father Leo; ITB; 1962
Full Moon for the Bride (Mac Liammóir); Potter; CBC; 1974
Gare du nord; Ibert; CBC; 1986
Golden Bell of Ko (Cumberland); Fleischmann; CBC; 1948, 1953, 1973
Golliwogs' Cakewalk; Debussy; INB; 1983
Golliwogs and Teddy bears; Kavalevsky; INB; 1983
Half Moon Street; Rossini, Respighi; CBC; 1954, 1967
Hansel and Gretel; Humperdinck; CBC; 1952, 1965
Haunted Inn; Khachaturian; CBC; 1954
Hommage à Chopin; Chopin; CBC; 1950, 1987
Hungarian Dances; Brahms; CBC; 1947, 1970
Hungarian Fantasy; Liszt; CBC; 1951
Invitation to the Dance; Weber; INB; 1983, rptd
La Giarra (Pirandello); Casella; CBC; 1965
La Gioconda; Ponchielli; IBC; 1981, rptd
Lugh of the Golden Arm; O Riada; IBC; 1977
Lullaby; Khachaturian; CBC; 1949
Macha Ruadh; Fleischmann; CBC; 1955
Masks; Kagel; CBC; 1970
Moy Mell; Potter, Gershwin; CBC; 1957
Nutcracker (reproduced); Tchaikovsky; CBC; 1948, 1952
Overture; Tchaikovsky; IBC; 1974
Papillons (Tilly Fleischmann); Schumann, Ó Riada; CBC; 1952
Pas de trois; Dvorak; CBC; 1954
Peer Gynt (Ibsen, Horne); Grieg; CBC; 1949
Period Suite; Morley; CBC; 1965
Peter and the Wolf; Prokofiev; ITB; 1959, rptd
Pilgrim's Progess (Bunyan); Bach, Gluck; CBC; 1950
Planting Stick; Fleischmann; CBC; 1957, 1966
Playboy of the Western World (Synge); Chieftains; INB; 1978, 1979, 1980, 1984, 1985
Polovtsian Dances from Prince Igor; Borodin; CBC; 1948, 1953
Prisoners of the Sea; Harty; CBC; ITB; 1961, 1970
Puck Fair; (Higgins) Maconchy; CBC; 1948, 1952, 1984
Pulcinella; Stravinsky; CBC; 1947
Rendezvous impromtus; Chaminade; CBC; 1952
Reputations; Lecocq; IBC; 1981 rptd
Rosamunde; Schubert; CBC; 1947
Saint Valentine's Day; Strauss; CBC; 1949, 1950, 1970
Scheherazade; Rimsky-Korsakov; CBC; 1952, 1976
Seal Woman; Harty; CBC; 1956, 1959, 1976
Singer (Homage to Pearse); Ó Gallchobhair; CBC; 1952, 1953, 1967
Slavonic Dances; Dvorak; ITB; 1962
Straussiana; Strauss; CBC; 1961

Street Games; T. C. Kelly, Moeran; ITB; 1959 rptd
Suite classique; Debussy; CBC; 1951
Suite symphonique; Tchaikovsky; CBC; 1953
Sweet Dancer (Yeats); Sibelius; CBC; 1989, 1991
Sylphides; Chopin; (reproduced) CBC; 1965
Táin; Fleischmann; IBC; 1981
They Come, They Come (Jack Yeats); Moeran; IBC; 1975, 1976
Three Hungarian Dances; Brahms; CBC; 1947
Trio; Beethoven; CBC; 1970
Valse triste; Sibelius; CBC; 1948, 1951
Vanity Fair; Offenbach; CBC; 1953
Vltava; Smetana; ; CBC; 1947, 1949, 1977
Voice in the Wilderness; Bloch; ITB; 1959, 1960
Wedding (Festival of Cork); Tradititional Irish Music; CBC; 1986, 1990
West Cork Ballad; Ó Riada; ITB; 1961, rptd
William Tell; Rossini; CBC; 1949

Opera Ballets:
Faust; Gounod; CBC; 1954, 1966
Fledermaus; Strauss; CBC; 1964
Il Trovatore; Verdi; CBC,IBC; 1954, 1966, 1983
La Gioconda; Ponchielli; IBC; 1980
La Traviata; Verdi; CBC; 1954, 1965
Orfeo and Euridice; Gluck; IBC; 1980
Samson and Delilah; Saint-Saens; IBC; 1979
Tannhäuser; Wagner; IBC; 1979

Musicals:
Camelot; Lerner, Love; CBC; 1986
Finian's Rainbow; Burton Lane; CBC; 1958
Guys and Dolls; Loesser; CBC; 1971
Land of Smiles; Lehar; CBC; 1973
My Fair Lady; Lerner, Love; CBC; 1970
White Horse Inn; Friml; CBC; 1959
Wizard of Oz; Arlen; CBC; 1973

(2) *Performances of JDM's Ballets in Chonological Order*

1947
Rosamunde; Schubert; CBC
La Calinda; Delius; CBC
Three Hungarian Dances; Brahms; CBC
Pulcinella; Stravinsky; CBC
Vltava; Smetana; CBC

Comus; Lawes, Purcell; CBC

1948
Nutcracker Act I (reproduced); Tchaikovsky; CBC
Valse triste; Sibelius; CBC
Bolero; Ravel; CBC
Polovtsian Dances Prince Igor; Borodin; CBC
Puck Fair; Maconchy; CBC
The Golden Bell of Ko; Fleischmann; CBC
The Fairy Queen; Purcell; CBC

1949
Lullaby; Khachaturian; CBC
Saint Valentine's Day; Strauss; CBC
Vltva; Smetana; CBC
William Tell; Rossini; CBC
Peer Gynt; Grieg; CBC

1950
The Fickle Princess; Handel; CBC
The Children of Lír; Friel; CBC
Saint Valentine's Day; Strauss; CBC
Hommage à Chopin; Chopin; CBC
Capriccio Espagnol; Rimsky-Korsakov; CBC
Pilgrim's Progress; Bach, Gluck; CBC

1951
Hungarian Fantasy; Liszt; CBC
Valse triste; Sibelius; CBC
Suite classique; Debussy; CBC
An Cóitín Dearg; Fleischmann; CBC
Coppélia Act II (reproduced); Delibes; CBC

1952
Nutcracker Act I (reproduced); Tchaikovsky; CBC
Les Rendezvous Impromptus; Chaminade; CBC
The Singer; Ó Gallchobhair; CBC
Papillons; Schumann; CBC
Scheherazade; Rimsky-Korsakov; CBC
Puck Fair; Maconchy; CBC
Hansel and Gretel; Humperdinck; CBC

1953
Suite Symphonique; Tchaikovsky; CBC
Golden Bell of Ko; Fleischmann; CBC
The Singer; Ó Gallchobhair; CBC

Vanity Fair; Offenbach; CBC
Polovstian Dances Prince Igor; Borodin; CBC

1954
Casadh an tSugáin; Ó Gallchobhair; CBC
Pas de trois; Dvorak; CBC
A la Degas; Delibes; CBC
The Haunted Inn; Khachaturian; CBC
Half Moon Street; Rossini, Respighi; CBC
Faust; Gounod; CBC
Il Trovatore; Verdi; CBC
La Traviata; Verdi; CBC

1955
Cameo; Tchaikovsky; CBC
Macha Ruadh; Fleischmann; CBC
Coppélia (reproduced); Delibes; CBC

1956
Carnaval des Glisseurs; Meyerbeer; CBC
The Seal Woman; Harty; CBC
The Big Top; Rossini; CBC

1957
Moy Mell; Potter, Gershwin; CBC
Capriccio Espagnol; Rimsky-Korsakov; CBC
The Planting Stick; Fleischmann; CBC (Cork Choral Festival)

1958
Casadh an tSugáin; Ó Gallchobhair; CBC (Gala Concert)
Finian's Rainbow; Burton Lane; CBC

1959
The Seal Woman; Harty; CBC
White Horse Inn; Friml; CBC
Peter and the Wolf; Prokofiev; ITB
Street Games; Kelly, Moeran; ITB
Voice in the Wildernis; Bloch; ITB

1960
Coppélia Act II (reproduced); Delibes; ITB

1961
Prisoners of the Sea; Harty; CBC/ITB
Straussiana; Strauss; CBC/ITB
Slavonic Dances Rhapsody; Dvorak; ITB

Valse triste; Sibelius; ITB
West Cork Ballad; Ó Riada; ITB
Cry Havoc; Roussel; ITB

1962
Devil to Pay; Ó Riada; ITB
Francis of Assisi; Father Leo; ITB

1964
Coppélia (reproduced); Delibes; CBC/ITB
Fledermaus; Strauss; CBC
Fairy Queen; Purcell; CBC

1965
La Traviata; Verdi; CBC
Les Sylphides (reproduced); Chopin; CBC
La Giarra; Casella; CBC (Clonmel)
Period Suite; Morley; CBC (Cork Choral Festival)
Hansel and Gretel; Humperdinck; CBC

1966
Faust; Gounod; CBC
Il Trovatore; Verdi; CBC
Thirteen Television Dance Programmes on RTE 'An Damhsa'; CBC

1967
A La Degas; Delibes; CBC
Catalysis; Roussel; CBC
Half Moon Street; Rossini, Respighi; CBC

1970
My Fair Lady; Lerner, Love; CBC
Coppélia (reproduced); Delibes; CBC
Prisoners of the Sea; Harty; CBC
West Cork Ballad; Ó Riada; CBC
Hungarian Dances; Brahms; CBC
Trio; Beethoven; CBC
Masks; Kagel; CBC

1971
Coppélia (reproduced); Delibes; CBC
Comedy Opus for 20; Prokofiev; CBC
West Cork Ballad; Ó Riada; CBC
Guys and Dolls; Loesser; CBC

1973
Land of Smiles; Lehar; CBC

The Wizard of Oz; Arlen; CBC
Golden Bell of Ko; Fleischmann; CBC

1974
Billy the Music; O Riada; IBC
Overture; Tchaikovsky; IBC
Devil to Pay; Ó Riada; IBC
Full Moon for the Bride; Potter; CBC

1975
They Come, They Come; Moeran; IBC

1976
Seal Woman; Harty; CBC

1977
Lugh of the Golden Arm; Ó Riada, de Buitléar; IBC
Vltava; Smetana; CBC

1978
Playboy of the Western World; Chieftains; IBC (Dublin)

1979
Playboy; Chieftains; IBC (Cork)
Playboy; Chieftains; IBC (New York)
Diúltú; Buckley; IBC (Dublin)
Samson and Delilah; Saint-Saens; IBC (Dublin)

1980
La Gioconda; Ponchielli; IBC (Dublin)
Orfeo and Euridice; Gluck; IBC (Dublin)
Blobs; Rivier; IBC
Playboy; Chieftains; IBC (London)

1981
Reputations; Lecocq; IBC
Táin; Fleischmann; IBC (Dublin)
La Gioconda; Ponchielli; IBC

1982
The Big Top; Rossini; CBC

1983
Golliwog's Cakewalk; Debussy; IBC
Il Trovatore; Verdi; IBC
Invitation to the Dance; Weber; IBC

Diúltú; Buckley; INB
Golliwogs and Teddy-bears; Kabalevsky; INB

1984
Playboy; Chieftains; INB (Dublin)
Puck Fair; Potter; CBC

1985
Playboy; Chieftains; INB (Rennes)
Fairy Queen; Purcell; CBC
Festival impromptu; Sullivan; CBC

1986
Wedding; Traditional Irish Music; CBC (Killarney)
Le gare du nord; Ibert; CBC
Camelot; Lerner, Love; CBC

1987
Hommage à Chopin; Chopin; CBC (Clonmel)
Castillan; Massenet; CBC (Clonmel)
Contrasts; Tradititional Irish Music, Jazz; CBC (Clonmel)
Pas classique; Bach; CBC (Clonmel)
Mardi gras; Massenet; CBC (Clonmel)

1988
Street Games; Kelly, Moeran; CBC (Everyman Cork)
Rinnce Mór and Washing Dance; Traditional Irish Music; CBC
Classical Variations; Glazounov; CBC (Everyman Cork)

1989
Overture; Tchaikovsky; CBC
Dissy Opus; Jazz; CBC
Sweet Dancer; Sibelius; CBC

1990
Wedding; Traditional Irish Music; CBC (Festival of Cork)

1991
Overture; Tchaikovsky; CBC
Dissy Opus; Jazz; CBC
Sweet Dancer; Sibelius; CBC

APPENDIX B:
CORK BALLET COMPANY

(1) PERFORMANCES

1947

Rosamunde; Schubert
La Calinda; Delius
Three Hungarian Dances; Brahms
Pulcinella; Stravinsky
Vltava; Smetana
Comus (Milton); Lawes, Purcell
(in association with A. R. Day and S. L. Horne)

1948

Nutcracker; Tchaikovsky
Valse triste; Sibelius
Bolero; Ravel
Prince Igor Dances; Borodin
Puck Fair; Maconchy
Golden Bell of Ko; Fleischmann
The Fairy Queen; Purcell
(In association with A. R. Day and S. L. Horne)

1949

Lullaby; Khachaturian
St Valentine's Day; Strauss
Vltava; Smetana
William Tell; Rossini
Peer Gynt (Ibsen); Grieg
(in association with A. R. Day and S. L.Horne)

1950

The Fickle Princess; Handel
The Children of Lír; Friel
St Valentine's Day; Strauss
Homage to Chopin; Chopin
Capriccio Espagnol; Rimsky-Korsakov
The Pilgrim's Progress (Bunyan); Bach, Gluck
(in association with A. R. Day and S. L.Horne)

1951

Hungarian Fantasy; Liszt
Valse triste; Sibelius
Suite classique; Debussy
An Cóitín Dearg; Fleischmann
Coppélia Act 2; Delibes

1952

Nutcracker; Tchaikovsky
Les rendezvous impromptus; Chaminade
The Singer; Ó Gallchobhair
Papillons; Schumann
Scheherazade; Rimsky-Korsakov
Puck Fair; Maconchy

1953

Suite symphonique; Tchaikovsky
The Golden Bell of Ko; Fleischmann
The Singer; Ó Gallchobhair
Vanity Fair; Offenbach
Prince Igor Dances; Borodin

1954

Casadh an tSugáin; Ó Gallchobhair
Pas de trois; Dvorak
A la Degas; Delibes
The Haunted Inn; Khachaturian
Half Moon Street; Rossini, Respighi

1955

Cameo; Tchaikovsky
Macha Ruadh; Fleischmann
Coppélia; Delibes

1956

Carnaval des glisseurs; Meyerbeer
Seal Woman; Harty
Swan Lake Act II; Tchaikovsky
The Big Top; Rossini

1957

Moy Mell; Potter, Gershwin
Giselle; Adam
Capriccio Espagnol; Rimsky-Korsakov

1958

The Sleeping Princess; Tchaikovsky

1959

Les Sylphides; Chopin
Pas de deux from Don Quixote; Minkus
The Seal Woman; Harty
Aegean Caprice; Verdi

1960

La fille mal gardée; Hertel
Voice in the Wilderness; Bloch
Nutcracker Act II; Tchaikovsky

1961

Swan Lake Act II; Tchaikovsky
Prisoners of the Sea; Harty

La Peri; Scott
Straussiana; Strauss

1962

Giselle; Adam
Petrouchka; Stravinsky

1963

Cinderella; Prokofiev

1964

Caitlín Bocht; Potter
Coppélia; Delibes
The Fairy Queen; Purcell

1965

Les Sylphides; Chopin
(inauguration of the new Opera House)
Hansel and Gretel; Humperdinck

1966

Thirteen Television Dance Programmes on RTE

1967

A la Degas; Delibes
Pas de deux from Don Quixote; Minkus
Catalysis; Roussel
Half Moon Street; Rossini, Respighi
Olympics; Sousa, Ferras

1968

The Sleeping Princess; Tchaikovsky

1969

The Sleeping Princess; Tchaikovsky

1970

Coppélia; Delibes
Prisoners of the Sea; Harty
West Cork Ballad; Ó Riada

1971

Giselle; Adam
Comedy Opus for 20; Prokofiev

1972

Swan Lake; Tchaikovsky

1973

Nutcracker; Tchaikovsky
The Golden Bell of Ko; Fleischmann

1974

Giselle; Adam
Full Moon for the Bride; Potter

1975

Les Sylphides; Chopin
Petrouchka; Stravinsky
Polovtsian Dances from Prince Igor; Borodin

1976

The Seal Woman; Harty
Viennese Caprice; Strauss
Scheherazade; Rimsky-Korsakov

1977

Vltava; Smetana
La Sylphide; Levenskjold

1978

The Sleeping Princess; Tchaikovsky

1979

Coppélia; Delibes

1980

Cinderella; Prokofiev

1981

Untitled Variations; César Franck
Petrouchka; Stravinsky
Polovtsian Dances from Prince; Borodin

1982

The Big Top; Rossini
Giselle; Adam

1983

Swan Lake; Tchaikovsky

1984

Puck Fair; Potter
Nutcracker; Tchaikovsky

1985

The Fairy Queen; Purcell

1986

Le gare du nord; Ibert
Giselle; Adam

1987

Swan Lake; Tchaikovsky

1988

The Sleeping Princess; Tchaikovsky

1989

Coppélia; Delibes

1990

Nutcracker; Tchaikovsky

1991

Cinderella; Prokofiev

1992

Giselle; Adam

1993

Coppélia; Delibes

(2) Cork Ballet Company – Guest Artists

1956 Swan Lake Act II:
> Domini Callaghan (Sadler's Wells), Peter Darrell (Festival Ballet); reproduced: Peter Darrell

1957 Giselle:
> Domini Callaghan (Sadler's Wells) Michel de Lutry (Sadler's Wells); reproduced: Michel de Lutry

1958 Gala:
> Anton Dolin, Margit Muller, André Prokovsky, (London Festival Ballet) Marina Svetlova (Metropolitan Opera House, New York)

1958 Sleeping Princess:
> Domini Callaghan, Michel de Lutry, Roger Tully, Christopher Lyall (all of Sadler's Wells); reproduced: Michel de Lutry

1959 Les Sylphides:
> Marina Svetlova (Metropolitan Opera House New York), Kenneth Melville (Royal Ballet); reproduced: Stanley Judson

1960 La fille mal gardée:
> Marina Svetlova (Metropolitan Opera House New York), Kenneth Melville (Royal Ballet), Stanley Judson (Vic-Wells/Royal Ballet); choreography: Stanley Judson

1961 Swan Lake Act II
> Chesterina Sim Zecha (Netherlands Ballet), William Martin (Royal Ballet); reproduced: Geoffrey Davidson

1962 Gala:
> Belinda Wright, Jelko Yuresha (London Festival Ballet)

1962 Petrouchka:
> Joahne O'Hara, Domy Reiter, John Cunningham (Irish Theatre Ballet); reproduced: Geoffrey Davidson

1962 Giselle:
> Domini Callaghan, Joseph Savino (Zürich Opera Ballet); reproduced: Geoffrey Davidson

1963 Cinderella:
> Joahne O'Hara, Domy Reiter (Irish Theatre Ballet); choreography: Geoffrey Davidson

1964 Coppélia:
> Joahne O'Hara, Joan Wilson, Deirdre O'Donohoe, Domy Reiter (Irish National Ballet); reproduced: JDM

1965 Les Sylphides (Gala Opening Concert Cork Opera House):
> Joahne O'Hara, Julia Cotter, Domy Reiter (Irish Theatre Ballet); reproduced: JDM

1965 Hansel and Gretel:
> Kay McLoughlin, Domy Reiter (Irish National Ballet); choreography: JDM

1967 Don Quixote Pas de deux etc:
> Joahne O'Hara, Domy Reiter; reproduced: D. Reiter

1968 Sleeping Princess:
Monika Knapp, Erich Zschach (Wuppertal Ballet); Alain Dubreuil, Jillian Shane (London Festival Ballet); reproduced: Michel de Lutry
1969 Sleeping Princess:
Beatrice Frauenfeld, Edgardo Hartley (Wuppertal Ballet), Ghislaine Thesmar, Peter Heusi (Paris Opera); reproduced: Michel de Lutry
1970 Coppélia:
Lavinia Anderson (Cork Ballet Company), Domy Reiter (Scottish Theatre Ballet), Sean Cunningham (Gulbenkian Ballet); reproduced: JDM
1971 Giselle:
Helen Starr (Royal Ballet), Alain Dubreuil (London Festival Ballet); reproduced: Michel de Lutry
1972 Swan Lake:
Sandra Conley (Royal Ballet), Alain Dubreuil (London Festival Ballet), Mary Hanf (San Francisco Ballet), Gerald Byrne (London Festival Ballet); reproduced: Helen Starr
1973 Nutcracker:
Helen Starr (Royal Ballet), Michel Bruel (Paris Opera); reproduced: Alun Rhys
1974 Giselle:
Joahne O'Hara, Patrick Hurde (Gulbenkian Ballet); reproduced: Michel de Lutry
1975 Polovtsian Dances Prince Igor, Petrouchka, Les Sylphides:
Prince Igor: Richard Collins (Irish Ballet Company); reproduced: Geoffrey Davidson
Petrouchka: Domy Reiter-Soffer (Irish Ballet Company); reproduced: Geoffrey Davidson
Les Sylphides: Domy Reiter-Soffer (Irish Ballet Company; reproduced: Geoffrey Davidson
1976 Scheherazade:
Julia Cotter (Cork Ballet Company), Richard Collins (Irish Ballet Company); reproduced: Geoffrey Davidson
1977 La Sylphide:
Lavinia Anderson (Cork Ballet Company), Babil Gandara (Irish Ballet Company); reproduced: Hans Brenaa
1978 Sleeping Princess Act II RTE 2 Gala Opening:
Kathleen McInerney, Richard Collins (Irish Ballet Company), Lavinia Anderson (Cork Ballet Company); reproduced: Michel de Lutry
1978 Sleeping Princess:
Kathleen McInerney; Richard Collins, Victoria Lee, Graham Goodbody (Irish Ballet Company); reproduced: Michel de Lutry
1979 Coppélia:
Lavinia Anderson (Cork Ballet Company), Babil Gandara, Sean Cunningham, (Irish Ballet Company); reproduced: Harry Haythorne

1980 Cinderella:
>Patricia Crosbie, Wayne Aspinall (Irish Ballet Company); choreography: David Gordon

1981 Petrouchka; Polovtsian Dances Prince Igor; Untitled Variations:
>Petrouchka: Sean Cunningham (Irish Ballet Company); reproduced: Geoffrey Davidson
>
>Polovtsian Dances: Wayne Aspinall (Irish Ballet Company); reproduced: Geoffrey Davidson
>
>Untitled Variations: Wayne Aspinall (Irish Ballet Company); choreography: David Gordon

1982 Giselle:
>Vyvyan Lorrayne (Royal Ballet), Paul Waller (London Festival Ballet); reproduced: Michel de Lutry

1983 Swan Lake:
>Frederick Jahn Werner (London Festival Ballet), Patricia Crosbie (London), Hedi Khursandi (London), Simon Clepper (Irish National Ballet); reproduced: Richard Collins

1984 Nutcracker:
>Nigel Burgoine (London Festival Ballet), Patricia Crosbie (London), Preston Clare (Irish National Ballet); reproduced: Richard Collins

1986 Giselle:
>Corine Beauvais (Vienna Ballet), Adrian Davies (Royal Ballet); reproduced: Richard Collins

1987 Swan Lake:
>Coleen Davis, Zoltan Solymosi (Dutch National Ballet); reproduced: Richard Collins

1988 Sleeping Princess:
>Coleen Davis, Zoltan Solymosi (Dutch National Ballet); Tina Kay Bohnstedt, Christopher Kettner (Munich); reproduced: Richard Collins

1989 Coppélia:
>Sheila Styles (Royal Ballet), Paul Watson (London City Ballet), David Gordon (Irish National Ballet); reproduced: Brenda Last

1990 Nutcracker:
>Coleen Davis, Alexis Manuel (Dutch National Ballet); reproduced Brenda Last

1991 Cinderella:
>Rachel Greenwood, Gilles Maidon (Cincinnati Ballet); reproduced: Richard Collins

1992 Giselle:
>Laurie Millar, Pablo Savoye (English National Ballet); Denise Roberts, Preston Clare (Scottish Ballet); reproduced: Brenda Last

1993 Coppélia:
>Misaki Watanabe, Pablo Savoye (Reiko Yammamoto Ballet, Tokio), Sean Cunningham (Irish National Ballet); reproduced: Brenda Last

(3) Folk Dance Group of the Cork Ballet Company
Choreography by JDM

1957 Cork Choral and Folk Dance Festival
  Planting Stick; Fleischmann;
  Cake Dance; Tradititional Irish Music
1958 Wewelsburg Festival, Germany
  Folk Dances; Traditional Irish Music
1961 Dijon Festival, France
  Folk Dances; Traditional Irish Music. Winners of Bronze Collar for
  Dancing, Production and Parade
1965 Dijon Festival, France
  Folk Dances; Traditional Irish Music. Winners of 2nd and 3rd Places
  for Production and Parade
1966 Festivals at Deidesheim, Dillenburg (Germany) and Berlin
  Annual Performances at Cork Choral and Folkdance Festival.

(4) Cork Ballet Company – 'An Damhsa'
Thirteen Television Programmes of Irish Folk Dances and Ballets.
Choreography by JDM

7 October 1966
  Rinnce Mór, Running Dance, The Yellow Beggar; Traditional Irish
  Music
21 October 1966
  The North Road, Washing Day, Fire Dance; Traditional Irish Music
4 November 1966
  Girls' Double Jig, Dancing the Baby, The Straw Boys; Traditional
  Irish Music
18 November 1966
  Cake Dance, Three Sea Captains, Harvest Dance; Traditional Irish
  Music
2 December 1966
  Gathering Duileasc, Saint Brigid's Eve; Traditional Irish Music
16 December 1966
  The Planting Stick; Fleischmann;
  The Evil Eye; Traditional Irish Music
30 December 1966
  West Cork Ballad; Ó Riada
13 January 1967
  Three Miniatures: Midir's Song for Etain, Fishamble Street, On the
  Bridge at Clash; Duff
27 January 1967
  Street Games; Kelly, Moeran
10 February 1967
  The Singer; Ó Gallchobhair;

The Wild Colonial Boy; Popular Song
10 March 1967
Puck Fair; Maconchy
7 April 1967
Devil To Pay; Ó Riada
21 April 1967
Seal Woman; Harty

APPENDIX C:
PROFESSIONAL BALLET COMPANIES

Entries give the name of the ballet, the name of the composer and the name of the choreographer [JDM = Joan Denise Moriarty].

(1) *Irish Theatre Ballet*

REPERTOIRE AND PERFORMANCES:
1959

Crown Diamonds; Auber; Stanley Judson
Spectre de la rose; Weber; Stanley Judson
Pas de quatre; Chopin; Stanley Judson
Peter and the Wolf; Prokofiev; JDM
Springtime in Vienna; Strauss; Stanley Judson
Street Games; Kelly, Moeran; JDM
Voice in the Wilderness; Bloch; JDM

1960

Coppélia Act II; Delibes; reproduced: JDM
Nachtstücke, Night Visions, Schumann; Stanley Judson
Nutcracker pas de deux; Tchaikovsky; reproduced: Judson
Les Sylphides; Chopin; reproduced: Judson
La fille mal gardée; Hertel; Judson
Voice in the Wilderness; Bloch; JDM
Nutcracker Act II; Tchaikovsky; reproduced: Judson
Carnival; Schumann; Yannis Metsis
Figure of Five; Ponchielli; Yannis Metsis
Giselle pas de deux; Adam; reproduced: Yannis Metsis
Narcissus; Debussy; Yannis Metsis
Sarabande; Debussy; Yannis Metsis
Swan Lake pas de trois; Tchaikovsky; reproduced: Metsis
Ballet Nonsense; Bartok; Denis Carey
A Country Lane; Lobos; Geoffrey Davidson
Bitter Aloes; Bernard Geary; Geoffrey Davidson
Il Cassone; Geary; Geoffrey Davidson

1961

Swan Lake Act II; Tchaikovsky; reproduced: JDM
Prisoners of the Sea; Harty; JDM
Straussiana; Strauss; JDM
Slavonic Dances (Rhapsody); Dvorak; JDM
Valse triste; Sibelius; JDM
West Cork Ballad; Ó Riada; JDM
Don Quixote pas de deux; Minkus; Domy Reiter-Soffer
Moods; Jazz; Domy Reiter-Soffer
Cry Havoc; Roussel; JDM

1962

A Kind Heart; Dohnanyi; Geoffrey Davidson
Eidolons; Fauré; Geoffrey Davidson
Francis of Assisi; Father Leo; JDM
The Devil to Pay; Ó Riada; JDM
Petrouchka; Stravinsky; reproduced: Davidson
Giselle; Adam; reproduced: Davidson
Cinderella pas de deux; Prokofiev; reproduced: Davidson
Cul de sac; Gerschwin; Domy Reiter-Soffer

1963

Cinderella; Prokofiev; reproduced: Geoffrey Davidson
Dark Enchantress; Copland; Norman Maen
Serefina; Khatchaturian; Domy Reiter-Soffer
Caitlín Bocht; Potter; Patricia Ryan
Giselle; Adam; reproduced: Geoffrey Davidson

1964

Caitlín Bocht; Potter; Patricia Ryan
Coppélia; Delibes; reproduced: JDM

(2) *Irish National Ballet*

REPERTOIRE:

Adagietto No. 5; Mahler; Royston Maldoom
Apsaras; Massenet; Peter Darrell
Beauty and the Beast; Ravel; Tony Hubbard
Biedermeier Dances; Beethoven, Schubert; Peter Darrell
Billy the Music; Ó Riada; JDM
Black Swan pas de deux; Tchaikowsky; reproduced: David Gordon
Blobs; Rivier; JDM
Bluebirds pas de deux; Tchaikowsky; Petipa
Brandenburg; Bach; Charles Czarny
Caprice; Tchaikowsky; Henrik Neubauer
Catalyst; Saint-Saens; Kathleen Smith
Celebration; Boyce, Pachelbel; Royston Maldoom
Chariots of Fire; Christou, Mamangakis, Xenakis; Domy Reiter-
    Soffer
Cinderella pas de deux; Prokofiev; JDM
Concerto Grosso; Handel; Charles Czarny
Contrast in Time; Handel, Jazz; Toni Beck
Corsair pas de deux; Adam; Jules Perrot
Devil to Pay; Ó Riada; JDM
Diúltú (Renunciation); Buckley; JDM
Diana and Actaeon pas de deux; Drige, Vynonen;
    reproduced: Richard Collins

Don Quixote pas de deux; Minkus; Petipa
Esmeralda pas de deux; Pugni, Drigo; John Gilpin
First Impressions; Mozart; David Gordon
Flames of Paris; Asafiev; Vynonen
Flights of Fancy; Bach; Patrick Hurd
Flower Festival in Genzano; Helsted; Bournonville
La Gioconda; Ponchielli; JDM
Grand pas gitane; Saint-Saens, Marenco; Peter Darrell
Invitation to the Dance; Weber; JDM
Images; Debussy; Toni Beck
Jingle-Rag, Jingle-Tag; Novak; Domy Reiter-Soffer
Konservatoriet; Paulli, Bournonville; reproduced: Hans Brenaa
Lady of the Camellias; Saint-Saens; Domy Reiter-Soffer
Laurencia pas de dix; Krein, Minkus; Chaboukiani, Petipa
Loveraker; Isang Yun; Domy Reiter-Soffer
Lugh of the Golden Arm; Ó Riada; JDM
Medea; Ginastera; Domy Reiter-Soffer
Miniatures; Stravinsky; Nils Christe
Naila; Delibes; Gordon Aitken
Offering; Dvorak; Toni Beck
Othello; Liszt; Peter Darrell
Other Days; Bob Downes; Domy Reiter-Soffer
Overture; Tchaikowsky; JDM
Paper Sunday; Bach; Sally Owen
Paradise Gained; Milhaud; Domy Reiter-Soffer
Party; Bruch; Royston Maldoom
Pas classique; Adam; Michel de Lutry
Pas de quatre; Pugni; Anton Dolin
Playboy of the Western World; The Chieftains; JDM
Pomes Pennyeach; Bach, Franck, Ravel, Satie; Domy Reiter-Soffer
Prisoners; Bartok; Peter Darrell
Raymonda Suite of Dances; Glazunov; Petipa, reproduced:
    Kathleen Smith
Reputations; Lecocq; JDM
Shadow-Reach; McCabe; Domy Reiter-Soffer
Study for Nine; Franck; Michel de Lutry
Sunny Day; Country and Western Music; Charles Czarny
Táin; Fleischmann; JDM
Ten!!; Donizetti; Jonathan Burnett
They Come, They Come; E.J. Moeran; JDM
Timeless Echoes; Vivaldi; Domy Reiter-Soffer
Timetrip Orpheus; Bewmann, Franke, Froese; Domy Reiter-Soffer
Valse; Ravel; Domy Reiter-Soffer
Ventana; Lumbye; Bournonville
West Cork Ballad; Ó Riada; JDM
Women; Boulez; Domy Reiter-Soffer

Yerma; Crumb; Domy Reiter-Soffer

La Ventana; Lumbye, Bournonville; reproduced: Hans Brenaa
Le corsair pas de deux; Drigo; Perrot
Lugh of the Golden Arm; Ó Riada, De Buitléar; JDM
Yerma; Crumb; Domy Reiter-Soffer

1978

Chariots of Fire; Christou, Mamangakis, Zenakis;
    Domy Reiter-Soffer
Concerto Grosso; Handel; Charles Czarny
Konservatoriet; Paulli, Bournonville; reproduced: Hans Brenaa
Offering; Dvorak; Toni Beck
Flames of Paris; Asafiev, Vynonen; Vynonen, reproduced:
    Richard Collins
The Devil to Pay; Ó Riada; JDM
Playboy; Chieftains; JDM

1979

Concerto Grosso; Handel; Charles Czarny
Othello; Liszt; Peter Darrell
Shadow-Reach; McCabe, Hartmann; Domy Reiter-Soffer
Study for Nine; Franck; Michel de Lutry
Playboy; Chieftains; JDM (Cork)
Playboy; Chieftains; JDM (New York)
Billy the Music; Ó Riada; JDM
Brandenburg; Bach; Charles Czarny
Othello; Liszt; Peter Darrell
Timetrip Orpheus; Bowman, Froese, Franke; Domy Reiter-Soffer
Yerma; Crumb; Domy Reiter-Soffer
Brandenburg; Bach; Charles Czarny
Study for Nine; Franck; Michel de Lutry
Billy the Music; Ó Riada; JDM
Samson and Delilah; Saint-Saens; JDM

1980

Brandenburg; Bach; Charles Czarny
Lugh of the Golden Arm; Ó Riada, Buitléar; JDM
Raymonda; Glazounov; Petipa, reproduced: Kathleen Smith
Timetrip Orpheus; Bowman, Froese, Franke; Domy Reiter-Soffer
La Gioconda; Ponchielli; JDM
Orfeo and Euridice; Gluck; JDM
Playboy; Chieftains; JDM
Blobs; Rivier; JDM (Rosc Exhibition)

February 1981

Adagietto No 5; Mahler; Royston Maldoom
Dance of the Hours; Ponchielli; JDM
Paradise Gained; Milhaud; Domy Reiter-Soffer

June 1981

Celebration; Boyce, Pachelbel; Royston Maldoom
Pas de quatre; Pugni; Anton Dolin

Medea; Ginastera; Domy Reiter-Soffer
Reputations; Lecocq; JDM
The Devil to Pay; O Riada; JDM
October 1981
Táin; Fleischmann; JDM
February 1982
Celebration; Boyce, Pachelbel; Royston Maldoom
La Ventana; Lumbye, Bournonville; reproduced: Hans Brenaa
Medea; Ginastera; Domy Reiter-Soffer
Paper Sunday; Bach; Sally Owen
August 1982
Cinderella pas de deux; Prokofiev; David Gordon
Flower Festival at Genzano; Helsted, Bournonville; Hans Brenaa
Women; Boulez; Domy Reiter-Soffer
The Party; Bruch; Royston Maldoom
The Prisoners; Bartok; Peter Darrell
Concerto Grosso; Handel; Charles Czarny
February 1983
Il Trovatore; Verdi; JDM
March 1983
Invitation to the Dance; Weber; JDM
Golliwog's Cakewalk; Debussy; JDM
Laurencia pas de dix; Minkus, Petipa; Brenda Last
Miniatures; Stravinsky; Nils Christe
Chariots of Fire; Christou, Mamangakis, Zenakis; Domy
    Reiter-Soffer
Black Swan pas de deux; Tchaikovsky; Petipa, David Gordon
June 1983
Naila; Delibes; Gordon Aitken
Diúltú; Buckley; JDM
La valse; Ravel; Domy Reiter-Soffer
Sunny Day; Country and Western Music; Charles Czarny
Golliwogs and Teddy-bears; Kabalevsky; JDM
August 1983
Beauty and the Beast; Ravel; Tony Hubbard
Catalyst; Saint-Saens; Kathleen Smith
Gipsy Dances Il Trovatore; Verdi; JDM
Sunny Day; Country and Western Music; Charles Czarny
Ten!; Donizetti; Jonathan Burnett
West Cork Ballad; Ó Riada; JDM
March 1984
Naila; Delibes; Gordon Aitken
Diúltú; Buckley; JDM
La Valse; Ravel; Domy Reiter-Soffer
Reputations; Lecocq; JDM
West Cork Ballad; Ó Riada; JDM

Carmen Dances; Bizet; Domy Reiter-Soffer
June 1984
Lady of the Camellias; Saint-Saens; Domy Reiter-Soffer
October 1984
Playboy; Chieftains; JDM
March 1985
Lady of the Camellias; Saint-Saens; Domy Reiter-Soffer
July 1985
Playboy; Chieftains; JDM (France)
January 1986
In the Mood; Glen Miller; Domy Reiter-Soffer
Beethoven Variations; Beethoven; Charles Czarny
Catalysis; Faure; David Gordon
Chopin Dances; Chopin; Gary Trinder
August 1986
Pie Jesu; Faure; Gary Trinder
Women; Boulez; Domy Reiter-Soffer
Bethoven Variations; Beethoven; Charles Czarny
Chopin Dances; Chopin; Gary Trinder
Catalysis; Faure; David Gordon
A Time Remembered; Mahler; Charles Czarny
Adagietto No 5; Mahler; Royston Maldoom
In the Mood; Miller; Domy Reiter-Soffer
1 September 1985
JDM resigned as Artistic Director of of Irish National Ballet; she was
replaced by Anneli Vourenjuuri-Robinson.
October 1986
Chopin Dances; Chopin; Gary Trinder
House of Bernarda Alba (Lorca); Ohana; Domy Reiter-Soffer
Dear Mr Gershwin; Gershwin; Domy Reiter-Soffer
February 1987
Symphonic Dances; Rachmaninov; Anneli Vourenjuuri Robinson
House of Bernarda Alba (Lorca); Ohana; Domy Reiter-Soffer
Dear Mr Gershwin; Gershwin; Domy Reiter-Soffer
Death and Transfiguration; Rosemary Helliwell
April 1988
Terrain Unbound; Vaughan-Williams; Domy Reiter-Soffer
Odd Man Out; Rossini; Rosemary Helliwell
Silverplay; Bach; Anneli Vourenjuuri Robinson
Paquita Suite; Minkus; reproduced: Anneli Vourenjuuri Robinson
8 February 1989
Oscar; Bax; Domy Reiter-Soffer

Appendix D:
JDM's Awards and Tributes

Champion Irish Stepdancer of England at the London Irish Step Dance Championship 24 April 1931. Gold medal

Second prize for solo war pipes at the Tailteann Games Croke Park Dublin 2 July 1932. Silver medal

87 marks for solo war pipes at a Scots Gathering and Highland Games at Morecambe and Heysham in Lancashire 15 July 1933

First prize for solo war pipes at Father Mathew Feis on 22 April 1934 in Cork: awarded full marks, 25 April 1934

Very highly commended (i.e. 3rd) for Irish dancing: Senior Slip Jig, Father Mathew Feis, 22 April 1934

Munster Open Championship in solo war pipes Killarney 1933

First prize for solo war pipes at the Father Mathew Feis, 6 May 1935

First prize for solo war pipes 1937 Kilcorney Feis, Co. Cork

Second prize for Operatic Soprano Solo at the Father Mathew Feis, January 1938

The Showcase Award 6 January 1972

The Publicity Club of Ireland Award 1975

Honorary Doctorate from the National University of Ireland, 5 April 1979

Silver Medallion of the Irish American Cultural Institute for the *Playboy of the Western World* at the Lincoln Center, New York 1979

Catholic Women of the Year Award 1980

The Mallow Hall of Fame Award 15 November 1980

Award of $10,000 by the Irish American Cultural Institute to assist the production of the *Táin* ballet, August 1981

Harvey's of Bristol: Theatre Award 15 May 1982, presented by Siobháin McKenna

Perrier Good Taste Award 12 October 1983

Variety Artistes Trust Society Award 20 November 1983

People of the Year Award 25 November 1983 with Sheila Goldberg, presented by the Taoiseach Garrett Fitzgerald

Registration Certificate of the Royal Academy of Dancing London for JDM as an officially approved teacher of ballet (under the rules which came into effect on 1 January 1986)

Anglo-Irish Bank Corporation Presentation October 1987

Special Presentation from Jack and Máirín Lynch 23 November 1987

Cork Arts and Theatre Club: *This is Your Life Tribute,* 24 February 1988, presented by Michael Twomey

Cork Ballet Company's Memorial Production of *Giselle* November 1992 commemorating JDM and Aloys Fleischmann, attended by President Mary Robinson

Critics' Award to the 1992 Cork Ballet Company production of *Giselle* at the Cork Opera House

Sculpture of JDM at Firkin Crane Centre unveiled by Jack Lynch in February 1993

Plaque set up in Broom Lane Mallow 1 July 1993 to 'The First Lady of Dance'

Commemoration in the Firkin Crane Centre in June 1997 of the 50 anniversary of the founding of the Cork Ballet Company opened by the Lord Mayor, James A. Corr.

NOTES

THE BALLET IN CORK

1   Aloys Fleischmann's account of the ballet in Cork, the Memorandum of 1971 to the Minister of Finance, and the unpublished article 'The Arts Council and the Dance' are among his papers in the Archives of University College Cork.

2   This article by Aloys Fleischmann was intended for a national newspaper, but he did not publish it as the Arts Council threatened legal proceedings. The contentious passages have not been included.

3   A degree *honoris causa* is the highest honour that can be awarded in Ireland. The Registrar of The National University of Ireland told the editor that there are three criteria: the person's achievement must be outstanding; Irish life must have been enriched by it; the conferring of the degree must honour the university as well as the person. The late Professor Colm Ó hEocha, a member of the Senate of the National University of Ireland at that time, told me that Miss Moriarty's nomination caused no surprise in the Senate, and that it was very widely supported.

4   Letter of 6 September 1983 from the dance officer of the Arts Council, to Peter Ryan at the department of the Taoiseach – see Arts Council ballet company files.

5   John Stephenson, quoted in Kennedy, *Dreams and Responsibilites: The State and the Arts in Independent Ireland*, published by the Arts Council, Dublin, n.d., p. 193.

6   Kennedy, *Dreams and Responsibilites* p. 264.

7   The following year the Arts Council was granted an increase in real terms of over 10%, but the damage had been done, and some of the work built up over a decade destroyed. Smaller theatre groups such as Everyman in Cork, Siamsa Tire in Tralee, the Hawkswell Theatre in Sligo were given grants out of the savings.

8   INB budget papers for 1984. Arts Council ballet company files.

9   Lansdowne Market Research, *Audiences, Acquisitions and Amateurs*, Dublin 1983, quoted in Kennedy, *Dreams and Responsibilities*, p. 210. (Figures just made available for Germany for 1998 are similar: only 9% answered 'yes' when asked had they been to an operetta or a musical within the last six months, only 4% had been to an opera or classical concert. Source: *Frankfurter Rundschau* of 10 March 1998).

10 See letter from the dance officer of 20 November 1980 to Richard Stokes in the Department of the Taoiseach.

11 See the contribution in this book by Loretta Keating Kleanthous, p. 190.

12 See letter from the dance officer of 20 November 1980 to Richard Stokes in the Department of the Taoiseach.

13 See Ballet Company board minutes of 23 June 1982 – Arts Council files.

14 Peter Brinson gave a lecture in Dublin on 25 July 1981 on dance in Ireland which was to become the 'bible' of the Dance Council of Ireland, the umbrella body set up in September 1984 to co-ordinate the work of the various dance groups. See Imelda O'Loan in: *Dance News Ireland*, Dublin, Summer 1985.

15 See Mary Clarke's obituary in *The Dancing Times* of May 1995 for an outline of his career; Brinson's 'Message to Members' on becoming director in *The Dancing Times* September 1968 for his plans; his foreword to Peggy van Praagh's *A Life of Dance*, Melbourne 1985 for his comments on de Valois and Rambert, whose authority among dancers he felt was excessive – he had a good deal to do with de Valois while he was working with 'Ballet for All' and during his year at the

RAD. The article by G. B. Wilson in the *Dance Gazette* of Spring 1969 outlines Brinson's plans for the RAD Archives: he set up an Academy library, collecting old books and visual material. However, to make room for them a bonfire was made of the entire correspondence of the director Kathleen Gordon's 44-year administration, crucial years for the RAD. There is only one document by Gordon in the library: an account of the British dance scene in 1979 written for the incoming director John Field. It illustrates how mistaken Brinson was to disregard this woman's insights and work.

16 See 'Peter Brinson' by G. B. Wilson in the *Dance Gazette* of Spring 1969.

17 *Ibid.*, p. 26.

18 The Brinson Report cost £14,000 – see Gaye Tanham, 'State Funding for Dance in Ireland' in: *Dance News Ireland* Winter 1989, p. 8. Peter Bassett, the archivist at the Laban Centre for Movement and Dance (where Brinson was director of research) told me that the Laban Centre paid half the cost; the London Gulbenkian Foundation (of which Brinson had formerly been director) supplied a secretary.

19 A memo written by the Arts Council dance officer was read out to the full council at the crucial meeting of 8 April 1988 at which the termination of Irish National Ballet's grant was decided. It erroneously stated that the 1985/6 cut in INB's grant amounted to 8%, the grant having been reduced from £325,000 to £284,000. An 8% cut would have been a reduction of £26,000; in fact, according to the council's own figures, £41,000 was removed; INB's grant was therefore reduced not by 8% but by 12.6%. The Arts Council tells me that confusion often arose because its financial year differed from that of the Irish National Ballet. The council gives INB grant figures (as per audited accounts) as follows – 1984: £344,900; 1985: £309,000; 1986: £295,000; 1987: £373,000; 1988: £285,000; 1989: £20,000; 1990: £25,000

20 From a statement of 2 April 1985 by James O'Donovan, chairman of board of Irish National Ballet, in response to a draft of the Brinson Report circulated before publication by the Arts Council to all dance groups. Arts Council files.

21 Brian P. Kennedy, *Dreams and Responsibilities: The State and the Arts in Independent Ireland*, p. 213.

22 See minutes of the meeting of 20 December 1984. Arts Council files.

23 Minutes of a meeting between the dance offcer, Miss Moriarty, Aloys Fleischmann and Pat Murray on 21 February 1985 in Cork – Arts Council files.

24 Two people I know of who were approached by Miss Moriarty with regard to taking over Irish National Ballet were Joahne O'Hara of the Royal Academy of Dancing, and Richard Collins.

25 I know of this from conversations with Aloys Fleischmann.

26 In the covering letter James O'Donovan sent to the council with INB's submissions on the report, he writes: 'Having only received the Brinson Report a few days ago, you can imagine how difficult it has been to have it circulated, and to arrange for an emergency meeting of the board while involved in our season at the Cork Opera House.' However (according to the memo drawn up by the dance officer for the director of the Arts Council) at a meeting with the INB board of 4 June 1985 the dance officer stated after hearing Fleischmann's criticism of the report: 'I said that we greatly regretted that the INB had not seen fit to present its comments on the report as fully as it was now doing in time for the April deadline which would have allowed Brinson to have their views in advance of the final draft being sent to the printer'. The memo does not record the board's response.

27 See letter from the Arts Council dance officer of 15 April 1985 to Peter Brinson,

Brinson Papers, Laban Centre, Goldsmith College of London University.

28 The White Paper on the government's cultural policy was: *Access and Opportunity*, Dublin 1987.

29 There are hardly any papers among the Arts Council files relating to the Brinson Report: not even Brinson's contract is there (the text of which is published in his report), nor are any of the written submissions mentioned in the report. Brinson bequeathed his papers to the Laban Centre for Movement and Dance in Goldsmith College, University of London; there is nothing among the collection relating to his work for the report on dance in Ireland, and only one letter and a policy document from the Arts Council. The London Gulbenkian Foundation has no material; the Arts Secretary wrote to me that Brinson's assistant may have it, as she believes he did most of the work, Brinson having been very busy [and ill] at the time. I have not been able to find Andy Ormston, the assistant.

30 INB files of 1985 (minutes of 20 May 1985). In a letter of 13 April 1988 to the chairman of INB, Donal Walsh, the dance officer expressly stated that the council had a 'prerogative not to comment on matters of artistic quality' so as 'not to interfere in the artistic integrity of any arts organisation'. He added that the council had its views on the subject and that such views 'formed the basis upon which decisions in relation to grant-aid are made'.

31 In a letter of 18 April 1988 to Irish National Ballet, the dance officer wrote that the reasons for not having 'come more into the open' about the grounds for the council's decision to terminate funding had been 'honourable as well as strategic'; he announced – probably due to the barrage of criticism which INB had let loose on the council – that as these reasons were now wearing somewhat thin, he might in future have to be be less reticent. Examples he gives of discretion practised are that no precise INB audience figures were released, that the name had not been mentioned of the new artistic director about whom the council had reservations, that the criticised artistic changes proposed had not been described (probably that INB danced for the Cork panto when its Dublin Grand Opera Society plans fell through, and did schools work when the Belfast Festival participation did not materialise). None of these issues constitute a discussion of policy, however.

32 The following summary of the Arts Council's case against Irish National Ballet derives from a memo written by the Arts Council director to the principal officer at the Department of the Taoiseach. The memo is undated but will have been written sometime in mid-March 1988.

33 From a letter of 29 April 1988 to Carolyn Swift from the Arts Council chairman. See Arts Council 1988 INB files.

34 The theatre had received two-thirds of Arts Council budgets in the 1970s; its share was reduced to just under 50% of the total budget in 1980 (see Kennedy *Dreams and Responsibilities* p. 202) – dance received a mere 7.6% (see Robert O'Byrne in: *Music Ireland* of July/August 1987). The theatre profited from the 1988 re-distribution after the abolition of professional dance in Ireland.

35 The figure for the Cork pantomime audiences of 1987 given by Aloys Fleischmann in an article in the *Cork Examiner* of 4 April 1988 was 57,000; in an RTE interview on 1 April 1988 Colm Ó Briain, a member of the INB board, stated that it was around 50,000.

36 However, the dance officer did not approve of the company's education programme, which may be a further reason for the negative approach. See his letter of 13 April 1988 to the chairman of INB justifying the council's decision to cease funding: he states that he had on several occasions expressed reserva-

tions about the quality of their schools' work – this was the work done by the new Finnish artistic director – and had offered (as an education expert) to discuss the development of a 'high-quality schools programme' with them, but was never taken up on his offer. In a letter of 13 October 1988 to Gemma Hussey, the director of the Arts Council called the schools work 'very old-fashioned'; the dance officer said it 'smacked of cultural imperialism': see note 43.

37 Quoted by Desmond Rushe in his 'Tatler's Parade' in *The Irish Independent* 20 June 1978, Fleischmann Papers UCC Cork. The visit to Derry in 1978 was sponsored by both the Protestant and Catholic bishops – see *Cork Examiner* 3 February 1978.

38 Memo of 8 July 1982 from the director of the Arts Council to the dance officer , Arts Council ballet files.

39 The aide memoire 'Thoughts' addressed to the dance officer is undated: it is to be found between files of 12 March and 19 July 1984, so was probably written in late spring or early summer of that year.

40 Letter of 17 February 1987 from the dance officer to Peter Brinson, Arts Council INB files.

41 Memo of 27 August 1985 from the theatre officer Phelim Donlon to the director of the Arts Council about an Irish National Ballet performance in Cork.

42 Miss Moriarty went on a visit to the Soviet Union in 1973: friends financed the trip as a present. I recall her being invited to a meal in our house on her return and her speaking with awe of the facilities given to the ballet companies there and of the cultural amenities given to working people.

43 Martin Drury, 'By Indirections Find Directions Out', paper to the First National Conference of Dance and Education at Thomond College of Education in Limerick, 24 March 1990, in: *Dance News Ireland* Spring 1990.

44 Brinson Report, p. 36.

45 The dance officer in an RTE radio interview on 25 March 1988 – the transcript is in the Arts Council ballet files. There is a tape of the broadcast in the Fleischmann papers, UCC.

46 The council objected in particular to two statements (though Fleischmann's text also contained a number of highly unflattering comparisons of which no mention is made): firstly that the council officers had virtually forced the newly elected Arts Council to accept their recommendation not to fund the ballet company, having made a 'cast-iron case for the abolition of INB', which the council 'had no option but to accept'. In fact, however, the officers were not at all sure they would prevail, and had prepared a statement for the eventuality that the council might decide against them. Secondly the council took exception to Fleischmann's statement in the proposed article that the executive officers had 'planned the demise of INB in 1985'. There is a transcript in the council files of a telephone call between the director and Fleischmann on 29 March 1989 (it only records what the director said) and also letters from them both on the subject. I have not been able to establish how the council came to see his text – he may have sent a copy, though I did not find one in the files.

47 Memo of 1 December 1986 to the council chairman, Arts Council ballet files.

48 Letter of 10 May 1988 from Peter Brinson, Arts Council INB files.

49 The dance officer in a memo to the director of the council of 6 April 1988. Arts Council INB files.

50 The dance officer on the role of the Arts Council in a memo of 17 June 1988. Arts Council INB files.

51 There was a lengthy period of unseemly haggling over who should pay the costs of winding up Irish National Ballet. The Arts Council had been greatly incensed at the intervention of the Taoiseach's Office and its grant of £120,000 given to keep the Ballet Company going until February 1989: the council felt this indicated a public documentation of the government's lack of confidence in the council's decision, and that it undermined the organisation's independence. The council suggested that the Taoiseach's Office should pay the debts, outstanding wages, fees and redundancy moneys as it had encouraged the Ballet Company to continue operating despite virtual insolvency. Ultimately the dancers, staff and the creator of *Oscar* only received a percentage of what they were owed. However, the Arts Council paid Miss Moriarty a modest pension after her resignation, although she had no legal claim to one, not having been a salaried employee. It must also be said that the council agreed that the source of the money should not be divulged to her, as she would otherwise not have accepted it. See Arts Council correspondence of 1986 with James O'Donovan on this matter. Miss Moriarty will have discovered where her pension came from after INB was disbanded. In her will she made a substantial bequest to the Arts Council for a scholarship to train an Irish dancer for a career in an Irish professional dance company. She decreed that if that should not be possible, the money was to go to the Cork SHARE organisation to build homes for the elderly.

52 The Ballet Rambert had visited Cork in 1951, and was entertained by the Cork Ballet Company; in 1958, after the burning of the old Opera House, it was in Cork for a week practising at Miss Moriarty's studio as the City Hall, in which the performances took place, had no practice rooms. Six members of the Cork Ballet Company danced in the *corps de ballet* with the Ballet Rambert, and one member of the company – Julia Cotter – was given a scholarship for a course with them in London. Marie Rambert and the Cork woman Alicia Markova were patrons of the amateur company; Ninette de Valois was patron of the professional company.

53 *The Collected Poems of W. B. Yeats*, London 1961, Last Poems (1936–1939) p. 340.

THE MUSIC FOR THE DANCE

1 Earlier ballets were *The Golden Bell of Ko, An Cóitín Dearg, Macha Ruadh, The Planting Stick*.

2 'Lugh was the Mercury of the Celtic Gods – light-footed, nimble, skilled in crafts, an inventor and protector'. Quoted from the programme notes for the 1980 production at the Opera House.

3 Tilly Fleischmann, *Aspects of the Liszt Tradition* (ed. Michael O'Neill), Adare Press: Cork, 1986; Roberton Wendover Aylesbury, Bucks., 1991. These editions are a shortened version of the original text, which is among the Fleischmann Papers in the Archives of University College Cork.

4 This account is taken from Joseph Gilmore, 'The Cork Ballet Company', *Threshold*, Vol.1, Autumn 1957.

5 Aloys Fleischmann, typescript on Ballet in Cork, pp. 14–15, The Fleischmann Papers, University College Cork Archive.

6 Aloys Fleischmann: script for radio broadcast (?), MS, n.d. (probably for weekly series *Composers at Work* broadcast by Radio Éireann in 1957)

7 Micheál Mac Liammóir, *Each Actor On His Ass*, London, 1961, p. 11.

8 Aloys Fleischmann, 'Seán Ó Faoláin – A Personal Memoir', *The Cork Review*, Seán Dunne ed., Cork 1991, p. 93.

9 Micheál Mac Liammóir, *et. al:* 'Design for a Ballet', *The Bell*, Vol. 4 No. 6, Sept-

ember 1942, pp. 394-403.

10 Letter from Micheál Mac Liammóir to Aloys Fleischmann, 15 July, 1946, The
Fleischmann Papers, UCC Archive.

11 From the programme booklet for the first performance.

12 Micheál Mac Liammóir, 'Design for a Ballet', *The Bell*, Vol.4 No. 6, September
1942, p. 339.

13 Letter from Kathleen O'Flaherty, assistant to the President of UCC, to Aloys
Fleischmann, 1 June, 1951, The Fleischmann Papers, UCC Archive.

14 Aloys Fleischmann: 'Ballet in Cork', *Music Ireland*, Vol. 2, No. 10, November 1987,
p. 15.

15 The legend is not discussed, for example, either by Douglas Hyde or Aodh de
Blácam, and is not included in the collections of P. W. Joyce or Lady Gregory.

16 This preface is unsigned, but it is not unlikely that Fleischmann himself is the
author.

17 Aloys Fleischmann, 'On Writing Music for Ballet', *Soundpost*, No. 4, October/
November 1981, p. 11.

18 Fernau Hall: 'Dublin Festival – *The Táin*,' *Daily Telegraph*, 8 October 1981.

FAMILY, ASSOCIATES AND FRIENDS

1 Owen Dudley Edwards, *The Quest for Sherlock Holmes: A Biographical Study of
Arthur Conan Doyle*, Edinburgh 1983, pp. 117–120 and 311.

2 The information in Thom's Directory was obtained from Richard Henchion of
Cork.

3 This is confirmed by Mr Dermot O'Mahony of Buttevant, involved himself in
plant hire, who regarded Jack as a highly intelligent, indeed rather a brilliant
man in his sphere. But Mr John Coulter of Mallow told me the Moriartys were
too trusting of people for their own good.

4 The information about Gus Moriarty's sporting abilities comes from Mr Tom
Redmond of Liverpool, whose father was a famous hurler (as was Tom
Redmond!) and a friend of Gus Moriarty's. Mr Larry Condon told me about
his good singing – he attended many evenings of music at Ballgarret House
near Mallow with the Moriarty family.

5 Letter of 1 May 1996 to Ruth Fleischmann from Jane Pritchard, Archivist of the
Rambert Dance Company. Fleischmann papers UCC.

6 Interview with Robert O'Donoghue in the *Evening Echo* of 4 January 1964.

7 See Obituary of Emily Moriarty in ISTD *Dance Journal* Autumn 1960.

8 Mrs Barbara Birdicon of West Kirby Wirral.

9 Tom Redmond told me that the Moriarty's Liverpool home was a grand house
in an area which was then a fine place to live.

10 I have this information from Mrs Esther Gyves of Mallow, who was a good
friend of Marion Moriarty's, and who worked until her marriage in 1938 for
Denis Moriarty the solicitor. According to the *Evening Echo* of 25 April 1931 the
Moriarty ladies were Gaelic supporters, having attended a hurling final in
London the previous day. Tom Redmond told me that Gus was a hurler of
such high ability that, though not a resident in County Cork, he was invited
to play on the Cork team – an unprecedented honour!

11 There are cuttings in Joan's scrapbook from the *Cork Weekly Examiner* going back
to 1928 (she kept a ballad about a hurling match of that year: 'When Mallow
Bate Blackrock'!) and from *An Phoblacht*. It was an ad she saw in the latter
(according to *An Phoblacht* of 25 April 1931) which gave her the idea of entering for the British Irish Stepdancing Championship. The *Telegraph* of 16 July
1933 states that she was a member of the Liverpool Scots Society; *The Cork*

Examiner of 28 April 1934 states that most of Joan's training in piping and Irish dancing 'was obtained in the Liverpool Gaelic League, of which she was a member for many years.' (JDM Papers.)

12 Joan's uncle Lord Justice Moriarty had a daughter Joan who married Kenneth Mackay, son of the first Earl of Inchcape; the family lived until 1992 in Glenapp Castle in Inverness.

13 This was written up in the *Evening Echo* and *An Phoblacht* on 25 April 1931, the latter speaking of her as 'Miss Molly Moriarty'.

14 She is written up in all the papers; somewhat belatedly in the GAA Irish language sports journal *An Camán* of 21 Samhain 1932 as Siobhán Ruadh Ní Mhuircheartaigh ó Learpholl.

15 *Telegraph* 16 July 1933, *Sunday Dispatch* 16 July 1933.

16 Letter of 6 May 1944 from Henrietta Evans of Clydaville, Mallow to JDM: JDM Papers.

17 In an interview on 16 September 1978 with Ciaran Carty of the *Sunday Tribune*, among others.

18 A message from Joan's old friend George Collins describing this fear was read out at the show given in Joan's honour *This is Your Life* of 24 February 1988 by the Cork Arts and Theatre Club. A video of the show is among the Fleischmann Papers in UCC.

19 In his speech, Aloys Fleischmann omitted this last phrase about his own death, which was to come six months later on 21 July 1992.

LIST OF CONTRIBUTORS

INDEX

270